Pursuing Equity in Medicine

Pursuing Equity in Medicine

ONE WOMAN'S JOURNEY

Catherine DeAngelis, MD, MPH

ISBN-13: 9781533341945
ISBN-10: 153334194X
Library of Congress Control Number: 2016908570
CreateSpace Independent Publishing Platform
North Charleston, South Carolina

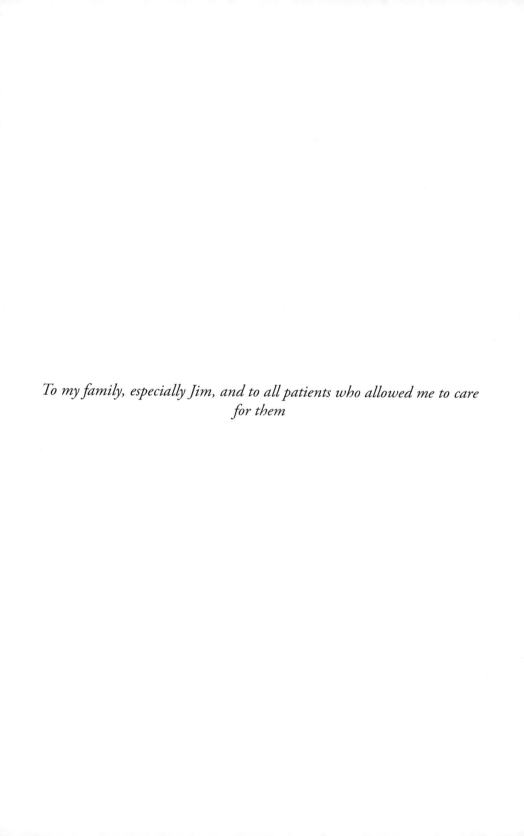

To my family, especially Jim, and to all patients who allowed me to care for them

Contents

Preface

~c~

EQUITY IS THE QUALITY OF being fair or impartial, of freedom from bias or favoritism. The basic issue for me as I began my career in medicine was, how could a woman achieve equity in the male-dominated field of medicine? My goal, as it became clearer with experience, was to help crack the glass ceiling without sustaining a severe concussion.

The profession of medicine is a vocation, not a job; it is a calling to which a future physician, woman or man, is drawn. The calling is to help people who are sick and suffering, using the knowledge and skills learned over many years and continuing throughout a physician's lifetime. Anyone who enters medicine without that calling is doomed to failure, because she or he will miss the precept of caring for caring's sake, and patients will suffer. Like all good physicians, I believe that very deeply and have tried to teach it by example, sometimes falling short but always returning to the calling to care.

So you might ask why I, or any woman, would settle for *equity* instead of *equality* with men. Women bring different qualities than men to medicine, and the contributions of both are essential, or else the profession would surrender half the available human ingenuity, intellect, creativity, and resources. Simply stated, women and men are not equal biologically. No man is equal to me, and I am not equal to any man. Further, until men are able to bear children, not presently foreseeable, men and woman will remain biologically unequal. Equity is another matter. To be clear, in certain circumstances, such as receiving equal payment for for equal work, equality is an integral component of equity. Payment for work must be ruled by equity, that is with fairness, impartiality, without bias or favoritism.

Many people and life-changing events have been intricately involved in my journey to pursue equity in medicine. I realized early in life that I needed to practice equity in dealing with others and to be treated with equity, in order to have a full and joyous life as a physician. Equity was what I chose to seek for myself and for all women and men. As I gained experience, I learned that there are four characteristic *T*s essential for any leader. These are *tough-mindedness, tenacity, thick skin*, and a *tender heart*. The latter two pose no problem when individuals view women; women are supposed to have these characteristics, right? However, the first two, when viewed through the opaque lenses of many, can cause problems for women seeking to advance or to assume leadership roles. That is where equity becomes vital. How I achieved equity is a long story composed of many ventures and adventures, which I relate in this book.

I hope this story will be helpful to other women, and men, aspiring to a career in medicine, or any other field that requires equity for the field to benefit fully from all who venture into it.

As I started on this journey, it was clear that how I was to achieve equity was not going to be easy, especially for a woman born in 1940 whose four grandparents and Father were born in Italy; who grew up in a small town, which was and is pretty much still unknown to anyone uninterested in pizza; and who grew up in a financially "poor" family (which I didn't realize it until I learned that fact in a college sociology class). However, I did achieve equity despite almost bleeding to death in Wisconsin; surviving a four-day comatose stay in a Turkish hospital intensive-care unit, after being held hostage by Chechen rebels; and eventually walking away after being hit by a Chicago Transit Authority bus, which resulted in a pelvic fracture and a brain concussion. I went on to found the Johns Hopkins General Pediatrics and Adolescent Medicine Division; to become vice chair of the Hopkins Department of Pediatrics; to be the twelfth woman professor in ninety-two years of Hopkins's history and the vice dean for Academic Affairs and Faculty at the Johns Hopkins University School of Medicine, after having been rejected for admission to that medical school; and to become the first woman editor in chief of *JAMA,* the *Journal of the American Medical Association.* The latter was an especially interesting achievement, since I had never been a member of the AMA until I became the editor in chief and had disagreed with almost everything the AMA had stood for after the mid-twentieth century.

I believe that Dante was correct: God is a comedian. And I'll add that (S)He has a peculiar sense of humor. How else can this world as it exists and my (and anyone else's) life be explained?

For full disclosure, this book contains no sex, but a lot of love and only a smidgeon, relatively speaking, of mostly psychological violence (especially in the introduction on what happened in Istanbul). However, if you are not looking for sex and violence, and you are curious enough about achieving equity in life and want a few laughs, and perhaps some tears, please read on (and note that, while the stories are real, the names of some patients have been changed to protect their privacy). Otherwise, I advise you to put this book back on the shelf and choose another book or something else to read online. I'll certainly understand. But for others seeking a vocation or career and hoping to find equity in that vocation or career, I feel that it will have been worth my time and effort to write this story for you about my journey. I hope you will find this shared adventure helpful.

ONWARD.

Introduction: Held Hostage in Istanbul

⁓

I KNEW THAT BEING THE first woman editor in chief of *JAMA,* the *Journal of the American Medical Association,* was going to be a great adventure. I just didn't realize how much of a challenging adventure it was going to be. One example of those challenges that became a very important part of me is what happened in Istanbul, Turkey, in 2001.

As a young physician who wanted to serve as a faculty member in a medical school (my ultimate dream being the Johns Hopkins School of Medicine), I anticipated there would be a great deal of travel involved in my life. I really enjoyed traveling, especially to new places, and meeting people from different cultures. However, I was not prepared for some of the foreign travel experiences that were to come. The first one for which I was not prepared happened in March of 2001, soon after I became the editor in chief of *JAMA.* The publisher and a few of his staff members, the *JAMA* attorney, our managing editor, my husband, Jim (that is Dr. James C. Harris), and I traveled for a meeting in Istanbul, Turkey.

Jim and I left for Istanbul on April 18, 2001, having no clue that five days later (and less than five months before the infamous 9/11 tragedy), we would be held hostage by Chechen rebels in an international hotel. Anyone who has been to the magnificent city of Istanbul, a city that straddles two continents, knows that beauty and intrigue are part of its essence. However, we had no inkling of just how intriguing our visit to that city would be. We had traveled there for a meeting of publishers who had relationships with *JAMA,* of which I had been editor in chief for only fifteen months. Being accompanied by several of our editorial, legal, and publishing colleagues, we all anticipated learning a great deal from other publishers. Little did we know exactly what we would learn and, more importantly, how that information was to be imparted.

HELD HOSTAGE

The meeting started on Friday, April 20, and the next evening we all had dinner at a Turkish restaurant. The food was delicious, and the atmosphere splendid, but on our walk back to our hotel, I began to have abdominal pain. That was a bit confusing because the pain was too early to have been caused by food poisoning, and no one else seemed to be having any problems. Most of that night and the next day I had severe abdominal pain, and when I began vomiting, I hoped the other end of my gastrointestinal system would also eject its contents to relieve the pressure that was causing the stretching of my gut, thereby causing the pain.

The human body is such an interesting model for self-healing. However, no such healing occurred, and I wasn't thinking well enough to realize that something more serious was taking place. Vomiting did relieve the abdominal pain, so some things were looking up (always remain positive). Over the course of the next two days, Saturday and Sunday, I could not eat or drink anything, but I continued to vomit with no diarrhea. This is never a good sign, especially when traveling in a foreign country. Sunday evening our group went on a dinner cruise up the Bosphorus (the Turkish strait), but naturally Jim and I stayed at the hotel because I was ill and feeling weak—very unusual for me. We could not have anticipated what was about to happen at the hotel.

Late that evening we received a phone call in our room from Annette, our managing editor, who had gone on the dinner cruise. When she and the others had tried to return to the hotel, they were turned away because the hotel was on lockdown. She warned us to turn out all lights and the TV, because our hotel had been invaded by Chechen rebels who were holding people in the lobby as hostages. It seemed so appropriate for Annette to be the one to call with the warning, because her motherly nature and nursing education were ever apparent no matter what the situation. We had no intention of leaving our room and needed no light or TV, so her suggestion was easy to follow.

However, an hour or so after midnight, despite our TV being turned off, a message appeared on the TV screen instructing us to call the front desk. I was concerned that something had happened to my father, who had not been doing so well. Jim and I had been traveling out of the country when my mother died, and I didn't want the same thing to happen with my father. I had instructed my sisters to call us if there was any change in his health. So Jim called the front desk, which turned out to be a bad mistake.

Shortly thereafter there was a hard knock on our door, and one of the hotel workers announced that we were to immediately come down to the lobby. Jim told the man that that was impossible because I was ill. The man replied that he was with two men who had guns and who would shoot the door open if we didn't comply.

I went to the door and peeked out the peephole to see two very young men who were holding what appeared to be hunting shotguns with the barrels pointed down. I told Jim that I doubted they wanted to hurt us, so we'd better follow them to the lobby. But I suggested that he should ask if we could first get dressed. They approved that request (a very good sign). I then put our passports inside my bra because I knew, or at least hoped, that Muslim men would not search a woman, and I wanted to protect our way out of the country if we could avoid being transported out in coffins.

When we stepped outside our door, I looked at one of the young men, who put his head down, but when he looked up I made a gesture indicating, "What's going on?" He smiled slightly and pointed his head down to show that his and his partner's gun barrels were pointed downward. I also had the feeling that he was as frightened as we were, but that might only have reflected my lesser-than-usual ability to think straight.

When we entered the hotel lobby, we saw hotel staff and several dozen other hostages from many countries sitting in the lower lobby, situated several stair steps below the level of the main entrance to the lobby. We later learned that there were 120 of us who had been held since around ten thirty that night. The lower lobby area had been a gathering place for hotel guests to sit and have drinks and snacks. Now it was the place where hostages were required to sit. The Chechen rebels had the hotel staff provide soft drinks, water, cheese, fruit, and bread for all (except I declined because I still could not keep anything down). We were also allowed to go anywhere in the lobby as long as we could be observed by the armed Chechens, who were seated in strategic places.

I noted that all of the front doors and windows of the hotel, that were (or rather had been) all glass, had been shot out, so there were glass fragments all over that part of the lobby. Jim found out that this was the result of the Chechens having raked bullets all across the front of the hotel, probably to gain the attention of the Turkish police. That act certainly worked. We could observe the Turkish police perched outside with guns pointed into the hotel lobby. I decided that the potential "rescue" invasion of the hotel by Turkish police might be at least as threatening as anything the rebels might do.

Jim and I found a place up against the short wall that separated the lower lobby longue where we sat from the front entrance of the hotel. That way, if the police were to shoot into the lobby, we would be below the line of fire, at least at first. Jim told me that if we heard gunfire, he would lie over me to protect me, but I flatly refused to allow that. I had no desire to live without him, especially knowing that he would have given his life to save mine. And so we sat leaning against the wall and held hands, knowing perhaps as never before how much we loved each other. I don't advise this experience as a test for anyone else, but that feeling is something neither Jim nor I will ever forget.

As it turned out, the only reason the rebels had invaded the hotel, which had so many international guests, was so they could gain world-wide attention. Before they would release the hostages, they demanded a news conference in which they could express their anger at the treatment of the Chechen people by the Russian government. By eleven o'clock Monday morning, after appeals from the minister of the interior and from local Chechens, the rebels surrendered and were taken from the hotel in a Turkish police van. Before the rebels left, their leader apologized for taking us hostage.

I can only imagine what happened to them thereafter, but the story appeared in many international newspapers. According to the BBC news report on April 23, 2001, the reason the Turkish police did not rush the rebels in the hotel was because of the risk of injuring hostages. Great decision, I think!

I have refused to refer to those rebels as terrorists, but who knows how I might feel if this had happened to us post-9/11. At any rate, we were happy to be reunited with our colleagues on Monday, one of whom had holed up in his hotel room. He had torn the sheets from his bed and tied them together in preparation for climbing down the sheet rope if he was asked to open his room door. Fortunately, that plan never needed to be tested, because there is doubt that the rope would have reached the ground or even close to ground level or that it would have held his weight.

The wife of another of our colleagues, who had stayed in another hotel the night of the hostage taking, was so frightened after hearing of the escapade in our hotel that she immediately arranged to take the next plane home. All but one of the others remained for another day or so to conclude the meetings and attend to the paperwork that was needed for the American Embassy and Turkish officials after the hostage episode. The person who remained in the city with Jim and me was Wayne Hoppe, the *JAMA* attorney, who stayed on as he had planned to explore the city. He was so very helpful to us and even took some of our luggage back to Chicago when he left.

Hospitalization in Istanbul

Because Jim and I had not done much sightseeing beyond the Blue Mosque and because my adrenalin levels were at peak levels, I suggested that we visit the Topkapı Palace Museum. The palace dates back to the mid-fifteenth century, and the current museum contains the opulent pavilion, a jewel-filled treasury and a sprawling harem, all of which provide a glimpse of the lives of the court of the Ottoman Empire that inhabited the palace for many centuries. Despite my interest in Topkapı, I don't recall much from that visit except that on the way home it rained, and by the time we reached our hotel room I was wet and very cold. I told Jim that I wanted to take a hot bath, which I'm sure I did, but I don't remember much of anything after getting in the tub except for snatches of conversations until I awoke in a Turkish hospital ICU many days later.

According to Jim, I had begun to act odd and somewhat disoriented after the bath. I can't imagine how he decided my behavior was any different than usual, but he claims that I was not making much sense (and that's different?). Apparently even though I was no longer complaining about abdominal pain, I still had not been able to hold down even small sips of fluids. Aisha, the wonderful Turkish publisher, asked a local physician to check me; he even had a portable ultrasound machine, which did not reveal a bowel obstruction. I do remember that someone gave me a liter of IV fluids in preparation for our planned return to the United States the following day.

However, Jim called a gastrointestinal specialist at Johns Hopkins who was a friend of ours and knew my history of having a congenital anomaly resulting in my having had a mesocaval shunt, an operation that rerouted the circulation in my abdomen around a blockage, many years previously. Apparently I spoke with her on the phone and was obviously very confused, so she told Jim to take me to a hospital emergency room immediately and suggested specific tests to be done. That's when Aisha became very involved, God bless her.

I was admitted to the hospital's intensive-care unit (ICU) from the emergency room, where I had been seen by a gastroenterologist. My ammonia levels were dangerously high, indicating that my liver was not functioning normally in clearing my body of this toxic product. I spent the next four days in a coma, being treated with the long-distance help of physicians at Hopkins who knew my medical history and who were close friends. They conveyed their advice for treatment via the phone with Jim, who met daily with my Turkish doctors. This was 2001, and we had no cell phones that worked outside the United States. Aisha kindly gave her European phone to Jim so he could keep in touch with our Hopkins and *JAMA* colleagues. Reportedly, I kept trying to get out of the ICU bed, so I was placed in four-point restraints—that is, my hands and legs were tied to the bed spread eagle to limit my movement. Jim did not leave my bedside until the late evening of my fourth day in the hospital, because I had by then woken up from the coma and actually had a logical conversation with him and Aisha. However, I remembered nothing of that conversation.

What I do remember is waking up early the next morning. It was pitch dark, except for a tiny light above a nearby door. I also noted a fan on the ceiling above my bed. I didn't know I was in a hospital intensive care ward with several beds. I was tethered in four-point restraints and could not move, and my back felt like an elephant had been sitting on it for days. I could hear people laughing and speaking in a foreign language and others who were crying out, apparently in pain. I immediately reached with the thumb of my left hand to feel my wedding ring, which was always a source of comfort to me because it reminded me of Jim. There was no ring! I now became panicked and imagined that the rebels (were they terrorists after all?) might have returned and taken Jim somewhere. I knew Jim would never allow anyone to take my ring.

I tried to get out of bed but could barely move because of the restraints. (In the United States, it is illegal to put a patient in such restraints unless there is someone sitting at the bedside, and I found out up close and personally why this is so important. It is frightening to be so tethered under any circumstances, but in a hospital it is horrible.) I took some deep breaths, tried to look around, and saw that I had a rigged IV running into my right arm. I realized then that I must be in a hospital, but how did I get there and where were Jim and my ring? I called out for someone to please come. When no one came, I called out louder several times with no response. Finally, I called out loudly, asking how anyone could be so cruel to not respond. This was a hospital, after all.

With that, a nurse from hell came to my side, squeezed the back of my leg, and said, "Keep quit." I assumed she meant "keep quiet," and with the pain she inflicted in the back of my leg, I certainly was going to do whatever she said. Let me be very clear; that nurse in no way personified the excellent, caring nurses who worked at that hospital (whom I had the pleasure of being cared by afterward). I guess she was having a bad night, or I might have given her a hard time while I was out of it. In any case, by comparison she made Charles Dickens's nurse in *Martin Chuzzlewit*, Sairey Gamp, look like Florence Nightingale.

I tried to move as much as I could to relieve my back, trying not to think about how dry my mouth was. In moving around, I noticed an older woman who was mopping the floor near my bed, and who was watching me. She looked concerned, so I smiled at her and said, "*Günaydın*," or good morning, one of the few Turkish words I knew. She returned my greeting with a most beautiful smile and came closer. She said something to me that I did not understand, and I shook my head and smiled. Apparently, she understood that I had pretty much used my entire Turkish vocabulary with günaydın. I licked my lips, and she went away and returned with a cold, wet cloth.

She squeezed a few drops of water (that tasted like liquid manna to me) on my lips and then used the cloth to wash my face and neck. I can never express properly how much I am indebted to that angel for her kindness. She is one reason I have tried to teach physicians the importance of including everyone who comes in contact with patients as part of the team, and to give them credit and thank them for their work. I tried to find that wonderful woman before I left the hospital but was unsuccessful. I know she was not a figment of my imagination, but no one seemed to know who she was.

I then tried to relax and to figure out where Jim was, hoping that he was all right and that I could soon be released from the shackles. Do you know how many Hail Marys can be said in a few hours before dawn while waiting for release? I guess my Mother's insistence on our saying the rosary so often when my sisters and I were children stuck with me and was a source of comfort even though I used my fingers instead of beads. In any case, she and my teachers, the sisters of No Mercy, were absolutely correct about the comfort that can be gained with prayer.

At dawn, the physician who had been caring for me in the ICU came to my bedside. I recognized his voice and remembered that he had previously asked me questions such as my name, where I was, what day it was, etc. to determine my state of consciousness. He'd apparently spent some time in an American hospital as a trainee, so his English was quite good. He came up to me and said, "I see you are awake," to which I replied, "Günaydın." It's amazing how far a few words can go.

He laughed and asked me if I knew my name; I told him I did and also that I was in Turkey. I also told him that I had no idea what day it was, but I sure was happy that I was awake no matter what day it was. At this, he knelt down by my bedside so he could put his forehead on my left hand that was still tied down, and when he arose he had tears in his eyes and said, "I am so happy that you are OK. We were so worried about you."

I asked him where Jim was, and he looked puzzled and asked if I'd been given Jim's note, which was supposed to have been given to me as soon as I awoke. He rushed off and returned in a few minutes with the note (which I still have) that informed me that Jim had gone back to the hotel to get a decent night's sleep and a shower and that he had my ring for safekeeping. He'd also written that he loved me, as if I needed such a reminder.

I asked the doctor if he would please release my hands and legs. He was upset that I had been put in the restraints with no one at my side and had not been released as soon as I awoke. When I was free to sit up,

I felt like an uncaged bird, but unfortunately I could not fly. He left to care for other patients, and I was left alone to wait for Jim.

Just before we had left for Turkey, Jim had had his loafers resoled, with a resulting squeak when he walked, probably from some air being trapped under the leather. He had planned to have it fixed when we returned home, but when I heard that squeak in the hospital corridor and knew he was near, it felt like bells ringing for a joyous occasion. We never did have the shoes fixed, and they've squeaked happily ever after.

By the time Jim came to my bedside, I'd washed up a bit and a kind nurse (not "keep quit," who thankfully had gone home) had combed my hair. Jim looked at me, not knowing what to expect. Before he came too near, I smiled and asked if he'd do me a favor. He said, "Anything." I asked him to please get me a pepperoni pizza. His response was a magnificent smile, a hug and a kiss, but alas no pizza. In fact, it would be quite a while before I could eat or drink anything, because as it turned out I did have a bowel obstruction. The physician who tested me in the hotel was using a hand-held instrument to determine whether or not I had an obstruction. I assume that instrument was not very accurate. The presence of an obstruction meant keeping a nasogastric (NG) tube in place until after I had been medically evacuated to Johns Hopkins Hospital. If ever there was a form of medieval torture, it is the NG tube for as long as it is in place, not to mention the insertion process. Inserting a rubber tube through the nose and down through the esophagus to the stomach requires that the patient (me) swallow while being gaged by the tube. Then the tube is taped in place until it is removed. The gaging sensation, while diminished, remains for as long as the tube remains in place.

Jim had discussed with a Hopkins physician how to manage the obstruction. With the help of his advice, Jim had decided not to transport me while I was comatose but to manage that condition in Turkey and then transport me to Hopkins for surgery. Jim also received advice from Dr. Andy Anderson, the executive vice president, chief executive officer (EVP/CEO) of the AMA, who had been a jet pilot. He warned that transportation was going to be very dicey, because if I was flown at too high an altitude there was a significant danger that, despite having the NG tube in place, my gut would expand and possibly rupture from the pressure. Therefore, the first move was to transfer me out of the ICU and into a private room to await transfer to Hopkins via a proper low-flying plane.

I was quite comfortable in the private room, and Jim could stay with me all the time. While I was there, the supposed richest man in Istanbul, who either owned or directed the hospital, visited me and brought three dozen roses and a big box of chocolates. We later gave the staff the chocolates since I couldn't eat them, and the staff certainly deserved a special treat. As it turned out, the gentleman was a friend of President Bill Brody of Hopkins, who was also our friend and who had bestowed a Hopkins honorary degree to the Turkish gentleman the year before.

My bed was situated so that I could look out in the distance and see the Hagia Sophia, which had been a major Christian church, built in the fifth century, and then a mosque, and then was secularized in 1935 as a museum. Jim placed a postcard of the painting of the Madonna and child from an inside wall of the museum and the three dozen roses in that window. I now had something beautiful to look at while awaiting my rescue home.

While I was awaiting evacuation from the hospital to the United States and doing quite well all things considered (including the NG tube), Jim was invited by the same Turkish gentleman to attend a reception one evening. At first Jim wanted to stay with me, but I convinced him that I was fine and that I'd be very happy if he would attend the reception. He went and was a bit surprised that the reception took place at a handbag museum that was directed by the sister of the kind gentleman. Probably the only person less interested in handbags than Jim is me, so we had nice time discussing the evening for which we both were very grateful, but had found ironic. That trip for Jim had involved a sail up the beautiful Bosphorus Strait and meeting many interesting people. So he had the adventure of the sail we'd missed.

FLYING HOME WITH THE BLUE ANGELS

My transport to Hopkins via air, after being in the hospital for ten days, was to be accomplished on a small medical-evacuation jet plane, the cost of which was to be covered by my AMA employment insurance. Much to our relief, Jim happily learned that while trying to determine how to mortgage our house to pay for that transport, which had been one more complication for him. In addition, the evacuation team had wanted to take me to Germany, the nearest medical center in their plan. Jim had to convince them that my "case" was very complicated, and that I had to be taken care of at Hopkins. I can only imagine the hell he went through while I was in a coma, oblivious to the world.

When the transport team of a physician and a nurse arrived, they were wearing blue scrubs, and I labeled them the "blue angels," not to be confused with the navy's Blue Angels, who are famous for their airborne aerobatics. While, thankfully, no aerobatics were involved in this flight, it was special in that the plane would fly low to prevent my gut from bursting—that is, no higher than eight thousand feet—which provided amazing views of the terrain below. We flew from Istanbul to Berlin, then to Greenland, and finally landed in Baltimore. And to my medical home: Johns Hopkins. That many landings were necessary because flying so low requires frequent refueling. I declined to travel reclined on a stretcher but sat up for the entire trip. I was feeling energized about going home and preoccupied by observing the medical equipment that the medical team had on the plane to provide continuous monitoring of my condition. I was also taken by the magnificent views below the low-flying plane. The earth is, indeed, a beautiful place.

HOSPITALIZATION AT HOPKINS HOSPITAL

When we arrived at the Baltimore airport, an ambulance was waiting, and I was once again reminded that I was a patient. The plane ride had given me sufficient distractions to disregard (if not remove) the obnoxious NG tube that had been part of my existence for too many days.

Having an NG tube feels like you are continuously being gagged, not pleasant to say the least. I was greeted in the Hopkins emergency room by the liver specialist who had been my friend and physician for many years and who had provided Jim, by telephone, valuable information about the care I needed in Turkey. Also present were a number of others whom I knew. Indeed, I was home!

It took only several hours for all pertinent tests to be performed and for surgery to be scheduled for first thing in the next morning. I had been the pediatrician for the surgeon's three sons, and he told me that because he had added my surgery as an early first case in the morning, he only needed to find an anesthesiologist in order to proceed. I responded that it was a good idea, because I was sure biting on a bullet was not going to do it for me. The next morning when I was wheeled into the operating room suite, it looked like a doctor and nurse's convention, because there were so many friends present, including several anesthesiologists. I felt so lucky.

Needless to say, the surgery was a success, and my sister, Grace the nurse, and my friend Phyllis, who wanted to be with me while I was recuperating, arrived while I was still in the OR. The next few days were wonderful, because I was with some of my family and friends. When I could finally eat, I must have been very protein deprived, because over the next week I consumed several dozen eggs, using three egg whites with one yolk for virtually every meal. Whatever else I learned from this experience, the kindness and care provided to me by family, friends, and strangers was sufficient to prove that people are truly wonderful, and the few bad actors we hear about or meet are the exceptions to this rule.

When I was recovering physically, I tried to deal with the emotional effects of almost having lost my life and consequently family, friends, and colleagues. I remember that the first day I was able to walk in the hospital, lugging an IV stand on wheels along with me, I ventured out on the fourth floor porch and looked up at the Hopkins dome. The rush of great feelings stimulated by that awesome (at least to me) sight lifted me to a level where I could now deal with the emotional turmoil.

That same evening, I was watching the movie *Finding Forrester* on TV, and I heard the Hawaiian singer, IZ, sing "Somewhere Over the Rainbow." The words, IZ's voice, and his banjo rendition of the song hit me so hard that I cried for the first time since the terrible episode started, thereby releasing a great emotional load. If you've never heard him sing that song, you are missing something very special. IZ died several years later, and his ashes were spread over the Pacific near his Hawaiian home, where rainbows are ever present. Wherever he is, he is responsible for at least one person's emotional recovery. To this day, I can't hear him sing that song without tearing up, and that from someone who never cries except when I am present when a baby is born (but only after I'm sure the infant is A-OK).

Another wonderful thing that happened was that our great friend, Dr. Terri Menke Hargrave, who sang at our wedding, traveled to our home from Syracuse, NY to sing for me. Terri's voice is angelic and always makes me feel so wonderful.

Considering the emotional roller coaster ride I was on, and all the love shown to me by so many people, I consider myself one of the luckiest people in the world. If I someday I win the lottery (which will never happen because I've never bought a ticket and have no intention to change that), I'll buy a TV station where good and bad news will be covered equally. There surely is more than enough good news to cover at least half of what's broadcast, and it might remind us of how many good people there are in this world and how many acts of kindness occur every day. Throughout this episode, equity was clearly on everyone's mind and in their actions, including the Chechen rebels'.

CHAPTER 1

My Family, a.k.a. La Famiglia

ON JANUARY 3, 2000, THE day after my sixtieth birthday, my husband, Jim, drove me to the airport for a one-way flight to Chicago. I was already feeing lonely, knowing that I would not go home to him from work that day and probably not for many days to come. I was on my way to assume the editorship of *JAMA*, the *Journal of the American Medical Association*. Never in my wildest dreams did I plan for this, so how did it happen? As I settled in my assigned seat and looked out over the terrain as the plane ascended, my thoughts went back to how had I arrived at this point in my life and in my medical vocation. It didn't take much thought to realize that my family and the environment of our home formed the basis for how and why I sought equity and made key life decisions. Considering that foundation built at home helped me to better understand why various experiences had become turning points in my life, leading to where I am now.

My thoughts went back to the place of my birth in 1940, in a not-very-auspicious place called Old Forge, Pennsylvania. The history of this little town dates back to 1789 and the founder, Dr. William Smith, an army surgeon. I did not know that, growing up there, but it was nice to find out later that there was a medical history in my hometown. Old Forge is actually not a town, but a borough (that's *borough* not *burro*, although there are those who believe the place is half-assed—but they are badly informed) was typical of the small villages, towns, and boroughs of northeastern Pennsylvania, where well over half the inhabitants were primarily of one ethnic group. In Old Forge, most inhabitants were, and still are, of Italian descent, and there's a pizza restaurant on practically every corner—thus the alternate name of "pizza town." You might have heard of it because of pizza fame and because Joe Biden and Hillary Clinton had relatives in the area. However, any fame for the place ends there.

I know of no better place to have been born, or a better family to have been born into, than mine. As I noted in this book's preface, we were supposedly poor—a fact I learned in a sociology course in college. I didn't consider the college-based definition to be credible in my case, although I've had much more than my share of excellent and worthy college education. If we were poor, the whole world should also be so poor. The definition of poor is obviously based on financial status, which is a terrible way to determine richness if you ask me. My family was and remains very rich in abundant love and happiness, mixed with just the right amount of ditziness.

The word *equity*, per se, was never spoken in our home. However, the words and concepts of fairness, impartial treatment of everyone, and pulling for the underdog were ever present. My father, first known as daddy and later as Poppie, was an amazing man. In my family, we are all called by the name used by the youngest members, a sign of how precious children are considered. My magnificent mother's name went from mommy to the much-revered Nannie. Neither of my parents had more than an eighth-grade education, but I was told by many of his classmates that Poppie was the smartest person in his class, and that he should have gone on to high school and college. But as the oldest child (and son), he had to work to help support his family. However, the lack of formal education didn't prevent him from gaining and transmitting his knowledge and expertise in many other ways.

Among other things, Poppie taught me how to work with numbers, for example by recalculating each beloved Yankee baseball player's batting average each time he came to bat. At first I did this using a pencil and paper, and later by calculating the new batting average in my head.

This occurred during the time Poppie and I spent on glorious summer evenings, sitting together on our porch listening to the games on the radio. He also taught me how to play poker not just by memorizing the cards but, astutely, by reading people's actions and facial expressions—for example, he would whisper in my ear, as I sat next to him while he played poker for pennies, "Watch Uncle Johnny's eye twitch; that means he's bluffing," and so on. I was enthralled.

That ability to read people has stayed with me throughout my life and has allowed me to help others or to prevent harm, depending on my perceptions about a person's actual feelings in various situations. It has proved to be invaluable, especially as a woman physician and even more as an administrator seeking equity. I continue to play poker almost every day as I size up situations.

During the first eight years of my life, our family, consisting of my father, mother two sisters, and me, lived in a three-room section of my paternal grandparents' duplex. Our home consisted of a large kitchen with a pantry, two bedrooms, and a half bath. Every Sunday night my parents would put a large galvanized-tin tub in the kitchen and fill it with hot water several times over so we could bathe. The rest of the week, we had sponge baths in the half bathroom. How spoiled we are now with multiple full bathrooms with tubs (even Jacuzzis) and showers.

During those years, I managed to fracture my right arm twice. The first time was when, at age five, I fell off the back of a tricycle while playing ambulance with my friends. The second time was when I fell out of a tree a week or so later and re-fractured the bones. I hated the cast that had been placed on my arm the first time, and tried to remove it by banging it against the porch bannister. So the doctor removed it probably a bit too soon. I had nightmares for weeks after the first fracture, because I was put under anesthesia with ether (not a very good anesthetic that thankfully is seldom used now), so the bones could be set. Ironically, I was afraid of doctors but also wanted to be one. That experience was probably a good thing, because I learned a lot about how not to do some things with patients, especially children.

Needless to point out, I was quite mischievous, and when I'd get in trouble with my mother, I'd run to Nonno (Poppie's father). He would hold me and say, "Catherina, *se voglio contenta, non pishata contra la ventra*." The translation is, "If you want to be content (happy), don't piss against the wind." When I was a little older, I told him that was only for boys. He laughed, and it became our joke, and in many ways my life's creed.

When I was eight years old, we moved to our very own house several blocks from where we had lived in the two-bedroom half of my paternal grandparents' duplex. I remember that early one morning, Poppie and two of my older male cousins moved all our furniture and belongings to the sidewalk. Then one of my cousins, a professional truck driver, rented a truck that the men and my mother quickly loaded with our stuff. He then drove the truck to our new house, where the men immediately unloaded everything from the truck onto the lawn, so he could return the truck immediately. As it turned out, Poppie had only enough money to pay for one hour of rent for the truck, and everyone cheered when my cousin returned in his car without having had to pay for any extra rental time. The men then moved everything into our house and my mother directed where to put everything.

Speeding tickets were unheard of in our town. People drove carefully because everyone knew everyone else, and no one wanted to harm neighbors. You can't beat having close families, and growing up in small towns. That's where I first learned that teamwork works wonders everywhere.

Our new home had a large kitchen with a pantry, a dining room, and a living room on the first floor. The second floor had three bedrooms and a full bathroom, so no more Sunday baths in a galvanized tub. My maternal grandmother, who had lived one block from us, now moved in with us so we could keep even closer watch over her. My grandmother was then legally blind and almost completely deaf. One of the three bedrooms was hers, my parents had the second, and my two sisters and I shared the third bedroom. It was wonderful to share with my sisters, at least most of the time.

My friends in the new neighborhood were just about equally divided between boys and girls. We played a lot of games together, and we used the boys' rules when we played baseball or basketball. (Girls did not play football, or Nannie, and probably most of the other girls' mothers, would have had a fit.) I later grew to appreciate that one-sidedness, because you had to play harder when many, and frequently most, of the participants were boys. Having to play by the boys' rules was good training for an equitable career in medicine.

While my sisters worked with Nannie, I spent most of my time helping Poppie cut down trees, reroof our garage, put in sidewalks, plant a garden, cut the grass (no motor mowers back then), etc. Some of my best memories are when he took me fishing and hunting for rabbits with him. He hunted for deer (venison) only with his buddies. Because there were so many other hunters in the woods, it was very dangerous, and while they looked out for one another, no child was allowed.

In the summer Poppie and I would wake up before dawn and drive to a lake as the sun was rising. We would then spend an hour or so picking blueberries, then fish and swim, and before we left we'd eat our packed lunch of tuna-salad sandwiches and pick more berries. We would always return home with the makings for a great fish dinner, several blueberry pies, and enough berries left to can a few quarts for winter pies. I learned much more from those chores and outings with Poppie than from doing the dishes and helping to clean the house, but the time I spent with both parents was special.

I actually did take my turn with the dishes and keeping our room clean. My special weekly cleaning time with Nannie was to wax the kitchen floor by following her as she scrubbed it; both of us did this by hand on our knees. She liked to listen to soap operas on the radio while we scrubbed the floor, and I liked to joke with her about the characters who never seemed to make progress or much sense to me.

With three daughters, Nannie was the disciplinarian armed with "the look" and a wooden spoon. Poppie hit only one of us (me) one time; usually all he had to do was unbuckle his belt, and we'd hop to whatever was requested. However, the one time he hit me was during the summer when I was thirteen years old and about to enter high school's ninth grade. I had met some new girlfriends, who had a much different attitude than to what I was accustomed. I decided to adapt their attitude of smart-mouthing everyone, including my parents.

One evening, Poppie and I got into an argument over a jar of mayonnaise, which he hated the very sight of and was never used in his presence. I smart-mouthed him, not for the first time, and he took off his belt, bent me over the arm of the living room couch and said, "Don't"—*whack*—"you ever again"—*whack*—"talk back to your mother"—*whack*—"or me"—*whack*—"like that again"—*whack*. As a pediatrician I am compelled to note here that this situation occurred in the early 1950s, and attitudes and practices regarding disciplining children have changed dramatically. While the whacks stung like hell, I knew that Poppie did not want to physically hurt me, but only get my attention and to get the message across. Mission accomplished: full attention and message received.

After the spanking, I ran to my room with my pride hurting much more than my backside. It was especially bad because the next morning Poppie and I had planned to go on one of our fishing and berry-picking trips. I thought that now he wouldn't want to do that. However, the next morning at five, per usual, he woke me and whispered, "Ready to go?" He had prepared the tuna sandwiches per our routine, with olive oil and vinegar—hold the mayo! We spent a glorious day together never mentioning the previous evening, and we never did thereafter.

In addition to both my parents teaching me to have respect for authority (I later modified that to "respect those in authority who *earn* that respect"), Poppie was the one who taught me to believe that I could accomplish anything if I really wanted it and was willing to work very hard to accomplish it. I knew I wanted to be a doctor since I was four or five years old. I saw how respected and admired our family doctor and our priest were, because they always seemed to care about and help us. Nannie had a special towel and a special pie for each of them when they came to visit our home, mostly to see my maternal grandmother once she lived with us. I knew I couldn't be a priest because I was a girl (that still bugs me), so I decided that being a doctor was the way to help people. Besides that, what doctors did seemed so much more interesting than what priests did. That observation became only one part of my desire for a career in medicine, because then I discovered the fascination of science. Combining that interest with my desire to help others, as I saw practiced every day by my family, was the final basis for my decision.

Every Christmas from the time I was four years old, I'd asked Santa (who I still believe exists in the very special way by which people seem to be more generous in spirit and action during Christmas) for a doctor's kit, but every year I'd receive a nurse's kit. When I was about seven years old, out of frustration I decided not to even open the nurse's kit on Christmas morning. After several days, Poppie asked me why I never played with the kit. I told him it was not a doctor's bag because it was pink (to this day I hate that color) and contained a nurse's cap with a red cross on it. A few days later, he brought me the bag, which he had painted black. He also gave me one of his old white shirts, upon which he had taped the red cross from the nurse's cap, on one of the sleeves. He then put the shirt on me, and declared, "Now you're a doctor." From that day on, I knew I would someday actually be a doctor. Incidentally, Poppie thought almost anything could be fixed with tape.

Soon after that episode, he took me for a walk to the drug store on Main Street and showed me some placards prominently displayed in the window, each one depicting an aspect of the history of Johns Hopkins Medicine. I have no idea where the drug store obtained those placards, and I have tried unsuccessfully to find others like them. Unfortunately, the owner of the drug store died many years ago, and the store has long been closed. I have seen nothing like them since, at least as they exist in my mind. I loved that display so much I made any excuse to walk past the window to look at it and dream of becoming a doctor. For many years thereafter, I assumed that Johns Hopkins was the only medical school in the United States. I now smile thinking about the naïveté of that belief, yet how much it influenced my career.

Nannie, on the other hand, supported my sisters and me by always seeming to find ways to help us achieve anything we really wanted. For example, my older sister, Seena (it's Thomasine, a name she has never used), and brother in law, Nate (actually, he was named Ignazio), later owned a bar and rooming house in Scranton. Lest you think they were wealthy, it took a great deal of time and effort for them just to pay the bills. When Nate tired of bartending and wanted to find another way to support his family, Nannie managed the bar every morning, allowing Nate to attend school to become a draftsman.

Soon after his graduation, Nate found a very good job and sold the bar. After their second son was born, it became clear that the neighborhood where their house was located was not a suitable place to raise children. So my parents exchanged houses with them, and the second floor of my parents' new house served as a boarding house. Nannie then assumed responsibility for maintaining the cleanliness of the three rooms in the boarding part of the house, which were rented to retired men. She also always made an extra pie, cake, or loaf of bread to share with these men. Obviously, they loved and respected her, like so many others whom she treated in the same fashion. She did not discriminate and simply nurtured everyone; talk about equity!

When one of the gentlemen who rented a room died in the rooming house, we discovered that he had left his body to me in his will, so it could be used to educate doctors. I was in medical school at the time, and obviously nannie had told him about me. I was shocked when she proudly called and told me about it (God love her!). Nannie had clearly touched this man's soul by her kindness. Fortunately, a faculty member at my medical school was able to arrange for the gentleman's body to be delivered to a Philadelphia medical school, which was much closer to Scranton, where my parents were living. So the gentleman's wish to contribute to the education of doctors was fulfilled.

One of the very best and most special talents I learned from Nannie was how to cook. She could make the most delicious meals with whatever happened to be available in the refrigerator, cupboard, or garden. One problem was that she never measured anything, so when she grew older and we wanted to write down her recipes, my sisters stayed with her as she cooked or baked, and when she took a "pinch" or "handful" of some ingredient, they would measure it. All three of us are very good cooks, but like Nannie, I never follow a recipe.

Nannie was a staunch Roman Catholic and made sure my sisters and I received all the sacraments of childhood, and we went to mass every Sunday. She insisted that we say the rosary almost every day, excepting the days she worked in the early evening, and could not fit that in between dinner and her leaving for work. Poppie's attitude toward religion was far different, but he made sure we followed Nannie's wishes. I remember his frequently eating meat (which is frowned upon by the Catholic church and actually is considered to be a venial sin (!) by the church), in the form of a pepperoni or salami sandwich, as a snack on Friday nights, when Nannie was at work. He made eggs for my sisters and me. When we expressed our chagrin at his eating meat, he'd make the sign of the cross over the sandwich and say in a prayerful voice, "You are not meat." When we'd giggle, he'd laugh and say if other men (priests) could do that, why couldn't he? Lest you misunderstand, Poppie was one of the most honest and kind persons on earth, but his spirituality did not include following religious rules that made no sense to him.

As proud as Nannie was of my becoming a physician and as hard as she worked to make it happen, I think of all the titles I have, the one that meant most to her was "Mrs.," signifying that she didn't have to worry about me anymore. Rather, she preferred to worry not only about my sisters and me, but also our husbands and our children. I'll never forget how excited she was when Jim (who was not yet my husband) came to visit us one Christmas morning. Although I'd had many male friends who had visited our home, she somehow knew then that he was very special to me. However, she was very concerned that he was "so skinny" and very quiet. I told her that with all the noise in our home, he couldn't get a word in edgewise, so of course he didn't say much. Poppie, a very quiet man (what can you expect being the only man in a household of five women?), thought he was terrific, although they didn't exchange more than a dozen words. Like recognizes like.

No matter how she felt about my prolonged unmarried state (I was thirty-nine when I married), and her thoughts about my spending so much time becoming educated and trained, she accepted my choices. She worked as a waitress long after she needed to, in order to help provide me with whatever she could throughout my many years of college and medical school. She and Poppie visited me in college (which was about fifteen miles away) every Sunday, bringing me laundered clothes (so I could spend more time in the lab instead of laundering clothes) and enough food to feed the entire dormitory where I lived. I kidded my dorm-mates by calling our car the DPW, that's the "Dago Picnic Wagon." Of course, only I could use that derogatory term for Italians. Nannie was a terrific cook, and when I was in medical school, she sent a big box of fresh baked and cooked food on a bus to Pittsburgh every Friday morning. God forbid my classmates or I should starve to death! She always sent an accompanying note that stated she was sending food to "keep up our morals." We knew she meant "morales," but I never corrected her for obvious reasons.

Nannie could solve any people-based problem or organize anything, and many individuals came to her with all sorts of problems, knowing that they usually would leave with a plan to solve the problem and always feeling much better. She organized the Parent-Teachers Association in our town and could wait on dozens of people in the restaurant where she worked, keeping all food orders straight and making each customer feel that he or she was the only one at the table to be cared for. In fact, she nurtured everyone that way. As a tribute to her when she passed away, there was a line of people, including the bishop, outside the funeral home that went two blocks, all waiting to pay her the respect she earned over her eighty-seven years of her life. Of course, the bishop was immediately invited to enter the funeral home without waiting in line.

I am the middle of three daughters. Actually there originally were four of us; another daughter was born after my older sister; but she died of pneumonia when she was a year old. The 1930s did not yet have the miracle of antibiotic cures of bacterial infections now readily available to all. At that time, only the rich could afford whatever medicine was available for pneumonia, so our family physician did not mention that possible treatment to my parents, knowing they could never afford it. As it turned out, that was probably a very good decision for many reasons, including possible brain damage resulting from the high fevers manifested by the illness. That is what happened to the son of another family from Old Forge, who was the same age as my sister and also had pneumonia at the same time, and who was treated with the expensive medicine available.

Seena was (and still is) the epitome of innocence. After high school she spent one year in business school and worked for a few years before getting married. She has devoted her entire adult life to her family and friends. She has two sons, one daughter, and seven grandchildren, all of whom are the delight and center of her life. She spends almost every day baking for birthdays, weddings, and anniversaries; shopping (although she never seems to buy anything for herself); or doing something artistic like wrapping gifts or decorating trees.

Despite her obviously enjoying our trips to foreign countries, her idea of a great vacation is going to New York City for a day or two and seeing a musical or comedy. She conveniently sleeps through violent scenes in movies or on TV. She has the personality of poppie's family, who are very bright but not outgoing. (For example, one of poppie's sisters deliberately flubbed an exam in high school when she learned that the valedictorian had to speak at graduation. She happily finished a close second in her class, relieved that she would not be required to speak.)

My younger sister, Grace, who trained as a nurse and is currently the family's chief organizer, has a completely different personality than Seena. She is known as Nana, a close second to Nannie in name and certainly in personality. Except for her education as a nurse, she is Nannie's clone, which means that she troubleshoots for everyone. Having three daughters, one son, and fifteen grandchildren by birth and two more children and five more grandchildren by unofficial adoption (the children and grandchildren of a very close friend, who is considered part of our extended family) makes for a whole lot of troubleshooting.

Her family is her life, and she raised her children as a single mother after her husband left. She worked very hard to care for and educate her children while still finding time to help others in need. Like with Nannie, others depend on her ability to assist them with wise advice and friendship. She also has a weird sense of humor, which probably keeps her sane.

Jim's mother and his brother, John, and sister, Nancy, were much different than my family. I felt closeness to his mother, Mary, immediately. She was a warm, educated woman, and we shared a love of football. She was an avid University of Alabama fan having grown up in Birmingham, where Jim was also born. John visits us frequently, and until her early death, we visited Nancy and her husband, Alan, several times a year to celebrate birthdays.

In 1999 after Poppie and Nannie both had strokes, Jim and I bought a house on the Delaware River in the Pocono Mountains of Pennsylvania so that my sisters, Nate, and Vlado, a wonderful gentleman from Slovakia who cared for Poppie, could care for them in one home. Nannie died unexpectedly a year later while Jim and I were at a meeting in Italy. Of course we flew home immediately. Poppie died two years later, and this time I was able to spend the last seven days of his life with him. He refused to eat or drink anything and only allowed me to put a few drops of a pain medication under his tongue. My sisters, Vlado, and I stayed with him only leaving his room to use the bathroom, bathe, or eat.

Amazingly, he maintained his wry sense of humor and peaceful nature right through to the end. The last thing he said to me was in response to my question, "Poppie, do you know who I am?" His response was to look at me, smile, and say, "Do you know who I am?" He and Nannie taught me how to live and Poppie taught me how to die.

My sisters and I remain very close and speak to one another every day or send messages when one of us (essentially always me) is out of the country. Because Seena refuses to use a computer, Grace and I communicate on those occasions, and she then tells Seena what's happening with Jim and me. All three of us, and various others including Jim, have traveled together to Israel (or as my mother called it, "The Holy Land"), England, Alaska, Italy, Greece, and Turkey, and although I have traveled to six continents, none of those trips were the same as those with my sisters. I tell people that I have traveled to seven of the eight continents, and when they catch me on their only being seven continents, I explain that I include incontinence, but that only occurred when I was in a coma in Istanbul, as I related in the introduction to this book.

The three of us sisters share everything possible, including my sisters sharing their children and grandchildren with Jim and me. Jim and I have no birth children having lost one in a miscarriage. I will explain that sad episode later in the book. The thing that keeps us so close is that, no matter what, we are always there for one another and contribute whatever we can for our family.

Notice I wrote *family*, not *families*; we are and have always been one big family. That's what makes it so special.

CHAPTER 2

Florence Nightingale Meets Sairey Gamp: Scranton State Hospital School of Nursing

FOR THOSE WHO ARE NOT familiar with Sairey Gamp, she is a character in Charles Dickens's Victorian novel *Martin Chuzzlewit* (1843–44). She is a gin-tipping, sloppy, patient-abusing nurse, a stereotype of the untrained, incompetent nurses of the early Victorian era, before Florence Nightingale, the founder of modern nursing, established the first nursing school in the world at St Thomas' Hospital in London in 1860.

SSHSON does not stand for SHH, SON (i.e., "Be quiet, young man,")—although this is not bad advice most of the time. It stands for Scranton State Hospital School of Nursing. Later the name was changed and General was added before Hospital, in order to distinguish it from most state hospitals, which care for psychiatric patients. However, at times the term State Hospital, sans General, seemed quite appropriate, not for the patients but for the staff, myself included.

My parents and I were told by my high school advisor that girls who wanted to become doctors had to be nurses first, which while not true is probably good advice for all doctors. However, in retrospect, I think the advisors rendered that erroneous advice knowing that my parents could never afford college, much less medical school, and not because the advisors didn't know better. In any case, little did they know my family or me.

Because I had entered nurses' training with the false understanding that it was the required first step for girls to become doctors, I was excited and eager to learn everything it had to offer. The hospital had about two hundred beds and served the poor and the rich of Scranton and vicinity. The classroom work was not difficult, and I read my way through the entire small library in the first six months, which was known as the "probation period" of training.

During that probation period, we were required to wear yellow uniforms in the classroom and on the general wards. However, we were not allowed on the private floor. I guess the administrators did not want a bunch of "canaries" (i.e., the yellow uniforms) roaming those hallowed halls of the well-to-do. Heaven forbid the patients, who could afford the price of private rooms, should be exposed to the yellow (perhaps green would have been a more fitting color) "probies," as we were called. I thought that term was much more fitting for proctologists, but I didn't dare say that to anyone in power, many of whom seemed to be devoid of humor.

In retrospect, some of the behaviors of the administrative nursing staff and of the students seems ridiculous, but I suppose it was acceptable, if not appropriate, for the late 1950s. For example, the director of nurses and her senior staff ate at a special table in the corner of the dining room that all students also ate our meals in. The director would ring a small bell, and a woman from the kitchen staff immediately would come to that table to wait on those seated there. The rest of us more appropriately went through a cafeteria line. The attitude of superiority demonstrated by these senior nursing directors, if not the action itself, was what made me very uncomfortable. On the other hand, the nurses who taught us in the classroom and in the hospital units were quite different. While they also commanded respect, it was by their attitudes and abilities, not their titles. They treated everyone, and especially the patients, with equity.

The hospital administrator was a jovial gentleman who had a great sense of humor. In my second year I hung an IV bottle and inserted the attached line into the trunk of the donated Christmas tree in the emergency ward. He thought it was funny; so did many others, and it was allowed to remain. If you had seen that scrawny tree, you would understand the humor.

My classmates were wonderful and almost as adept at mischief as I was. We drove the housemothers (yes, housemothers—this was 1957, after all) crazy with our antics in the dormitory, where we were required to live. What else could be expected from mostly eighteen- to nineteen-year-olds (I was seventeen), who had to be in our rooms with lights out at 9:00 p.m.? Of course we prowled the halls after hours. When the housemother made her rounds, one of us would be on guard near the bathrooms and would quickly flush three toilets in a row as a warning that "the enemy" was about. That maneuver was known as "the sign of the flush."

I remember having a glow-in-the-dark statue of the BVM (Blessed Virgin Mary) given to me by some "devout" person. One night after lights out, I sneaked into the room of an especially renown do-gooder who was asleep in a very dark room. While lying on the floor beside her bed, I began to hum the "Ave Maria" while slowly moving the statue closer to her. When she suddenly awoke, the scream that ensued was heard all over the dormitory, and we all scampered to our rooms and slipped under the covers, pretending to be asleep as the housemother came rushing up the stairs to see what was going on.

The dormitory rooms for first-year students were on the second floor, and the upperclassmen's rooms were on the third floor. The housemothers sat at a desk on the first floor near the entrance door, ostensibly to protect us from any intruders, especially of the male gender. That was surely the idea of someone who had no knowledge about the physical abilities of the sixty-five-plus older women, who served as housemothers. Of course the guards were only a phone call, and a very long distance, away.

In any case, on the night in question with the BVM statue, we all claimed not to have heard anything. Because the poor classmate was so relieved that she was in no danger from anyone but us, she joined the denial. The poor housemother was so confused, she returned to her desk mumbling something that I doubt was a prayer.

Once we were past the probation period, we donned our stiffly starched white uniforms and caps at a special ceremony. Each hospital school of nursing had its own special cap, and in the days when nurses still wore caps it was possible to know from which institution they had graduated. By the time of the capping ceremony, we had learned many things from books and papers. For example, we could make trash containers from paper bags that hung from the patients' bedside tables and make a bed so tight that a quarter could bounce off the cover sheet; our nursing instructors had all served in the army during World War II. To this day, I refuse to make our bed at home; that's one of the few household chores that is the responsibility of my husband, Jim. I told him that I had made enough beds while a nurse to last at least two lifetimes. I've not tried to bounce a coin off the sheets of the beds he makes, and really couldn't care less as long as *I* don't bounce off.

I remain very close friends with a number of my classmates. Many of us dated together and spent our time off at one another's houses. While I was in nurses' training, I met a special young man with whom I maintained a friendship for many years. But I knew I wanted to be a doctor, and that along with other reasons precluded my marrying him, no matter how much he tried to convince me otherwise, which continued for years after I finished nursing school. Sadly, he died several years later while I was working in Wisconsin. Because of a very bad snowstorm, I couldn't attend his funeral. However, many years later, Jim and I visited his gravesite to finally complete the relationship, if ever a special human relationship could be completed.

During one of the classroom seminars of my first year, I was presenting a paper and suddenly fainted. I was then admitted to the hospital and underwent surgery for what was thought to be appendicitis but which turned out to have been a ruptured ovarian cyst. To be a patient was interesting but one I wished to never experience again. Little did I know what the future held for me regarding my personal bouts with illness and resulting hospitalizations.

The real training and beginning of knowing that we could indeed help the sick occurred when we started working on the wards. We worked from seven in the morning until noon, and then from three thirty until seven thirty in the evenings, thereby assuring we were on the wards during the peak workload times. Because it cost us financially nothing for the training, I considered this a real bargain. Since there was only one chief resident physician, who covered the entire hospital, nurses pretty much ran the hospital. The physicians in private practice, who admitted their patients to the hospital, were normally only present in the mornings to round on their private patients. I can't begin to explain how wonderful it was to learn during that time from association with some of the finest nurses I've ever encountered. Their dedication, work ethic, sense of equity, and integrity were truly something I wanted to emulate.

I also learned a great deal from the physicians who were in private practice and made daily rounds on the patients they'd admitted and from those who performed surgery on their patients. Because I was more interested in learning than in resting, in my second and third years of training, I spent many of my afternoon off hours helping in the emergency room and in the operating rooms. The physicians were very kind and were happy to have two more hands, so no one stopped me from spending extra time in the hospital.

The one thing that was routine for nurses that I refused to mimic once I had graduated from nursing school was to stand up whenever a doctor entered the ward or room or to give up my seat for the "lord master" doctor. I certainly felt and showed my respect for the doctors and later, in medical school, to my physician teachers and colleagues, but I did so by other means.

When I finally graduated from nurses' training, I was only twenty years old. Because Poppie refused to sign the necessary papers, I would have to wait until I was twenty-one to proceed with my next planned step, which was to become a Maryknoll missionary nun. So in the meantime I planned to join one of my classmates and applied for and was accepted for a job at Columbia Presbyterian Hospital in New York City. Columbia Hospital was a short train ride to Ossining, the home of Maryknoll Sisters.

The caliber of my nurses' training was evident during that first job as a nurse at Columbia. Despite being surrounded by nurses with academic degrees but my having only a hospital certificate diploma, I was allowed to work in areas requiring great nursing skills, which I certainly had. I envied the nurses' book knowledge, but what they lacked was the ability to act appropriately and quickly in various clinical situations. Of course that would come with their clinical experiences, as would my book knowledge in the future.

I began working on a general medical unit for male patients but soon, at my request, was transferred to the postsurgical cardiac intensive unit. The patients there were very sick and required a great deal of attention. The goal was for them to recover from surgery sufficiently to be transferred to private rooms.

Pain was a big problem for the patients. This was before the days of self-controlled devices, where the patient could press a button to have pain medicine delivered intravenously (only up to a level that assured no overdosing, of course). It also predated the many types of pain medication, now available, that have mostly replaced the self-administration machines. What was available was pain medication that could be administered every few hours according to orders written by a physician.

Many times, the patients would ask for more medicine because of the pain that was obviously present. I used a number of ways to try and divert their attention, including playing their favorite music on a portable radio I had; the New York radio stations had a wide variety of music from which to choose. However, the diversion that seemed to work best was holding the patients' hand and talking about their families, especially their children. Fortunately, usually only two or three patients were present in the unit at the same time, and I could manage to take care of their medical needs and have the time for the type of extra comforting necessary to alleviate pain.

I had an experience later, while I was a medical student, that showed just how pertinent my nursing training and experience were in making me a better physician. I'll write about that later, in better context.

At Columbia I longed to join the head nurses and doctors as they made rounds on the patients, and I promised myself that I would do that someday. Many years later, when I returned for my first academic position as an assistant professor in the Columbia University College of Physicians and Surgeons, I spent the day before my official start on the very wards in the hospital where I had worked as a nurse. On that occasion, I joined the doctors and nurses on their rounds. What a glorious day that was. But for now my mind was set on working in a large hospital close to the Maryknoll Sisters mother house in Ossining, New York.

CHAPTER 3

Marys and Marias Everywhere: The Maryknoll Sisters

COLUMBIA PRESBYTERIAN HOSPITAL PROVIDED ME with an excellent work experience in a large, academic hospital and was situated an easy thirty-mile train ride from Ossining, New York, home of the Maryknoll Sisters. After all, my dream since childhood had been to become a doctor, specifically to work in Africa with the Maryknoll Missions.

I was now twenty-one years old and no longer required Poppie's signature to become a Maryknoll Sister. As I mentioned before, Poppie had refused to sign the papers necessary for me to enter Maryknoll. He said that I had stopped listening to him when I was two years old, even though he was wise, so he knew I'd never stay in an organization run by a group of men who made no sense at all to him. Poppie was one of the most Christian persons I've ever known, but he had problems with some of the rules of the Roman Catholic Church. Many years later, I recognized his wisdom about the rules set by some men who wore long black dresses...but I get ahead of myself.

So soon after beginning work at Columbia, I found myself on the train to Maryknoll in Ossining, New York. I was filled with anticipation of fulfilling my life's dream of becoming a Maryknoll nun and doctor. Like so many Catholic girls, I had read the famous *Bernie Becomes a Nun* book about the young Sister Bernadette Lynch, MM (Maryknoll Missions), published in 1956 by Sister Maria del Ray Danforth, MM, and George Barnes. The book had followed a very popular article presenting religious life as an attractive option for young women, one that

35

had been published in 1954 in *Cosmopolitan* by the famous photographer George Barnes. The article was complete with photographs of Sister Bernie. This is somewhat ironic because Barnes had also photographed stars like Marilyn Monroe and Elizabeth Taylor.

I even knew that I wanted to work specifically with Sister Mercy, MM, in Rebecca Hospital, in what was then called Tanganyika (now Tanzania), Africa. I had read about her in a *Maryknoll Magazine* when I was in high school.

When I arrived for my prearranged interview with the novice mistress, I learned that she was ill but that another sister would interview me. I was somewhat taken aback by the nun who entered the room to interview me, because she was very old and reminded me of all the joke stories I'd heard about the so-called "Sisters of No-Mercy", the supposed opposite of the wonderful order of nuns, the Sisters of Mercy. I decided that God worked in strange ways, and there was probably a good reason why this woman would interview me. Indeed, God, the Great Comedian, was at work.

I told the sister (I eliminated her name from my memory almost immediately after meeting with her) what I wanted to do. After a brief interview, she told me that because the Maryknoll Missions needed nurses, and I already had that training, I could potentially make a valuable contribution as a nurse, but not as a doctor. However, she was concerned that I had had no "formal" Catholic education. That there was no parochial school in our town, that I certainly had attended all classes to receive communion and to be confirmed, and that the nursing training at the local Catholic hospital was inferior to that at the hospital where I'd trained were not considered in her assessment.

She expressed concern that my lack of formal religious education would hold back my class of sisters, because the others would have better foundations in Roman Catholicism. Indeed! So she suggested that I spend the next year taking courses in religion at a Catholic college or university and then return to be interviewed for possible entrance to Maryknoll.

If ever there was an interview to deflate, this one was masterful. However, I knew that this sister had probably labored long and hard in the missions, and this encounter was simply a matter of her being in the wrong place at the wrong time. Or perhaps she was in the right place and time, and I owe her a great deal. In any case, God bless her, because she was responsible to a great degree for a turning point in my life.

On the train back to New York City I felt horrible. Rejection and dejection are powerful stimulators for deep thought. By the time the train pulled into the New York City terminal, I thought it was ironic that "terminal" was the correct word, for what had happened to my dreams about becoming a Maryknoll Sister. I realized that, in truth, I wanted to be a doctor more than a nun, and that as a physician, I could help many people in my own country and pretty much anywhere else in the world if I so chose.

The very next weekend I returned home and visited my high-school chemistry teacher, Edward W. (I was convinced his middle name was "Work") Clause, who knew of my long-time desire to be a doctor. He was excited with my news that I was ready for premed courses in college. He immediately took me to meet the admissions officer at Wilkes College, who arranged for me to matriculate there that fall, based solely on Mr. Clause's word of my worthiness. Of course I subsequently took tests, to make sure I wouldn't hold back the class (I say that with humor and no disrespect to the interviewing sister at Maryknoll). However, I'm getting ahead of myself. Stream of consciousness is not a habit solely of James Joyce.

So now I had about nine months to work and earn enough money to pay for the first year of college. Poppie was so excited with my decision. He told me that he and Nannie had been saving whatever they could to help pay for my college expenses, because he was sure I would be a doctor someday and would need the money. Where they found those dollars remains a great mystery to me, but I know they did without many things. I signed on to work double shifts from 3:00 p.m. to 7:00 a.m. five days a week at Columbia, because there was an extra supplement for working evening and night shifts. So with that money, what my parents had saved, and the scholarship Wilkes provided, I would soon be on my way.

EVENING AND NIGHT SHIFTS

However, I still had to wait and continue working at Columbia Presbyterian Hospital for nine months. I was now working sixteen straight hours a day, five days a week. I spent the evening shift on a general medical unit and the night shift on the postoperative unit. The postoperative unit essentially served as a sort of intensive-care unit, where postoperative and a few nonsurgical, critically ill patients were admitted. I was the only nurse working there at night and was assisted by a nurse's aide. Of course, I could call for backup help if things became too hectic for me to handle. I loved that work, because while I didn't have a college degree in nursing, my training in caring for patients had been outstanding.

The house staff anesthesiologist who was on-call for that unit at night slept in a corner bed. He or she was to be called if I had any questions about the patients. I soon learned their methods of handling the problems that arose, so instead of waking them for what I considered to be routine issues, I handled them myself. Early the next morning, I would report what I'd done when I woke him with a hot cup of coffee and buttered toast. Since childhood, I had learned it doesn't take much to be part of a team, whether it involved sports or caring for patients. It only requires each team member functioning as well as possible in his or her capacity and giving extra consideration to the other team members' needs to help them to function better.

MARIA

One fateful night I had only a few postoperative patients, who required little care, and one critically ill woman. Maria was twenty-two years old and the mother of three children, all under four years of age. She had become pregnant once again, and she knew that she and her husband, who already had two jobs, could not possibly afford another baby. They lived in a three-room, cold-water, third-floor walk-up apartment and could barely afford to feed the children they had. So despite her and her husband being staunch Roman Catholics, she had decided to terminate the pregnancy using a coat hanger. This was 1960, pre–*Roe v. Wade*.

As a result of her efforts, she had developed sepsis, a serious complication of an infection with inflammation throughout the body. Sepsis can cause blood clots and block oxygen from reaching vital organs, resulting in organ failure and even death.

When I first saw Maria, she was lying on an ice blanket and had the strongest antibiotics available being delivered to her intravenously. Despite this, her temperature was 106 degrees Fahrenheit, and she was deliriously coming in and out of coma. Fortunately, that night I had time to spend with her, because the few other patients were mostly sleeping and needed very little of my direct care. Because there was no one else to comfort her, I tried to do so by spending all the time I could at her bedside, holding her hand.

At one point, she was alert enough to tell me that she was very frightened, because she knew she was going to die and would go to hell for doing what she had done. I told her that I, too, was a strong Roman Catholic woman who believed very deeply in the sanctity of human life. Yet I could not believe that God would not understand and forgive her. The look on her face as she stared at my eyes and said, "Do you really believe that?" was heartbreaking. I told her truthfully that the God I knew would embrace her and that she was not to worry. I then held her, and she died in my arms, I hope peacefully. I'll never forget the way I felt when she took her last breath.

I had surprised myself by my reaction to Maria. All the teachings of my religion on the subject of abortion were overturned by my faith in my conviction about what I believed would be God's reaction to Maria. As I have gone forward in life, I have never participated in anything that would terminate a pregnancy. That includes my own refusal to even have an amniocentesis, much less an abortion, when I became pregnant at forty-three years of age. Jim and I made that decision even though we knew the pregnancy was seriously putting my life at risk. I'll write more about that later.

Because of Maria, I will never judge a woman's right to make such a decision based on the circumstances surrounding her pregnancy. Over the years I have discussed the issue of abortion with various individuals, including priests. I especially remember such a discussion I had, as part of a Newman Club meeting with Hopkins medical students, as a member of the faculty. Newman Clubs, inspired by the nineteenth-century writings of Cardinal John Henry Newman, provide pastoral services and ministries to Catholic students. The Hopkins Hospital Catholic chaplain sponsored a monthly meeting, inviting any catholic student who wanted to attend. He provided soup, sandwiches, and soft drinks and held the meetings in his living quarters, which were located in one of the Hopkins buildings.

The priest with whom I was to "debate" the issue of abortion was a theologian from Catholic University in Washington, DC. I began by telling the group about Maria and my feelings about not judging any woman who has had an abortion because of my interaction with Maria. The looks on the faces of the students, the chaplain, and the theologian told me that they were moved. I was pleasantly surprised by the equity of the theologian and the profound discussion that followed, allowing for all opinions to flow freely. I hope that Maria inspired for the student doctors consideration, or reconsideration, about the issue of abortion, as she did for me.

In any case, I owe so much to Maria, to Sister Whomever at Maryknoll, and to Mr. Clause, and will be forever in their debt for the influence they have had on my life as a physician and as a person.

CHAPTER 4

Scholarship by the River: Wilkes College

AFTER BEING ACCEPTED TO WILKES College, pretty much on the word of Mr. Clause, I became a twenty-one-year-old freshman who hadn't ever really studied for anything with the exception of the Scholastic Aptitude Test (SAT), which I had taken after acceptance to Wilkes. Of course, I might have scored low on the SAT or, worse, failed out of Wilkes after a semester or two if I didn't produce. So I had to make sure that I scored high on the SAT and perform very well in classes, in order to maintain Mr. Clause's confidence in me, and my reputation.

I scored high on the SAT, but achieving and maintaining high grades was going to be no easy task for a number of reasons: I shared classes with mostly very bright students who had great studying habits; I played on the women's varsity basketball team, which I dropped, much to the chagrin of the coach, one game short of receiving a letter; and in addition to carrying twenty credits a semester, I had a twenty-four-hour-per-week job working in a research lab. This lab was led by Dr. Sheldon Cohen, an immunologist-allergist, who had one of only two National Institute of Health (NIH) grants given to nonacademic medical center laboratories at that time. In actuality, the grant was through the Wilkes-Barre Veterans Administration Hospital, but the main laboratory was located at Wilkes College.

Even though I had to drop basketball because of the time constraints (I learned firsthand the importance of sleep), I maintained my avid interest in college sports. Later, much to my delight, because of the generosity of Coach Agnus Berenato, who coached at the University of Pittsburgh (Pitt) for years, I even served as a guest coach for a women's basketball game at Pitt, where I serve on the board of trustees.

The first semester at Wilkes was not my best, but I learned to study, although my study habits to this day are considered to be very unusual. I need to have a lot of background noise (it's my Italian upbringing, I guess) and to deal with at least two subjects or projects simultaneously. I work on each project usually for a half hour or so at a time, and go back and forth until I am satisfied. (As an aside, my psychiatrist husband tolerates my need for noise, even though he requires absolute silence when reading or concentrating. At first we worked in different rooms. Later, much to my joy, he bought me a set of wireless headphones, which keep the room quiet, and I can have all the noise I want.) I functioned especially well using those study and work habits later, when I became the editor in chief of the *Journal of the American Medical Association* (*JAMA*), which involved a very chaotic environment, mostly of my own instigation.

By the second semester and on, I was able to take twenty credits a semester, work twenty-four hours per week in the lab, and even start a health service for students three evenings a week. The college provided a room above the bookstore where students could come with their health problems, most of which I could easily care for with over-the-counter medications, a hug, or a shoulder. If someone was really sick, I had the backup of a physician whose office was a block from campus. There was no charge to the students for my care, but Wilkes provided me with free room and board, because the arrangement provided a health service and kept the students in class. This helped me a great deal financially, because I also worked on holidays as a private-duty nurse, to earn spending money in order not to depend so much on my parents.

Dealing with the problems of college students—who were mostly homesick, had minor trauma from playing sports, or were dealing with issues of sex—stimulated my interest in adolescent and young-adult medicine. I was surprised that so many young men, primarily freshmen, were concerned about their own sexuality because of physical encounters with other males that gave them pleasure. I had little difficulty in eliciting these concerns from the young men. I was an experienced nurse, I was older than them, I listened and did not judge, and they knew I would never reveal anything said to me in the health room without their permission.

I usually smiled when they told me about the incidents and asked them why they were surprised by the pleasant feeling, no matter who provided the stimulus. I assured them that one, or even a few, such encounters did not mean that they were gay. I told them that if these encounters continued and they wanted to discuss it further with me, I would be there. A second visit only happened with a few young men over the years, and I tried to help them the best I could, mostly by listening and not judging. Remember, this was the early 1960s. If ever fairness and acceptance of differences was essential, it was in those situations.

It really was not surprising to me that even the kind and effective physician in private practice, who offered to cover me with the students' health problems, was very uncomfortable dealing with such problems of adolescents and young adults. I was to learn a great deal more about that, later in medical school, where I discovered that adolescents and young adults, who didn't have physically serious illnesses, mostly fell through the health-care cracks. Ultimately, I decided that, in reality, an adolescent medicine specialist is a psychiatrist who also performs pelvic exams and sports physicals.

My four years at Wilkes College were incredible. I was able to obtain a sound foundation in science and also take many courses in literature, history, political science, psychology, sociology, German, and even music appreciation. Why German? you well might ask. Four semesters of a foreign language were required for graduation, and I was told that scientists needed to know German. This was foolish advice, because I have never needed to read a paper in German or use it in any way, except for traveling in Germany or fumbling my way through speaking with a few German people. So much for advice from those individuals who are in advisory positions but know little about the field about which they are advising.

I also enjoyed being president of the student government. I had learned in high school that girls are expected to be secretaries, whereas boys are the presidents. Talk about nonexistent equity. I told all that I couldn't type (I really still can't unless you count twenty words a minute with thirty mistakes as "typing"…I'm exaggerating only a little), and my handwriting was terrible, even before medical school, when it became illegible even to me. So I couldn't possibly be the secretary, but I could certainly be the president. This proved to me that there are some benefits even from some inabilities.

There were so many excellent teachers at Wilkes that I hesitate to name a single person, but one who remains in my thoughts to this day is professor Charles B. (or just plain "Chuck") Reif. He was the chair of the Biology Department and an avid outdoorsman. The experience of his "lab," in which we sounded the local lakes by chopping holes in the ice and dropping measuring and sampling devises through the holes, was very exciting to me. It compared with the excitement I felt later in being able to bring a diabetic patient out of coma with the careful use of insulin and fluids. Until his death, Professor Reif sent every current and former student of his an annual update of the department. His integrity and generosity to everyone was so admirable. Much of the hope of our future rests with such inspiring professors and teachers.

I also learned in the botany course, taught by another great professor, just how smart Poppie was about nature. Except for the taxonomy, I didn't really learn very much in that class that Poppie hadn't already taught me during our walks in the woods in my early childhood. In fact, I received extra credit on the final exam by answering a question about finding a way out of the woods, based strictly on what Poppie had taught me about examining the bark on trees and about what plants grow on the north, south, east, and west sides of trees. Those experiences further instilled in me that the promise of our future rests greatly on parents teaching children what they know, including how to treat others.

Another great thing about Wilkes was my friends and classmates. The first year, before I received free room and board for working in the "infirmary," it cost a great deal to live in the dormitories. However, it was worth every penny, because I lived twenty-four hours a day with individuals who were not part of my birth family. While I had a similar experience in nursing school, this was really a new experience, because the environment, including having men around (except living in the dame dormitories), was different. Over the years, all my roommates were from New York or New Jersey, and because I wanted to change my coal-region dialect, I adopted theirs. My roommate and classmates in medical school from New York enhanced this new dialect, resulting in many people now mistakenly believing I'm a native *Nu-Yorka*. However, I tell them to *fuhgeddaboudit*.

I spent the summers working full-time in the Wilkes research laboratory and taking the required physics courses at the University of Scranton, which was located a few blocks from my parents' home. I would return from working the lab at Wilkes, eat dinner, and then walk to my physics class. All my classmates for those two courses were young men studying to be engineers. It was interesting to learn how differently they approached problems.

By having taken the two required physics courses over the summers, I could really enjoy my junior and senior years, because by then, I had taken all courses necessary for medical school entrance. Hence, by the second half of my junior year, I was free to take more liberal arts classes and to have more free time, even though I continued to work in the laboratory, in the health room during the semesters, and as a private-duty nurse during the holidays.

I spent some of the later part of my junior year studying for and taking the Medical College Aptitude Test (MCAT) and interviewing at various medical schools to which I had applied for entrance. I had included Johns Hopkins and Harvard (the "preparation Hs"), knowing

I'd never be accepted, and of course I wasn't accepted to either one. Many years later, I wished I had kept my rejection letter from Hopkins, which was kindly worded but still a rejection, after all. If I had kept it, I would have placed it on the wall in my Hopkins office in 1985 next to a letter stating that I was now a Hopkins professor. As it turns out, I have never placed any diplomas or such things on the walls of my offices or anywhere. In fact, I have no idea where they might be physically, but they are stored securely in my heart, never to be lost.

There are two medical-school interviews that remain in my mind as if they occurred yesterday. The greater one was my interview at the University of Pittsburgh, to which I'd only applied at the strong suggestion of my research mentor, Dr. Cohen, who had completed his fellowship in allergy and immunology there. Almost all of the doctors I knew from northeastern Pennsylvania had trained at the Philadelphia medical schools, but none in Pittsburgh. However, I fell in love with the University of Pittsburgh School of Medicine, where several wonderfully colorful persons interviewed me. One interviewer was an amazing woman, who sat in a chair next to mine (no behind a desk for her), and lit a pipe that had a diamond chip in the bowl. Dr. "Penna" Drew was elegant and taught me so much about how to interview someone and to never to judge a person because something he or she does seems peculiar.

On the other hand, the interview from hell occurred at a Philadelphia medical school that will go unnamed, out of deference to the current faculty there. I entered the room, and the man (a gentleman he was not) gestured to a chair across the desk from behind which he was sitting. He opened with, "Miss DeAngelis, I don't know why you are wasting my and your time with this interview."

Now, I had become accustomed to the usual "Why is a woman taking up a spot in medical school when she will drop out to have children and can't compete in the sciences anyway..."

So I responded, "And why is that, sir?"

He then said, "Because we already have our share of guineas." I felt like someone had just punched me in the solar plexus, because while I'd heard that denigrating term used for Italians, I never expected it from a doctor, especially during an interview. What a smug, sorry soul he was.

I immediately stood up, told him he was correct that I was wasting my time there, and walked out the door. Fighting back tears, I thought of how hard my parents had worked so I could be a doctor, and I made a vow in their honor that I would never set foot in that place again. And I have not, even many years later, when I was invited to interview for the position of the dean of that medical school. I have also refused to speak in that school's buildings, despite many invitations to do so over the years. Such reprehensible behavior would never be tolerated today and should never have been in 1964. Disrespect of race, creed, color, or disability is simply unconscionable, nevermind inequitable.

Of the two memorable interviews, the one at the University of Pittsburgh was overwhelmingly warm and positive and fortunately had occurred after the Philadelphia fiasco. You can then imagine my joy when, only one week after my interview, I received my letter of acceptance to the University of Pittsburgh School of Medicine. I remember exactly where I was when I read that letter and was so excited I blurted out the news to my friends sitting at the dinner table with me in the Wilkes cafeteria. In true Wilkes spirit, word spread rapidly, and after one of my friends at another table stood up and yelled, "Congratulations to the future Dr. DeAngelis," everyone in the cafeteria stood up and cheered. What a great day that was.

Of course I had, immediately after the interview from hell, withdrawn my application to that Philadelphia school, but I was accepted to several other Philadelphia medical schools. However, I ultimately decided that I would best be educated and trained to be a doctor at the University of Pittsburgh School of Medicine. Now I had only to wait a few months until I would enter the magic world of medical school.

CHAPTER 5

MD or MD-ity?: The University of Pittsburgh School of Medicine

YEAR ONE

MY FIRST DAY OF MEDICAL school was like walking into paradise. Oh, I knew getting through the next four years would be arduous, but after such a long time in preparation, I was finally actually a medical student well on my way to becoming a doctor.

The first day of class, we were asked to introduce ourselves, naming the colleges from which we had graduated. I was awed, because the vast majority of my classmates were from Ivy League schools or other famous colleges or universities. When I announced that I was from Wilkes College, only a few seemed to know where that was, but happily that didn't seem to matter to them. I was accepted for myself, not from where I'd graduated. That was my introduction to a group of people who were to become my family for the next four years and, for some of them, long thereafter. By the time I graduated, I knew that the unassuming acceptance of everyone in our class by all in our class had formed a foundation for long-lasting friendships.

During my first year, I lived in the building for nursing students. I didn't mind staying there because, except for sleeping and some studying, I spent very little time in my room, and the cost was well within my budget. I had purchased a dinner-only plan available for all University of Pittsburgh students. Like many other students, I saved a sandwich and fruit from dinner, which I ate for lunch the following day. I was fairly certain the university administration was well aware of the practice and yet made no move to curtail it. This was a true spirit of charity in its best form. That was one of many reasons I have had great respect for Pitt, which remains to this day.

I was very happy to find a job that was to begin in my second year; it entailed covering the Veterans Administration (VA) Hospital medical library evenings and weekends, along with two other medical students. In return, we received free room and board and also saved on buying books, because we could use the books in the library. Even better, I could study in the library, because all I had to do was put books away that had accumulated during the day and assist the few physicians who came to the library in the evenings or weekends. Also, the women who worked in the kitchen made sure we ate well and even prepared a hearty bag lunch that I shared with one of my classmates. Talk about being lucky!

I would be lying if I said I had enjoyed that first year of classwork. I loved learning new things, but it felt like year five of college, because it involved no clinical experience. (I remembered that many years later when I led the initiative to change the Johns Hopkins's medical school curriculum and made sure there would be patient-based experiences beginning the first week of school.) An important issue involved how a few (fortunately there were only a very few) of the instructors treated women. Equity was not in their vocabulary. My experience with one of the "bad guys" had a profound effect on me, as I will explain below.

ERRONEOUS BELIEFS ABOUT WOMEN STUDENTS

One Friday afternoon during my first semester, I was preparing to spend the weekend studying for a final examination scheduled for the following Monday. At that point, every member of my class had received a grade on a physiology paper we had submitted earlier. Each of those papers described a research project we had designed for the physiology class. My paper was graded as an F. However, there was no comment other than a note that I was to have a new paper on the instructor's desk first thing Monday morning. Failing to do so would result in failing the course. Now, one thing I knew (and knew that I knew!) was how to write a research project. After all, I had spent four years, including three summers, working in the research laboratory of a National Institute of Health (NIH) researcher, Dr. Cohen, at Wilkes College. I simply could not understand the failing grade on the paper.

I had read the papers prepared by my group partners (all males) in that class and knew mine was easily as good as theirs. I also knew there was no way I could prepare another time-consuming paper and also have time to study for the final exam in another subject. I wasn't sure what I could possibly do to remedy that situation, so I went to my room and tried to study, sitting at my desk. I fell asleep and then awakened in the middle of the night feeling sick with worry. I went down the hall to the bathroom. While I was washing my hands, I noticed that someone had broken the mirror above the sink, and a sharp shard of glass was in the sink. At that point I was so distraught that I stared at the glass. I momentarily contemplated cutting my wrists and holding my hands under hot water so I could bleed to death faster. I couldn't imagine living if I was about to fail out of medical school, especially because of the ridiculous circumstances that would cause my failure.

Fortunately, that frightening thought lasted only a very short time. I then became very angry, knowing that I had been driven to that desperate state of mind by an unfair (inequitable) decision by one instructor. That instructor had a reputation for being biased against women medical students. Women constituted only seven percent of my entering class, pretty much par for that time. I went back to my room, determined that I would not accept that unfairness without a battle. Consequently, I slept deeply for four hours (not unusual for me), and except for Sunday mass, meals, and sleep, I spent the entire weekend studying for the exam and doing nothing with my physiology paper.

On Monday morning, I first took the exam for the other course, and did well, and then marched to the office of the physiology instructor. He was in his office, and as soon as he saw me, he began berating me because

I was late. I ignored his comments, and slammed on his desk the paper he had graded with the F. He looked at me with a shocked expression as I told him that I knew my paper was worth at least a B. I told him that he could either grade my paper fairly or I was going to the dean of students' office, where I would ask that my paper, and those of the five men in my lab group, be given anonymously to three faculty members to grade. I had asked permission of my lab partners to do so, and they had agreed with enthusiasm. These young men certainly understood equity.

To my amazement, the instructor quietly and gently asked me to sit down. He then proceeded to tell me that I had just proven that he had been correct in thinking that I was different from other women (really?). He said he believed that I would probably make a good doctor. In response, I told him that I didn't think I was different from the other women students, and then I told him about what had happened to me the previous Friday night. He was shocked and said he certainly didn't want to harm me in any way and that he was only testing me. I told him that testing someone in such a cruel way could lead to a disaster that would make him and many others very sorry. Amazingly, he agreed with me and apologized.

I wonder how many other students have been harmed by such teachers, who mean no harm but harm anyway. In any case, with a smile he marked an A on my paper. I'm not sure if he really understood how harmful his inequitable behavior was, but trying to be fair, I gave him the benefit of the doubt. We exchanged Christmas cards for many years thereafter, which was interesting because he was not Christian. That experience taught me a lot about how to handle situations, which were many, involving unfair treatment of women.

LOSS OF CLASSMATES

By the end of the first year, several of my classmates, including two women, left, never to return. I knew one woman failed out, but I don't know why the other left. At least one man, who was extremely bright and had received good grades, also left. He never wanted to attend medical school in the first place and had done so only to please his parents. I think he wanted to show his parents that he tried, but he simply did not want to be a doctor. I was especially saddened by his leaving because he had been one of my close friends and had introduced me to the music of Edith Piaf. Along with a few other friends, we had spent several Saturday nights listening to her magical voice in his room. I thought especially of him and the effect Piaf's music had on me, when my husband and I, many years later, visited the apartment where Piaf had lived in Paris. The current owner had made it a sort of museum and allowed visitors by appointment.

ELECTIVES

As my fellow classmates and I neared the end of our first year and thought about the rest of our time in medical school, we realized that Pitt was one of the very few medical schools that allowed for no elective time. Because many of us wanted to have experiences outside the set curriculum, we decided to request a meeting with the dean of students to discuss our having some elective time. We scheduled a meeting one evening, at which all except one of our classmates were present. The missing classmate was in the hospital recuperating from an appendectomy. A faculty member showed up to meet with us, and when he saw the crowd of students in the filled classroom, he called the dean of students. The result of that meeting with the dean was that we were allowed to have three months' elective time in our third or fourth years. Sticking together for an important cause can have great results.

A SERIOUS HEALTH PROBLEM

Toward the end of my first year, as a class exercise, we drew blood from one another in hematology lab, so we could learn about certain blood tests. That occurred on a Friday afternoon. On Saturday morning, one of my classmates told me that the instructor (a hematologist) was looking for me and suggested I call her. I did so, and the instructor told me that she wanted to repeat my blood tests on Monday because my hemoglobin and platelets were very low.

Knowing what that might mean, I went to my room to examine my lymph nodes and abdomen. To my horror, I found that that my spleen was enlarged. Like so many medical students, who believe they have almost every disease they are studying at the time, I went through the possible reasons for such findings. The immediate possibilities that came to mind in the differential diagnosis were leukemia, lymphoma, or similar bad diseases. (Is there such a thing as a good disease?) That weekend was one of the most frightening I've ever spent, because I didn't want to discuss it with anyone until I was sure of the diagnosis. Being alone when worried greatly compounds the problem, and I lost my appetite (unheard of in people of Italian descent) and had trouble sleeping.

Early Monday morning, I saw the instructor and told her about my enlarged spleen. She immediately arranged for me to have a complete evaluation by a clinical hematologist. After an extensive work-up, it turned out that I had Banti's Syndrome, which is congestive enlargement of the spleen. This enlargement results in destruction of blood cells and platelets, but the cause of the enlarged spleen was not obvious.

The memory of one diagnostic procedure that remains with me is the bone marrow aspiration taken from my sternum (the breast bone located in the center of the chest). The procedure involved driving a needle into my sternum and aspirating bone marrow. When the physician pulled back on the syringe to aspirate the bone marrow, it felt like my heart was being pulled out through the needle. I knew that was not happening and that I was in the hands of an excellent and compassionate physician. So I wasn't really frightened but was awed by the feeling. Fortunately, that procedure has essentially been abandoned, and bone marrow is now aspirated from the pelvic bone. That procedure is not nearly as dangerous or frightening to most patients. I later also had that procedure, along with a biopsy, as part of my medical evaluation.

Over the summer vacation from school, I had my spleen removed. I lost a lot of blood because of the many collateral blood vessels that had formed around my spleen. However, I was very grateful to the skilled hematologist who made the diagnosis and to the surgeon, who managed the bleeding. I was very thankful that I didn't have leukemia, lymphoma, or a similar disease. Little did I know what was to follow, years later, as a result of this necessary surgical procedure.

Because of the surgery and recovery, I missed two weeks of working in the research lab of a professor in the School of Public Health. This was my second summer working in his lab. He had tried to convince me that, instead of clinical work, I would be much happier doing research the rest of my life, because of my supposed talent for research. I had told him that I felt greater satisfaction in keeping laboratory animals alive for days after I'd removed their adrenal glands (in order to complete the experiment) than I did collecting the data.

The professor told me that anyone could operate and keep the animals alive, and that the experimental results were more important. However, when I returned to the lab after having been away for two weeks, I made an interesting discovery: none of the staff had been able to operate on and keep alive any guinea pigs—out of fifty—which they tried to do while I was away. Only ten were necessary, so they had operated on five times the number needed for the experiment. I finished the experiment by having success in keeping alive all of the next ten animals that I worked on. Thereafter, there were no more discussions about my career choice. It is interesting that my surgical skills ended the "debate" about a research, rather than a clinical, career, but I never became a surgeon. I'll write more about that decision later.

YEAR TWO

Year two began with a get-together the night before classes began; it included a number of my classmates. While I was dancing with one of my classmates, I noticed that he had markings on his lower neck, which signified to me that he was receiving radiation treatments. My heart sank. Remembering how distraught I had felt when I first discovered that *I* might have had a lethal disease, I proceeded to tell him about my health experiences over the summer. I hoped to encourage him to tell me about his health problem, if in fact, he had one. He then told me that he had a neoplastic disease (cancer) with a very bad prognosis. He wanted to remain in class as long as he was able, and over the next months, our group of close friends tried to support him as best we could. When he finally went home to die, we felt—up close and personally—the devastation of losing a dear friend. Later, one of our group and her husband named their son after him. Losing that friend significantly contributed to how I worked with patients thereafter.

Except for that experience with my classmate who died, the second year was much more enjoyable than the first. The courses were more directly clinically related, and we began to have contact with patients. Our group, consisting of a half dozen or so close friends, continued to travel to West (by God) Virginia every few weeks on Saturday nights to hear real bluegrass music. None of us had much money, so we chipped in for gas and to buy several pitchers of beer and bowls of peanuts. We shucked and pitched the peanut shells on the floor of a barnlike building where the music was played. That seemed to be very bad manners to me, but that was the custom. So I joined the crowd. Those experiences engendered my love of bluegrass music, which remains to this day.

We also had dinner together every so often. I cooked most of our dinners together, which consisted of spaghetti with meatballs, garlic bread, and a half gallon of cheap, poor-quality Chianti wine. (I later learned from my Italian relatives that you should never buy cheap Italian wine in a straw-covered bottle.) You'd be amazed at how a good meal can be cooked for a dollar or two per person. Of course we couldn't afford napkins, so we substituted toilet paper effectively. However, unlike our bluegrass forays, nothing was thrown on the floor.

Years Three and Four

Years three and four were exactly what I wanted medical school to be. The hours were very arduous and long, but the various clinical rotations were interesting and fulfilling. Unfortunately, I found myself in trouble with one of my first clinical rotations, when I was assigned to an outpatient internal-medicine clinic.

On the first morning, I arrived at the 8:00 a.m. general medical-clinic site to which I'd been assigned. I was greeted by a waiting room full of mostly older patients, but there were no doctors present. The nursing staff told me that the doctors would arrive after morning conference, which was held from 8:00 to 9:00 a.m. This was the pattern every morning. So I asked why the patients were there so early and was told that there were only 8:00 a.m. or 1:00 p.m. appointments, and patients were given numbers as they arrived. They then were seen in the order of those numbers, in the morning and afternoon sessions. I asked if the place was a clinic or a bakery shop and was told to wait for the doctors to arrive so I could discuss it with them.

I did wait and discussed the issue with the senior resident who arrived first; he told me that was the custom. He advised me just to see the patients to which I would be assigned and not to be concerned about how the clinic was managed. I told him that I refused to be part of treating people like that, and I went to the library, knowing what was likely to happen. As expected, after a few hours, I was paged to the office of Dr. Ken Rogers, one of my favorite faculty members. He was one of the faculty who had interviewed me when I had applied to medical school. He was a self-described "old navy man," who had a rough outer core that unsuccessfully hid a very tender heart.

He asked if I wanted to be a doctor, to which he very well knew the answer. He told me that if I did, I had to complete an outpatient clinic experience. I told him that I thought he knew it was not right to treat patients as they were being treated in that clinic. I knew the medical care provided was very good, but the appointment system was disrespectful and wrong. He agreed but told me I had to pick my battles better, and then he asked how fluent I was in Spanish. I told him I didn't speak Spanish, at which point he handed me a small book on medical Spanish. He then told me that he had arranged for my new outpatient assignment to be joining one of my classmates and a faculty member in Nicaragua, vaccinating children using "vaccine guns."

I told him I had no money to pay for such a trip, and he said that he had arranged for me to attend a meeting that evening. I was to attend and convince a group of nurses that they should provide me with a small grant to cover my expenses. I thought he was kidding, but he wasn't, so I spent the next few hours planning my presentation. As it turned out, that group of nurses, from one of the local community hospitals, provided scholarships and small grants for special projects, always to nurses. Dr. Rogers, who frequently provided lectures to the group, refusing compensation, had explained my situation to them, including that I had been a nurse before entering medical school. God only knows what else he told them, but they provided me with the grant. In return, I made several following presentations to them, including the first on my experience in Nicaragua. I will be forever grateful to those nurses, for their kindness and understanding.

Because of their generosity, I spent three weeks vaccinating children from the back of a jeep in Nicaragua. I learned so much about the beautiful spirit of people who had so few material goods. I was struck by how proud the mothers were when they presented their children for vaccination. Every child wore a clean shirt (mostly patched T-shirts) and was freshly bathed with hair combed. I was told that this was a sign of the respect they had for the *doctora* who was helping their children. What a wonderful lesson that was for me, and it solidified my belief that a reciprocal respect in dress code was appropriate for doctors toward patients.

I had bilateral conjunctivitis (red eyes) and "the GI's" (diarrhea), throughout my stay in Nicaragua, even though I tried to eat only boiled rice and cooked vegetables and to drink only cola from capped bottles. There was no bottled water back then. Unfortunately, Santo, the public-health gentleman who was my guide wherever I went, sought to assure my health by removing the caps from the bottles. He would then wipe the tops of the bottles with his bare hand. He was so protective I didn't have the heart to stop him from doing that. No matter the physical discomfort, I would never exchange that wonderful experience for anything.

Later in the third year, while on vacation at home, I developed stones in my common bile duct, resulting in a cholecystectomy (gall-bladder removal). A surgeon performed the procedure at the hospital where I'd attended nursing school in Scranton. The stones were the result of the destruction of so many blood cells in my enlarged spleen, which had been removed the year before. Counting a tonsillectomy and adenoidectomy in second grade and the appendectomy in nursing school, that was my fourth surgical procedure. I thought this was getting to be a very bad habit.

TIME IN AFRICA

There were so many valuable experiences in my clinical years of medical school. The one I remember best is the almost three months I spent with one of my classmates, Randy, working in a bush hospital in Liberia, Africa. During our first year of medical school, Randy and I had discussed our desire to work in a developing country during medical school. We had arranged to join a program organized by the Columbia College of Physicians and Surgeons for their students. We were able to be part of that program, from mid-September to mid-December of 1967, our third year of medical school, because there were no Columbia students scheduled at that time.

While in Liberia, we worked in a two-hundred-bed hospital managed by the Firestone Rubber Company outside Monrovia. The hospital was situated in the middle of a rubber-tree plantation, on land rented from the Liberian government by the Firestone company. There were hundreds of workers, and the hospital was set up to care for the workers and their family members.

The doctors and nurses, who staffed the hospital and clinics, were from the United Kingdom and were inspiring professionals and teachers. Randy worked with the adult patients. I worked in the "belly camp" (the obstetric unit, including the delivery room) and the pediatric unit, which had fifty beds but a hundred patients (usually there were two patients in a bed). It is difficult to describe how much I learned in that setting, because often our responsibilities were much like those of interns in the United States. However, the attending physicians were never far away and were happy to provide consultation to assure the safety of the patients.

The staff that maintained the hospital and our living quarters were very thorough. They assured all the wards and rooms were spotless and that we ate well. I remember how thrilled they (and we) were to trade our canned pineapple for the fresh African version. The staff could sell in the market one can of the fruit, exchanged with the fresh version as we requested, for several days' pay, even though the fresh fruit was more delicious than the canned version. That surely was proof that different folks have different tastes. The staff also did our laundry. I was amused and delighted one morning when I found that someone had sewn pockets inside my bras. Apparently they had seen me putting money in my bra when I traveled, because I had no pockets in my skirts or blouses. Unfortunately, no matter how hard I tried, I've never found similar bras in the United States. Now, there's a business idea for someone.

The Belly Camp

I was taken by surprise the first time I walked into the belly camp. I was greeted by silence, but a patient would occasionally raise her arm and snap her fingers. I assumed she was signaling for someone to come to her, but in fact she was expressing labor pains. This was a curious and important cultural lesson for me, on how different people express pain in different situations.

Another amazing cultural lesson involved my observation of mothers and their babies. Very often the women would gather just outside the hospital, either waiting for their children or themselves to be seen by a doctor. They always engaged in the seemingly ever-present "palaver"—that is, discussing whatever was of interest to them at that time. I very soon learned that this palaver was very important for engaging patients in this culture, and to some degree in all cultures.

Each mother carried her baby in a long cloth tied to her back, with the naked baby sitting or lying in the cloth in the mother's front, much like a sling. I had noticed that these sling-like cloths never were soiled, which I found unbelievable. However, I observed that every once in a while, while a mother continued her participation in the palaver, she would remove her baby from the sling and hold him or her away from her body. The baby would then urinate on the ground. The mother would then wipe the baby girl's bottom with her hand or gently shake the baby boy's penis, and replace the baby in her sling. The palaver continued, and no one, besides me, seemed to be surprised or to even notice.

I asked many Liberian women how they knew when the baby needed to urinate, and they all looked at me like I was either kidding them or simply not well trained as a woman. The latter was, and continues to be, very true, because to this day I cannot understand how the mothers knew. I assume this is another form of ESP, elimination sensory perception. This is yet again another of life's great mysteries of motherhood, and that God is indeed a Great Comedian.

Sundagar, The Child with Scrofula

There were many memorable experiences with specific patients, but the African child who remains in my mind most clearly is a scrawny little boy, Sundagar. This little tyke had scrofula (swollen lymph nodes of the neck, in his case, caused by tuberculosis). In addition to medications, he required weekly drainage of the tubercle mass on the right side of his neck. That treatment is no longer performed, but at that time, on

Friday afternoons one of the two operating rooms (ORs) was used for that purpose. That allowed the room to be scrubbed three times over the weekend, when no scheduled surgery was performed. This was to prevent spread of the bacteria that caused tuberculosis. Over the weekend the other OR was used for emergency surgeries.

I'm not sure who took Sundagar to the hospital, and no one was certain of his age. However, I think he was six or seven years old. (Because the hospital and clinics served the workers and their families and the care was so good, many workers seemed to have several "wives" and dozens of children. We never checked but simply cared for all who came.) Sundagar had the biggest brown eyes I've ever seen, and he would never cry or even whimper while he was being treated.

He often followed me when I made rounds on the ward, saying nothing but seemingly missing nothing. He always gave me the brightest smile when I looked at him, especially when I rubbed his nearly bald head. When he was discharged, after weeks of care and gaining over ten pounds, he hugged me. He then proudly handed me the Liberian penny he always had with him and said, "Thank you," in English. I treasure that coin and believe the hug and the penny to be among the most rewarding payments I've ever received.

Extracurricular Activities

While Randy and I worked in the hospital many hours each day, often including weekends, all at our own discretion, we also had a great deal of fun. One ritual that seemed vital to maintaining the spirits of the male medical and other staff, was the Friday afternoon rugby game. At first I was unfamiliar with this game, but I love essentially all sports, so I went to every match. Randy played with one of the teams, and I immediately became the medic on the sideline, whose job it was to attend to the injured players.

One example of how seriously the players took these contests was that many of the usual injuries involved cuts that I had to suture. The first time a player came to the sideline for a "quick sew up, Doc," I began to prepare some medication to numb the area. I was quickly admonished with, "Are ya daft? That will take too much time, and we're one man short!" So I sutured as fast as I could, and the player immediately ran back into the fray sans a bandage. Men!

After the game we all retired to the clubhouse, where there were kegs of cold beer, soft drinks, and tonic water. I assumed the tonic water, which contained quinine, was a favorite throwback to the days when quinine was a treatment for malaria. While I developed a taste for tonic water, Randy and I continued to take our weekly prophylactic malaria medicine.

Another experience involved a festive ritual dance, to which Randy and I were invited. We were seated in front, given cups of palm wine, and treated to some of the most magical chanting, with drums and dancing, I have ever witnessed. I'm not sure how much the palm wine affected my perception (I drank only one cup), but I can understand why the Africans would consider this ritual more than mere entertainment.

Heading Home
Just before leaving Liberia, I had spent a full afternoon bargaining for gifts for my family, much to the amusement of the villagers. They laughed at my telling taller tales than the Charlie. (That was the name given to the salesman who came to villages to sell wares he had purchased from other villagers.)

I had learned that the villagers looked forward to such sessions, and they gathered around Charlie and me to enjoy the show. One of the women served tea, and the show began. Charlie first asked an outrageous price for the goods I had chosen, and I countered with a ridiculously low price. He then told me about the many children, plus a wife and his parents, he had to feed. I countered with a tall tale of my poor, sick parents and sisters, whom I had to support. We went on like that for about an hour, adding more ridiculous scenarios about our poverty until we finally settled on an agreeable price. The observers judged our stories by clapping, laughing, or making other sounds, easily distinguished as disbelief or "good one."

I was able to purchase small ivory elephant sets for my parents and sisters, a wooden statue, a mask, and a blanket that I had watched being made from the start in a nearby village. It had beautiful bright red, yellow, and white wool woven into a black wool background. I still have that blanket and remember the glorious time I had in Liberia every time I see it.

I decided to exchange my return-home plane ticket from Africa for a ticket on the merchant marine ship on which Randy had secured free round-trip passage, by his serving as a "pharmacist mate." The option of pharmacist mate was only open to men, but I was allowed to pay for my passage home. That return trip was memorable for many reasons, including learning how to use a sextant to determine our location at sea. I studied and demonstrated that skill in order to prove to Dimitri, the Greek navigator, that a woman could do so. He was very surprised, but seemed pleased, and subsequently allowed me to watch him as he navigated the ship. I consider that to be an example of equity earned.

Another special memory was shore time in Sierra Leone one night with three young, crazy merchant marine officers from the ship and Randy. They took me to a nightclub, which featured an exotic dancer, who had a shape the world should be in. Her exotic (to put it mildly) dancing was something to behold, and I was very happy there were several other women present. Needless to say, the guys were in heaven. I remember returning to the ship by walking along the dark streets where thousands of bats hung in the trees along the way. It is now believed that these bats may have had a significant role in the spread of Lassa and Ebola infections in humans. One never knows what lurks in so many dark places.

Nights at sea were beautiful and serene, except for one occasion when the ship encountered a storm and rode the waves like a roller coaster...only much wetter. Much to the chagrin of the captain, the young officers, Randy. and I tied ourselves to a post near the inner wall of the ship. We wanted to experience the thrill of riding the wet waves on the big ship. That we did such a crazy thing is unbelievable to me now, but it was the most exciting ride I've ever had. Fortunately, we all lived to tell the story of this adventure.

We docked in Norfolk, Virginia, a week before Christmas. Randy and I took a taxi to the bus station after trying, by force of habit in Africa, to bargain with the driver for less payment than that shown on the meter. He thought we were crazy but laughed when we told him how much money we had and that we had recently docked from Africa. He kindly accepted a lesser fare, and that made it possible later for us to buy some coffee and doughnuts before we got on the bus home. Kindness is everywhere.

The bus drive home from Norfolk was much different from the bus trips in Africa and Nicaragua. On US buses, there is plenty of room not shared with too many people and various animals. In addition, Randy and I sat in comfortable seats, and not on benches or hanging on the side or back of the vehicle. However, I must admit that the trips in Africa, Nicaragua, and subsequently in other developing countries were much more exciting and interesting. In any case, I arrived home with the sum total of eleven cents in my pocket, but feeling so very rich, especially in spirit, which indeed I was!

Going to the grocery store in the United States was another almost overwhelming experience after the small shops and stalls in Africa. It was hard to get reaccustomed to having all sorts of food and groceries and having many brands and types of each from which to choose. How spoiled we are in the United States.

Even though I had a wonderful time with my family over the holidays, returning to medical school after vacation was a happy time. It was fun to exchange medical stories with my colleagues about treating patients with exotic tropical diseases after making diagnoses with the help of little more than a microscope, a plain-film X-ray machine, and other simple devices. I soon realized how much my clinical abilities had been honed by physicians who, for example, could determine whether a child with dehydration needed more or less sodium by the feel of the skin. I had experienced the art of medicine at its finest.

As the Great Comedian would have it, as soon as I returned to Pitt, one of the first patients I cared for, as a student on my clinical rotation in hematology and oncology, was the son of the hematologist's secretary. He had been admitted for a work-up of an unremitting fever. After learning that he had recently traveled through Africa, I took a smear of his blood, treated it with a stain, inspected it under a microscope, and immediately diagnosed malaria. The hematologist expressed doubt and thought I'd been in Africa too long. However, he was a fair man and asked a tropical-disease consultant, who affirmed the diagnosis. Some days it's worth getting out of bed.

THE STUDENT AMERICAN MEDICAL ASSOCIATION

At the end of my third year, I was elected to be the president of the student government. Because of this position, I was invited to have dinner with some members of the board of the American Medical Association one evening when they were in Pittsburgh for a meeting. That meeting was an eye-opener for me. Although the gentlemen (they were all men) were very polite, almost all of the dinner conversation dealt with payment to doctors. There was no mention of patient care. I was very disappointed.

When I reported that meeting to my classmates and others, we all decided not to join the Student American Medical Association. That was not the best introduction to the AMA for someone who would one day become the editor in chief of the *Journal of the American Medical Association*.

THE ROLE OF NURSING IN MY TRAINING TO BE A DOCTOR

My training as a nurse had a significant influence on me and made me a better doctor. I had not been all that aware of the profound effect until one day a patient made it very clear to me and others. During my third year, I was assigned to work in one of the male inpatient wards (remember, this was 1968) at the Pittsburgh Veterans Affairs Hospital, an affiliate of the School of Medicine, which was only a few block away.

One morning we were "rounding"—that is, going from one patient to another—during which a resident would present pertinent information about patients. The patient usually was in bed or sitting at his bedside. The attending physician would then examine and discuss the patient with the residents and medical students in the presence of the patient. When done properly, these were very effective teaching occasions for the young doctors and, one hopes, for the patient. During the morning in question, we were interrupted by a small commotion in the far corner of the ward.

A patient, who had been discharged, was arguing with the head nurse. He refused to leave until he said good-bye to his nurse. The head nurse tried to explain to him that the nurse who was at her side *was* his nurse. He refused to believe her. I realized that the patient was someone to whom I had been assigned and who had been in and out of a coma for days. I asked permission of the attending to say good-bye to the patient and to try to calm him.

When I reached the patient's side, he immediately reached out to me and said, "Here's my nurse." The head nurse said that he was mistaken, because I was the student doctor who had taken care of him, not his nurse. He looked at her and said, "She talked to me like a nurse, touched me like a nurse, and treated me like a nurse. She is my nurse! I want to thank her and hug her." I then hugged him and explained to all that indeed I was a nurse training to be a doctor, so he was correct. That was a great double lesson for me: that nursing prepared me well for patient care and that patients in comas can hear and feel a great deal. My personal experience of hearing and feeling while in a medical coma ratified that lesson.

RESIDENCY MATCH TIME

Very soon after returning to Pitt from Africa, I began applying for residencies. I had decided on the specialty of pediatrics and not surgery, which had been my first thought. I had tried to resist choosing pediatrics, because that's what women were expected to choose, and I did love surgery. However, working with children was my first love, and it would have been foolish to choose something just to go against the expectations for women. Despite my choice of pediatrics, during my fourth year of medical school I took call for the pediatric surgeons every third night. The surgical chief resident was always available to help me if necessary. He taught me how to do routine surgical procedures, which could be performed outside the operating room. I was pleasantly surprised that the pediatric residents did not object, but they had grown to trust me, and I never tested that trust.

As a result, the hospital's chief surgeon asked if I would return to Pitt, after my pediatric residency, to do another residency in pediatric transplant surgery. He believed my background in immunological research combined with pediatrics would be an excellent foundation for what he proposed. I told him I certainly would accept that unbelievable offer and would keep in touch with him over my pediatric residency years. My friends told me I was crazy, because I would be close to forty years old by the time I completed all my training. I told them, "At that time, I'll be almost forty, no matter what I'm doing." So I was going to do what I thought was best, no matter how long it took.

On match day, the day we found out where we had been accepted for residency, I was shocked to discover that I had not matched at any of the places to which I had applied. Even though I had applied to very good places, I had at least one place I'd assumed was a "sure thing," Children's Hospital of Pittsburgh, but I didn't match there.

As I tried to understand what had happened, I remembered my interview at one place where the interviewer had handed me the envelope containing my records, including the letters of recommendation from the dean and two instructors. He had not sealed the envelope, as he should have, but instead suggested that I read the letters on my way to the next interviewer. Also I was to be sure to I seal the envelope, before I met with the next interviewer. The two letters from my instructors, who knew me, were very good. However, the one from the dean, who was a pediatrician but had no real knowledge of my work, was damning with faint praise. He had only recently become the dean, and I'd never worked with him when he was in pediatrics. I was very surprised but thought that the other letters from the faculty who knew me would offset the dean's letter. Little did I know how damning the dean's letter would be.

Because I had spent three months in Africa, my time was cut short for working at Pitt before I began interviewing for my residency positions. During my time away was when letters of recommendation were written. So I assume the dean's letter was written quickly (he had to write over a hundred of them) and with no real effort to know students with whom he'd had little contact. I never cease to be amazed by the deleterious effects people in power can have because of disinterest or carelessness. In any case, the instructors who knew me took me aside as soon as I opened my match letter. They said they were very sorry, and they couldn't understand what had happened.

I felt betrayed, and my first reaction was to get as far away from that dean and Pitt as I could. The instructors knew that I was hurt and angry, and they were shocked when I told them about the dean's letter. However, they wanted me to stay at Pitt and do my residency at the Children's Hospital of Pittsburgh. The dean already had paid for an extra position for me. I think they then understood why the dean had done something so unusual, in making allowance for my staying there. Perhaps the dean realized that he had made a serious mistake when writing my letter of recommendation and was trying to amend the error. I tried to be fair and understand the dean's position, but it was very difficult at that point.

The instructors told me there were two other good positions open that I could have, but I needed to make a decision right then, or the positions would be lost. However, they told me, and I knew, that the position at Pitt was much better. So after swallowing my pride and anger in favor of better training, I agreed to stay. That proved to be a very wise decision. It allowed me to have very good training and to reach an opinion of the dean that was fair to him.

GRADUATION
CLASS PLAY

Probably the only "creative" thing in which I participated during medical school was the class play. As in many, if not most, medical schools, our senior class put on a play close to graduation time. At Pitt this has been a very special occasion lasting three evenings, including the official dress rehearsal, the first night open to anyone, and the last night produced especially for the faculty, other medical students, and the alumni.

In fact, Pitt has a special Scope and Scalpel Society open to any member of the senior class, which is responsible for the show. Alumni and faculty contribute money to purchase material, rent lights and the like for the play, and to pay for the bash that follows the final evening show. They also receive tickets for the show and party. The official faculty advisor for this group was "Bebe" Miller, an obstetrician-gynecologist and Broadway-theater enthusiast. He and his wife, Gwen, opened their home, including refreshments, to the class writing group that met almost weekly for a year. The result was an hour-and-a-half musical production that we named *Medic Hair*. You might recall that *Hair* was a Broadway hit at that time, and we rewrote the lyrics of many of the songs from that show, mostly to make fun of the faculty and of ourselves. It was all done with an understanding that no one should be offended by what was said or sung.

Every one of our classmates participated—either as a writer, actor, member of the full orchestra (we had a number of very good musicians in the class), stage hand, or usher for the production nights. Many of us participated in several of these activities. I directed the show, once again learning how talented and cooperative my classmates were. It was not easy to coordinate a show that included some substantial song-and-dance routines, but because we worked so well as a team we had a great deal of fun. A number of faculty and alumni members told us that the play was one of the very best shows ever put on at Pitt. I'm not sure how true that was, but we all agreed that it had been well worth the effort involved.

GRADUATION CEREMONIES

In anticipation of spending the next year in Pittsburgh, my classmate Diane and I rented an apartment in a house near the medical center and moved in a few weeks before graduation. I couldn't believe the day had finally come. Diane and I planned a garden party for our families and friends and their families, who would come to the graduation ceremony. The day before the official ceremony, which included all graduates, their families, and a few friends, there was a small ceremony. At this meeting, including only the medical school graduation class and some faculty members, the faculty announced various awards. I skipped that meeting in order to prepare for the party arranged for the next day.

When Diane returned from the meeting, she told me that the class had voted me the outstanding graduate of the year. I couldn't believe it; I certainly wasn't the smartest or the most talented, so I was flabbergasted but greatly honored by the news. I can still remember the look on my parents' faces when that award was announced at the official graduation. Memories like that remain throughout a lifetime.

A few weeks before graduation, Poppie told me that he and Nannie wanted to buy me my first car, for which they had been saving for many years. When Poppie and I went to look at used cars, I saw a fairly new, beautiful, green Firebird convertible. I knew they couldn't afford an expensive used car, so I convinced Poppie to allow me to cover the difference. After all, I would soon actually be receiving a paycheck and could well cover the monthly payments for the relatively small difference. Poppie liked the car so much that one day I saw him sitting in the driver's seat with a glowing smile on his face. I'll write more about that car later, but now it's time to go on to my internship (or first year of residency, as it is now known).

CHAPTER 6

Finally, I'm a Doctor: Internship at the Children's Hospital of Pittsburgh

As it turned out, my decision to stay at the Children's Hospital of Pittsburgh for my first year of residency (then called internship) was very wise. The faculty; my colleagues, including the doctors, nurses, and all other health-care staff; and patients and their families allowed me to learn in surroundings that maintained the Pitt spirit of excellence in a caring environment.

How to Be a Jewish Homemaker
Diane had married just before graduation, but her husband, Mal, had moved to Canada, where he was offered a very good job. Of course that meant Diane would be away from Mal for most of a year. In addition, being Jewish she wanted to prepare for her family-to-be by keeping a kosher kitchen. This was to be a new experience for both of us. Needless to say, because of the kosher rule not to mix dairy with meat, our dishes and cutlery spent most of the time in dirt. I'm not sure why that was supposed to cleanse them, but I followed what Diane told me. It was an interesting experience, especially since we had not much time at home, with our every-third-night on-call schedule at the hospital.

While I learned a great deal about kosher cooking, this was another example of the Great Comedian's peculiar sense of humor: a nice "Italian" woman sharing a kosher kitchen with a nice Jewish woman. I

72

believe this proved that there is not much difference between the two, regarding the importance of food. In fact, there really is only one difference between a Jewish and an Italian mother: if a child won't eat, the Jewish mother says, "Nathan, if you don't eat I will kill myself," but the Italian mother will say, "Joey, if you don't eat, I will kill you."

My Jalopy Vacation

We were given a two-week vacation during internship. Mine was scheduled for the end of January, during which time I spent one week with one of my intern colleagues who lived in Canada. Our vacations had been scheduled for the same period, so we had a wonderful time resting and touring. At the end of the one week I spent with her, I left her home in Canada driving my new (to me) Firebird. I looked forward to a leisurely drive to my parents' home, where I planned to spend the final week of my vacation. That was a great plan, but about two hours from my colleague's home, I hit a large patch of black ice. I spun out of control, and ended up facing the opposite side of the road, having hit a post. Fortunately, there was no traffic on that road at the time, and I had not been driving very fast, so I was not injured. However, my car had to be towed to a nearby garage.

The owner of the garage told me the car needed repairs that required it to be left there for a few days. After I called my insurance agent, the garage owner arranged for a ride to the bus station for me. He said he'd call me when the car was ready for pickup. He also said that, because I was a doctor and was time constrained, he could even arrange for his son to deliver the car to me at my parents' house, for a modest fee. His young son was obviously enamored with the car from the moment it arrived at the garage. I checked with my insurance agent, who approved all arrangements.

A few days later, I received a call from my insurance agent. He told me that my car had been declared totaled. The insurance company would reimburse me for an amount not nearly enough to pay what I still owed on it; the amount also did not include sufficient funds for a new car anywhere near as nice as the one I had been driving. I told him that my car was certainly not totaled when it was towed. There was only some front-end damage that I had been led to believe was going to be fixed. I also told him that I thought the garage owner's son now owned a very nice car. I also asked how the car could have been declared totaled when I had the deed. Also, I had not given permission for them to declare the car totaled. My insurance agent told me that I could fight it in Canadian courts, but I had little chance of winning. I was not a Canadian citizen, and he said that I'd have a difficult time obtaining car insurance in the future. This was a clear case of unfair treatment that, unfortunately, is probably not all that unusual.

Whether or not what my agent said was true or fair, I decided this was not a battle I wanted to fight at that point in my life. I also tried to give the owner and his son the benefit of the doubt. So after I received the check from the insurance company, I went to the used car dealer in Scranton where I'd purchased my beautiful Firebird. I bought an old Pontiac GTO that I could afford. I decided that mourning the loss of a car, or any material thing, is simply not wise. That has always proven to be true for me.

SOME EXPERIENCES WITH PATIENTS

I can best project that internship year's professional experience by discussing what happened with two patients for whom I was privileged to have provided medical care. The first was an eighteen-month-old boy whose care was turned over to me when I returned to the hospital after a two-day Christmas holiday. He was the child of a couple who had spent almost twenty years trying to conceive and carry a baby to birth. They both had worked at low-paying jobs, saving for the child they wanted so badly. The mother had quit her job when the baby was born. Two days before I first saw the boy, he had developed a high fever and had trouble breathing. After a complete medical work-up, he had been admitted to the hospital and put on intravenous antibiotics. Despite this regimen, his condition gradually worsened. He was moved to a unit for sicker patients, which had more nursing staff. This was before the days of pediatric intensive care units.

I had closely watched him over the course of the day, while caring for other patients. That evening it was apparent that the child would probably require intubation (putting a tube down his trachea) and probably a ventilator, because his breathing had become so labored. I asked the nurse to prepare for the procedure of intubation. When I looked deeply at the back of his throat with a laryngoscope, I discovered a mass swelling that for some reason had not been apparent on an X-ray taken several hours before. The swollen mass was very inflamed and appeared to be quite boggy.

While keeping a prayer in the back of my mind (I did that frequently in situations like this; I figured I needed all the help I could get), I asked the nurse for a 20-cc (two-thirds of an ounce) syringe with a long needle, usually used for spinal taps. With her assistance in making sure the child did not move, I inserted the needle into the mass and withdrew so much pus it almost filled the syringe. My prayers of pleading for guidance turned to prayers of thanksgiving, because when I withdrew the needle and the laryngoscope, the child began breathing restfully.

We watched him very closely the rest of the night. I had spoken with his mother several times over the previous day and late evening and had received her permission to intubate him that night, in her absence, if necessary. At that earlier time, I believed I would not have very good news when she arrived back at the hospital early the next morning. I had not called to tell her that I hadn't intubated her little boy, because I didn't know if that might become necessary over the next hours, during the night, even though he seemed to be doing very well. It always seems that bad things happened during the night, so I was taking no chances.

Early the next morning, the nurses bathed the child and put on him a clean hospital gown. Then he sat up in the crib, crying for his mother.

Sometimes, in situations like this, the cries of a child can be a wonderful sound. When his mother saw him looking so cute and reaching out for, her calling her by name, she started to cry. She was joined by many of us who had trouble hiding back our tears of joy. The child was discharged from the hospital on New Year's Eve, two days before my birthday. When both parents came for him, they gave me a box of chocolates. Clearly the now-healthy child is one of the best birthday gifts I've ever received, and I think of him and his parents every time I see a box of chocolates. To me this is another reason why chocolate is so great.

Now there might be some doctors and nurses reading this and wondering why I didn't call a surgeon, who would have performed the procedure in the operating room. To those who wonder about this, I suggest you consider that this episode took place in 1969, more than forty-five years ago—or, in medicine, forty-five light years ago. Like all doctors, I had been taught to respond to emergencies as soon as possible. The child was in respiratory distress, and I certainly knew how to intubate him. I had no second thought about aspirating the boggy mass, with the laryngoscope protecting the child's airway. This was one time when the adage "Don't just do something; stand there" was just plain wrong.

The second patient representing an important incident in my internship year was Bobby. That is not his real name, but it is how I remember him. He was admitted eight days before I was to leave for my residency at Johns Hopkins. Before being admitted to the hospital, four-year-old Bobby had a few days' history of fever, fatigue (almost always of concern in a four-year-old), and bruising.

After a brief evaluation, the diagnosis of acute lymphoblastic leukemia was made, and we began treatment with medications that made him feel even sicker than when he was admitted. He was a very brave little kid, and it was painful to watch his parents suffer with him. He was their only child, and at that time (unlike today, thank God), leukemia cures were not common. Like so many parents of children with leukemia, they wanted so badly to believe their child would be one of the rare children who would be cured. That hope was what kept so many of us able to care for these very sick children and their families every day.

Bobby's treatment required frequent blood drawings and keeping IVs open to deliver the medications. To make matters worse, like most children with leukemia at that time, his veins were difficult to enter with a needle. They also easily infiltrated (the fluid escaped from the vein and accumulated in the surrounding tissue), requiring additional insertions into another vein. I had had a lot of experience inserting needles into tiny veins while working in the Wilkes College laboratory with rabbits, so I was very good at it. However, these children presented a challenge to even the very best. To somewhat allay the fears of children undergoing painful procedures, I would sing a silly "owie" song with the child. That song allowed the child to sing (or yell), as loud as he or she wanted. However, the song did not make the needle insertion any easier.

Like so many children, Bobby dreaded going to the treatment room, because he knew it meant another needle insertion usually requiring several attempts before the needle could be secured. The development of venous catheters was to come, but not in time to help Bobby and others like him. Bobby had a lucky dime his grandfather had given him, and he would hold that dime whenever he required a painful procedure.

One day, after two attempts by me to insert a needle, Bobby, who was usually very stoic, had tears in his eyes. He opened his hand with the dime, and asked me if I would take his dime and stop with the "owies." I held him for a few minutes, but I had to leave him in the treatment room with a nurse for a while so I could regain composure. When I reentered the room, he told me that he was better and that he wanted the medicine to help him. I had no idea what the nurse had said or done to calm Bobbie, but I later told her how grateful I was. So Bobbie and I again sang the "owie" song and, thankfully, the next attempt to insert the needle was successful. The bravery of some children can be simultaneously both heartbreaking and heartwarming.

I spent much time with Bobby over the next week, but it did not look like the medication was helping. When I had first met Bobby and his parents, I had explained that on June 29 (one week after his admission), I had to leave, because I was going to be a resident at Johns Hopkins in Baltimore. However, I promised them that I would work as hard as I could to "make Bobby better," and if that didn't happen by the time I had to leave, another resident, who was very good, would take over Bobby's care.

My last day at the hospital, I went to see him as soon as I arrived at the hospital that morning. I reminded him and his parents that I had to leave for Baltimore early that day, and I introduced them to the resident who would take my place. I anticipated a sad good-bye, and judging by how badly Bobby looked that morning, I knew he was not going to live much longer. I had started work at 6:00 a.m., anticipating being able to leave at noon. I had parked my fully packed car in the hospital parking lot to save time, so I would have time with Bobby and his parents before I left.

I had worked an extra weekend in order to leave a day and a half earlier, so I could drive to Baltimore in the daylight, the day before I was to start my residency there. This plan to drive in daylight had become even more important, when a week before, one of our beloved senior resident colleagues, who had been driving to a fellowship position in Boston, had left in the evening. He apparently had fallen asleep while driving, hit the back of a trailer truck, and was killed.

The day I was to leave, in addition to taking care of my patients, I had to make sure all records were in pristine shape and that the resident who would take over my patients was properly informed. It was now about three o'clock, and I knew that only if I left immediately could I make the drive all the way to Baltimore in daylight. That meant that I would not have a lot of time to spend with Bobby and his parents.

So after a brief, and tearful, good-bye with Bobby and his family, I made the decision to leave. Even though I arrived safely, if exhausted, in Baltimore at dusk, I have always regretted making that decision. I know I could not have done any more for Bobby, and that by staying longer I would have endangered my life by driving in the dark while being very tired. However, when I found out that he died two days after I left, I felt a great sadness. I think of him often, still with regrets that I had not stayed much longer for the last good-bye.

ON TO HOPKINS

Lest you think my intern days were all sad, it is important to assure you that I had many happy and fulfilling days and nights. I would not have traded that experience for anything. There were many days of gratification and even joy. However, I had made the decision to spend my second and third residency years at another institution. So, early in the academic year, I had sent applications to a few pediatric residency programs that I learned had openings for second-year pediatric residents.

One of them was a relatively new program in community pediatrics, at Johns Hopkins. While it was not the famous Harriet Lane program, and most of the experience would occur at what was then the Baltimore City Hospital, all the faculty were Hopkins professors. Also, a number of the rotations could occur at the famed Hopkins Children's Center. This seemed like a wonderful opportunity for me to finally experience Hopkins medicine. About halfway through my internship year, I had interviews at Hopkins and the Children's Hospital of Colorado programs, which were my first choices. A few weeks later, I received an acceptance letter from the Colorado program. They requested that I let them know as soon as possible, because they had several other doctors seeking that position.

Rather than simply accepting the Colorado position, I decided to call Dr. Robert Cooke, the chair of Pediatrics at Hopkins. I wanted to know if I would be accepted to their community program. This was a brazen act, but in fairness to Colorado, I had to make a rapid decision about where I would spend the next two years of training. I was shocked that Dr. Cooke personally answered my call. Before I could say anything except for introducing myself, he asked if I had already received the letter he had sent to me, a day or two before. My heart sank, believing that it was a rejection. Instead, he told me that he wanted me to accept a position in the Harriet Lane program, which had just become available. I almost fainted with joy, and of course I accepted immediately. I could only imagine what wonderful days lay ahead for me at Hopkins. Of course, I immediately called the program director in Colorado, respectfully declining their kind offer.

Many years later, we discovered that the Harriet Lane position that had become open was originally offered to my later-to-be husband, Jim, before it was offered to me. He was returning from his experience in the National Public Health Service as a Peace Corps physician in Thailand. Jim had decided to accept a position at the University of Rochester for one year, and the following year he would come to Hopkins, where I met him. The Great Comedian was at work again.

CHAPTER 7

My First "Preparation H" Experience: Residency at the Johns Hopkins Children's Medical and Surgical Center

My first day at Hopkins was a mixture of happy fulfillment; sadness for having left Bobby, other patients, and colleagues back in Pittsburgh; and confusion. The Hopkins Children's Medical and Surgical Center, or CMSC, is huge, with several buildings interconnected to the rest of Johns Hopkins Hospital. There were so many new people to meet, including the patients, my fellow residents (all of whom had been together for a full year), other residents and fellows, nurses, child-life workers, the maintenance and diet crews, social workers, and the myriad of others who comprise a health-care team. (Note that I include patients first as part of the health-care team; in fact, the patient, for whom all decisions are made, should be made should be the center of the team.)

I could hardly believe that I was actually in the esteemed Harriet Lane program and not the community program, to which I had originally applied. To those not familiar with the history of the program, it is named after Harriet Lane, the niece of bachelor president James Buchanan. She had served in the role of First Lady of the United States from 1857 to 1861. She later married Henry Elliott Johnson, a Baltimore banker. After they lost two young sons to illnesses, she donated a generous sum to found the Harriet Lane Home for Invalid Children, which served as the first hospital for children in the United States. In gratitude, to this day her name has remained on the pediatric outpatient clinic and the pediatric residency program at Johns Hopkins.

The wisdom of her gift has been proven. The Hopkins Department of Pediatrics, in many ways, became one of the meccas of US pediatrics because of the quality of education, research, and clinical care provided there. In fact, arguably the highest award in pediatrics is named after Dr. John Howland, the second chair of pediatrics at Hopkins. He set the scientific course of pediatrics and established how a "modern" pediatric clinic should work. The first Howland awardee was Edwards A. Park, the Hopkins chair of Pediatrics at the time. It would be incorrect to think that this award and the first awardee were contrived by Hopkins folks. The award was established and awarded by many non-Hopkins pediatricians who were active at the time in the American Pediatric Society, which sponsors the award.

When I became a Hopkins pediatric resident, we worked every other night, which really meant thirty-six of every forty-eight hours. If we were lucky, we could take calls from our homes during the night. For those who had been on duty (i.e., awake) during the previous night, there was a scheduled one-hour naptime; it was called noon conference.

Because residents worked an every-other-night call schedule, we were required to live within a very short distance of the hospital. In addition, the hospital was situated in a less than ideal place to live, in the eastern part of Baltimore. Most residents lived in a hospital-owned living facility called The Compound (an odd name for an apartment complex, I thought). The Compound consisted of a group of apartment buildings across from the main hospital. I rented a studio apartment, and it took me exactly two minutes to walk from my door to the hospital's main entrance.

To this day, anyone who enters the main hospital entrance, under the famous Hopkins dome, is met by a magnificent ten-foot, marble statue of Christ, The Consoler or The Divine Healer. The statue is a replica of the Christus Consolator, sculpted in 1838 by Bertel Thorvaldsen, which stands in the Church of Our Lady of Copenhagen, Denmark.

The statue is a symbol of hope and healing. Jim and I have been very taken by that statue, so much so that we made a special trip to see the original a few years ago. We have a small replica of the statue in our living room. It truly is a magnificent work of art.

Johns Hopkins Hospital and the entrance area have changed substantially since my residency years. However, the Christ statue remains under the magnificent dome entrance, where it was placed in 1887, when the hospital opened. People of all religions continue to touch His right foot as they pass by. When called back to the hospital in the middle of the night, I—and so many other residents, patients, and visitors—felt a sort of comfort performing this ritual. In fact, the statue's right foot has been worn smooth by the touch of so many. In addition, people leave poignant notes and flowers at the base of the statue.

Working essentially thirty-six of every forty-eight hours for two years meant that we celebrated birthdays, engagements, many holidays, and various other happenings at the hospital. I had many dinner dates there with guys who thought it was cool, except perhaps when I was paged (no beepers then), to see a patient.

When I first arrived, I wondered why there was always a Hopkins security guard on duty, in a tiny shelter at the end of the street that led from the hospital, to the entrance of the compound, where I and many residents lived. I found out why late one night, after a very long and tiring day. When I was walking home from the hospital, three adolescent boys, who probably lived in the neighborhood, were following me.

They started calling me dirty names and using foul language. I kept walking and looked down the street for the guard, but he wasn't there. As the boys drew closer and started to encircle me (one had a knife), my fatigue vanished with a rush of adrenalin, and I became angry. I stopped and opened my overcoat, to reveal my white coat. I then told the boys that I had just spent all day taking care of their brothers, sisters, and neighbors. I also said that if they wanted to hurt me in order to feel powerful, they certainly could, because I was hardly capable of fighting off three of them. I stood there with my arms outstretched and faced them. The boy with the knife put it away and called off the others. I began walking very fast toward my apartment. They kept following me, but now at a distance, all the way to my door.

I went inside and locked and bolted the door. While my heart was still pounding, I called the security desk and found out that the guard had stepped out "for only a minute." When I told him what had just happened to me, he was very upset, mostly with himself. I promised not to report him, and he promised to never leave his post unattended. Fair exchange, I thought.

SOME EXPERIENCES WITH PATIENTS
OUTPATIENT EXPERIENCES
Once again I will use stories or situations involving patients as examples, this time of my Harriet Lane experiences. I was the only woman among the nine residents in our group. Whereas that made no difference to my colleagues or me, I sometimes found myself in curious situations. Such was the case when I spent time in the so-called emergency room (ER). The ER also served as a walk-in clinic, especially during the daytime, because many East Baltimore families had no private doctors. No doctor wanted to set up a private practice office in that dangerous neighborhood. The "east Baltimore rod and gun club" usually met at night and on weekends and contributed greatly to the capacity of the ER after dark.

As I saw patients in the ER during the day, I noticed that I was seeing many girls between the ages of ten and the early teens. (Those older than eighteen usually were seen in the adult ER and were mostly admitted to the adult units, rather than to the adolescent unit in the Children's Center. This changed years later as adolescent medicine became part of pediatrics.) I was curious, so I discussed the number of teenage girls I was seeing with the triage nurse. The nurse put the patients' charts in the various boxes that were situated outside the room where each patient was to be seen by a resident. She told me that she routinely put the charts in the boxes in the order of when the patients were registered, unless one doctor seemed to be taking a lot of time with a sick patient.

I then noted that many of the girls *I* was seeing had a chief complaint of abdominal pain and realized that my male colleagues seemed to be uncomfortable and probably felt unprepared to care for them. That was clarified when I discussed it with my colleagues. They admitted exchanging patients assigned to me for girls assigned to them who presented with problems situated between the navel and knees.

On reflection I realized that much of my knowledge in general adolescent medicine came primarily from my personal relationships with my sisters, my female friends, a bit from nurses' training, and some from my experience as a nurse at Wilkes College—not much of it was from my training as a doctor. That realization was the stimulus for my interest in adolescent medicine and why I started an adolescent medicine program when I returned to Hopkins years later. I also noted that, although our residence training and experiences were excellent for hospitalized patients, outpatient care seemed to be treated as being of secondary importance. I read a lot about adolescent medicine and outpatient care during my residency and became more and more interested in what was to become known as primary care. This interest was surprising to me because I had planned to return to Pittsburgh to complete another residency in transplant surgery.

My first encounter with a young mother-to-be happened when I saw a twelve-year-old who was complaining of abdominal pain. When I examined her, it was obvious that she was in labor but hadn't a clue about what was happening. When I went outside the examining room to speak with her grandmother, who had brought her to the ER, she told me that she had thought that was the case but was not sure. The child (and she was indeed a child) did not live with her grandmother, but the girl had gone to her when she had the pain. I returned to the examining room with the girl's grandmother and found the young girl hugging a doll that she had brought from home.. I explained what was happening, but she obviously didn't completely understand. Her grandmother agreed to stay with her while I had the girl admitted to the obstetrics unit. She was still holding her doll when she was wheeled to the unit.

After I was finished in the ER, I went to the obstetrics unit and found the girl's grandmother waiting for her granddaughter, who was in the labor room. Later that night, the girl child delivered a baby child. Thankfully, the grandmother agreed to take care of both the new mother and her baby. That episode began my plans for setting up an adolescent program for mothers and babies, who would be seen together.

A humorous patient-centered incident involved the mother of a child whom I had seen the previous evening. When we wanted a patient to be followed up the next day, we would fill out a slip of paper that indicated that the appointment was to be with the doctor we designated as "F/U" (for follow-up). That was done because we weren't always sure who might be the designated follow-up resident the next day. We were amused that many parents came to the ER asking to see "Dr. Fu," but one mother caused a laugh-out-loud situation when she asked to see the "hippie woman doctor." As it turned out, she was referring to me, because my hair was so long I could sit on it, and she thought I was a hippie, even though (or perhaps because) I wore it pulled back with a colorful scarf. It's amazing how sometimes we present to others and remain clueless to the presentation.

A not-so-amusing incident occurred in a different outpatient setting. I volunteered to work in a nearby storefront free clinic every other Tuesday night, when I was not on call. One evening, as I was parking my car outside the clinic, the volunteer nurse came to the car along with an older woman, who was holding a sick toddler in her arms. They had been waiting for me just inside the door of the clinic. One look at the very sick child and I asked the woman (who turned out to be the grandmother) to get in my car. I asked the nurse to call the Hopkins pediatric ER and warn them that I was bringing in a very sick child. I wanted an IV set up, and I'd see the child immediately while the grandmother was registering him.

Taking care of the child was routine, because what he obviously had was pneumonia. He had a very high fever, was breathing with difficulty, and required oxygen and IV antibiotics. Like so many children with pneumococcal (the type he probably had) pneumonia, he was afebrile and running around the ER within eight hours after treatment. We sent him home to be followed up the next day.

He was healthy and happy when I saw him the next day, and although his grandmother looked like she could use a good night's sleep, she also was very happy. When I noted that she lived only two blocks from Johns Hopkins Hospital, I asked why she hadn't taken the child directly to the pediatric ER when he first became sick. She replied that she didn't have the two-dollar "down payment." I had no idea what she meant, until the front-desk staff pointed to a sign that recently had been posted in the pediatric ER. The sign stated that a two-dollar fee was required before a patient could be seen.

I was very upset and immediately removed the sign, and I told the staff to have anyone who objected call me. Later that day I was called by Dr. Cooke, the chairman of Pediatrics, who wanted to know why I had removed the sign. I told him the story of the child with the pneumonia, who could have died without antibiotics. He understood my point, but stated that the hospital needed to charge something. Many of the patients didn't have insurance and used the ER like a doctor's office, many times for small problems that did not require a doctor's care, much less an ER.

He said he was going to have the sign replaced. I told him that I understood the reason for the sign, but if it was replaced, I would resign. He didn't believe that I'd actually do that until he looked at me and realized that I wanted no part of such a program. There had to be another resolution to the problem. I knew in his heart he also did not like the policy, and I told him exactly that. He sighed and agreed, and the sign was never replaced. However, the staff did try to collect whatever they could from the patients. They also referred appropriate patients to a social worker, who could help them acquire medical assistance insurance. Seven years later, I returned to Hopkins with a plan to take care of that problem, which I'll relate later.

That incident was a turning point in my career and sparked my decision to withdraw from returning to Pittsburgh for the transplant surgery residency and fellowship. I determined that for every child I could help with a transplantation, there were thousands who could benefit from my application of medical service, research, education, and organization of better outpatient care, with the continuation of coordinated inpatient care when necessary. In other words, I wanted to organize a program to teach residents how to care for children, the way every pediatrician should practice every day in the office or clinic. I wanted to change the method of training future pediatricians by no longer treating hospitalization as "in-house" medicine versus outpatient care as "out-house" medicine. I believe both are incredibly important, and better outpatient care should lead to fewer hospitalizations.

INPATIENT EXPERIENCES

Stories about two hospitalized children may provide some insight about that aspect of my Hopkins residency. The first involved "Jimmy," a five-year-old boy who was admitted with a diagnosis of rhabdomyosarcoma, a relatively rare form of cancer that had a very poor prognosis. After many weeks of unsuccessful chemotherapy and radiation therapy, Jimmy was admitted to the hospital for what is now known as palliative care. That care consists of reducing the physical and emotional pain and stress associated with serious illness when the patient is near death. For Jimmy, the physical part included pain-relieving medication and oxygen, because he was having trouble breathing. His parents wisely had refused to have him intubated and put on a ventilator, because they knew that would only prolong his suffering.

As with so many parents whose children have bad diseases, his were completely devoted. At least one of them stayed with him at all times. They had received special permission from the hospital administration to do so, because their child was very sick and believed to be near death at the time of his admission. This special permission was necessary, because this incident happened before the institution of the current practice, which *encourages* parents to stay with their children, and provides chair/beds (that is, chairs that could be made into beds) in every room for family members. Sometimes wisdom prevails with time and experience.

I tried to spend as much time with Jimmy as possible, attempting to comfort him and his parents while not neglecting my other patients. There was not much more I could do beyond making sure he received sufficient pain-relieving medication and oxygen. After several days watching Jimmy gradually growing weaker and having more trouble breathing, his parents asked if they could speak with me privately. Of course I agreed but was decimated by their request. They wanted me to give Jimmy something to end his suffering forever. When they perceived my reaction of sadness and shock, his father fell to his knees, took my hands in his, and tearfully begged me to please do as they asked. I was shaken but softly and carefully explained that I simply couldn't do what they wanted. I left the room to try and regain my composure.

No one had ever made such a request of me, and this occurred long before the idea of euthanasia was openly discussed, certainly never in any medical conference I'd attended. My religious background and medical professionalism made even considering such an act impossible. Or so I thought. For the next few hours I attended to the needs of my other patients, but I kept thinking about the little boy down the hall, obviously suffering, as were his parents. Was my vocation not to relieve pain and suffering? Yes, but was deliberately shortening someone's life an accepted way of achieving this? I wasn't sure.

I kept thinking of ways I could end this suffering, such as giving the maximum dose of pain medication—which could well suppress Jimmy's respirations—and turning off the oxygen. These disturbing thoughts stayed with me while I attended to the needs of other patients.

However, after making final rounds for the night and signing my other patients out to my colleague, I returned to Jimmy's room. I had decided that I just couldn't do such a thing. Instead, I stayed with him and his parents all night, to provide them with succor, even though I was officially off duty.

The next morning, I went home to shower and change clothing and then returned to Jimmy's room. His condition continued to decline that day and the next, until finally he took his last breath, while being held by his mother and father. I was also in his room at that time, knowing that the end was very near. His parents and I then held hands and said a prayer for him, and I silently added one for them.

Three days later I attended Jimmy's funeral. As we walked away from his gravesite and said good-bye, his parents hugged me and handed me a small box that they asked me to open later. The box contained a small silver silhouette charm of a child's head, which looks very much like Jimmy. I have kept that charm in a music box that, unlike Jimmy, continues to play.

The other story of one of my patients involves "Candy," an eleven-year-old girl who was hospitalized for evaluation of fever, anemia, low platelet count, high white-cell count, and splenomegaly. It didn't take very long to make the diagnosis of acute lymphoblastic leukemia (shades of Bobby in Pittsburgh) and to begin IV chemotherapy. When the situation was discussed with her understandably distraught parents, they insisted that their child not be told the diagnosis. Of course, we all agreed to honor their wishes, even though some of us were not sure "protecting" the child in this way was a good idea.

Our routine was for the on-call resident to make rounds on the patients with the residents going off duty at 10:00 p.m. This was to make sure all necessary procedures had been performed and medical orders written before we went home for the night. Remember that we all lived only a few minutes away from the hospital, and one resident slept in the single on-call room, to handle all emergencies until the resident for that unit could be present.

One night, as I was about to leave, I passed by Candy's room and heard her crying. I went into the room, put my arms around her, and asked why she was crying and had looked so sad all day. I asked, "Do you have pain?" to which she replied "Only in my heart, Dr. De." I was taken aback by that mature response from such a young child and asked her why her heart was hurting. Her response taught me a very important lesson, which I carry to this day. She said, "Because no one will tell me the truth. I know I have leukemia, and that's a very bad disease, and that I am probably going to die. But I can't talk to my mom or dad about it because they won't tell me, and I don't want to hurt them. But I am very scared, and I really want to talk to them."

I told her that, with her permission, I would tell her parents what she told me. I thought they would want to know, so they could talk to her about anything she wanted. I also asked her if she wanted to talk to me. We then had a long and honest discussion about her illness, and about her dreams of what she wanted to be when she grew up. I made sure she had an honest but good reason to believe that she well might go into remission with the new medicines she was receiving. Also, with all the progress that was being made, she might even be cured someday.

I knew well that it is wrong to lie to a patient (which I hadn't) but also very important to always leave her or him with hope. I stayed holding Candy's hand until she fell asleep. The next morning, I told the attending physician what had happened, and we both met with her parents as soon as they came into the hospital. They actually were relieved and, through tears, related their frustration and sadness that they hadn't been able to properly support and encourage their child. Candy did go into remission, but I don't know how long that remission lasted. My hope is that the remission lasted long enough for the medicines soon to be discovered that have led to so many cures of leukemia in children.

There were so many other patients and incidences that made my residency such an educational and wonderful experience, but the examples I've provided will have to suffice. When I think of the many sad endings, I remember the wisdom of Bishop Romero when he observed that many important things can only be seen through eyes that have cried.

Plans for The Future

Because I had made the decision to make a 180-degree change in my career plans, I had to first call the surgeon at Pittsburgh to tell him that I would not be coming for the surgical residency in his program. He was shocked that I had made that decision. He said that he had offered me a chance to "make history." How true was that prediction when one considers the incredible transplant program that developed and expanded at Pittsburgh. The surgeon also said that I was throwing it away for something that was not nearly as exciting and would not be as rewarding to someone like me. I told him that he might well be correct, especially about the exciting possibilities of transplant surgery, but I hoped he was wrong about the rest. He kindly wished me well, as I did him. In retrospect, knowing what happened later with ground breaking transplant surgery at the University of Pittsburgh, he was absolutely correct about making history. However, I have never regretted my decision, and I have been very happy with the choice I made.

Where and How Next?

Now I had to determine where and how I might obtain the knowledge and training for something that didn't quite exist at that time. I wanted eventually to develop and implement an academic general pediatrics and adolescent medicine program. Such a program would include the clinical, teaching, and research rigor that was present in the subspecialties. At that time, there existed bits and pieces of what I needed in various places, but none had what I felt would be right for me. I knew that I needed to know much more about the economics of medical care, because the dollar seemed to be a major factor in decisions about where to spend resources for programs. I also needed to find out more about the legal aspects of care.

I was told that Harvard had some of the best resources for obtaining such training. So I visited there to meet with a few professors in their School of Public Health. They all advised me to come there to study. They told me that I could obtain a fellowship grant from the National Institutes of Health (NIH) if I applied first for entrance to the Harvard School of Public Health to obtain an MPH (Masters in Public Health) degree. I applied for the NIH grant and to the Harvard program, even though I didn't really seek another degree. After all, as I told my friends, no matter how many degrees you earn, you can never match the number of degrees on a thermometer, and you know where that instrument ends up. However, amazingly to me, I received a grant to cover my tuition and a small stipend that easily covered my needs, living frugally but well. I considered myself to be one lucky person!

My decision to do this, instead of choosing one of the several offers for subspecialty fellowships at Hopkins, was met with chagrin by many Hopkins faculty members. Despite that, at the end of June, upon completion of my residency at Hopkins, I would be off to Boston. I would have ten weeks before I matriculated at Harvard in September. A faculty member in the Hopkins School of Public Health, who had heard of my treasonous decision to attend the other "preparation H" school, asked if I would like to do an eight week "fellowship" in Peru. Surely the Great Comedian's sense of humor was working overtime.

CHAPTER 8

Peru and My Second "Preparation H" Experience:
The Harvard School of Public Health

WHAT MIGHT THE HARVARD SCHOOL of Public Health (HSPH) and
Peru have in common, as far as I was concerned? Well, I had ten weeks
of unplanned time between my residency at Hopkins and matriculating
at the Harvard School of Public Health. I needed to contemplate what I
would do in those ten weeks, and over the following nine months while
I would be earning my MPH degree. That included deciding where I
might spend the ten weeks, and then what courses I would take and the
experiences I might seek at the HSPH.

After having spent three years of working thirty-six of every forty-
eight hours, I knew vacationing and doing nothing useful for ten weeks,
and then only sitting in class for nine months, would drive me crazy
with boredom. This would happen no matter how enjoyable the vacation or interesting the courses would be. So I decided to accept the
offer from the professor in the Johns Hopkins School of Public Health,
who happened to have been born in Peru. I would spend eight of the
ten weeks in Lima, working at a hospital in which he had organized a
project involving nutrition research for children. So plans for my "vacation" were set.

I wanted the specific knowledge and experience that would be
offered at the HSPH and to avoid what I had already studied in medical
school. So just before I left for Peru, I was able to arrange to opt out of
the only two required courses for a physician seeking the MPH degree at

the HSPH. They were epidemiology and biostatistics (more accurately described as *biosadistics*). Fortunately, what I remembered from medical school was sufficient to pass the opt-out tests. That was a wonderful surprise to me, but I was not about to argue. I had other plans for use of the time I would have spent in the classroom taking those courses. But for now, I was off to Peru.

PERU

My two months in Peru were full of life-enhancing experiences, including a heavy dose of public health in the raw. I lived in a pension in beautiful Mira Flores, a suburb of Lima. It was a far cry from the place where I would spend a great deal of time, working with the native people. That place was Ciudad de Dios, in English translated to "City of God." It was well named, because only God would allow His name to be associated with it. Ciudad de Dios, where I worked in a makeshift clinic, was located on a hill just outside Lima. It was a poor excuse even for a barrio, with ramshackle living quarters constructed of pieced-together loose cardboard, tin, wood, and whatever else could be used to keep out the elements and allow for some privacy. The water supply was community barrels, filled twice a week by a city truck. The people who lived there tried their best to keep the water supply clean, but I knew better than to drink it.

The road from Lima to Ciudad was paved all the way to the bottom of a hill, where the road came to a fork. A dirt road led the way to Ciudad, and the continued paved road led to the other side of the hill, to a place called Monte Rico, that is "Rich Mountain." Rich it was indeed, with watered grass and flowers around very nicely constructed homes. The contrast was startling, and far worse than the difference between where the rich and the poor lived in the United States. At least in the United States the vast majority of poor people have reasonable, if not elegant, shelter and clean water.

My official fellowship involved making rounds and teaching in the Anglo American Hospital's Nutrition Research Unit, sponsored by the

Hopkins School of Public Health faculty member who had provided my fellowship. That fellowship paid for my travel and a stipend sufficient to cover all my living expenses. It also provided some extra money, which enabled me to visit local sites and travel on weekends to other parts of Peru. I easily completed my hospital responsibilities in the morning, and I then spent the rest of the day working in the Ciudad clinic.

I had brought some antibiotics, vaccines soon to expire, and a few *pistolas de la pas* ("pistols of peace,") as they came to be known, similar to those I had used in Nicaragua while in medical school. The pistolas were for rapid and painless injection of the vaccines; I also had some syringes for the injectable antibiotics. These medications and supplies were generously donated by the Hopkins Hospital, and I had the pistolas left over from my Pitt Nicaragua experience. I had been allowed to keep the pistolas "for possible later use." Little did we know at that time how well they would be used.

My Spanish was rudimentary at best and mostly consisted of medical terms I'd learned in Nicaragua years before. So I was looking for someone fluent in Spanish who might be willing to help me distribute the vaccines and translate in the clinic. The driver who transported me back and forth from the hospital to my pension also transported me to Ciudad. He told me to find "Madre Phillips," a Maryknoll nun (here we went again with Maryknoll) and nurse, who worked in the Ciudad.

When I found her in the Ciudad, she was teaching a group of mothers about nutrition and the importance of vaccinations, of which the clinic had none. I walked up to her (she was not wearing a habit then or ever since then) and told her that I was a physician and had some vaccines and some antibiotics. She looked at me as if I was an angel, definitely an erroneous assumption. Over the next forty-plus years of what became a very close friendship, it was the only time her assumption of my being an angel (despite my name) ever happened. She obviously got to know me better.

Madre Phillips (née Phyllis Autotte) and one of her coworkers, a native Peruvian woman named Carmen, organized the distribution of vaccines. I also set up an afternoon clinic where I could see children screened by Phyllis and Carmen. My Hopkins fellowship mentor was delighted that I wanted to work in the clinic. He even asked that I admit malnourished children to the Nutrition Research Unit of the hospital. Care would be provided for the children, with parents' permission of course. When I returned to the United States, Phyllis continued to give vaccinations at the clinic, sans physician, and we continued to correspond by mail.

Cusco and Magical Machu Picchu

One weekend in August I decided to travel to Machu Picchu and to Cusco. That involved traveling on what was then the highest train in the world (now the highest train is in Tibet). I recently investigated what is now involved in making such a trip and was amused to see the difference from what I experienced. While the current trip involves a very comfortable train for tourists, complete with dining facilities, it does not include the striking scenery or the same high-mountains experience. Too bad, because the trip I had was so memorable.

In 1972 the train to Cusco started in Lima and ascended to La Galera, a tin mine situated at a little over 15,800 feet. This is more than half the height of Mount Everest. I had been forewarned to stay as quiet as possible on the train and not to eat anything, in order to preserve oxygen. It was also important to suck on hard candy to maintain my blood sugar at high-normal levels. I experienced the wisdom of this advice as I watched other tourist passengers being given oxygen from a very large rubber bladder and *coramina* (a drug that stimulates circulationof the blood) tablets, which were carried by an attendant.

I was able to turn down both and even managed to be the only foreign traveler who got off the train at the highest point to take pictures of the amazing vista. However, I was unable to muster the energy needed to step back onto the train without the assistance of two Peruvian men. They were very surprised that I'd actually gotten off the train and had done so without passing out. Of course, hours later, when we arrived at our destination at a much lower altitude, I had a bad headache. Happily, the headache dissipated after a few hours' nap. Peruvians called this headache and fatigue *soroche* (altitude sickness). Understanding the physiology of this condition, I kiddingly described it medically as "the handle falling off the sodium pump."

I knew it was very important to sleep in order to regain the energy needed to fully tour Cusco. The only hotel space available was a two-bed room I had to share with a young Peruvian couple and their two young children. Of course I had the bed with the two children, one of whom wet the bed. Fortunately, there was a shower, and I had brought a change of clothes. The couple and their children, especially the bed wetter, were so delightful I didn't mind the inconvenience. What pediatrician would?

That family and I shared breakfast, and then I went off to tour the many wonders of Cusco before I traveled to Machu Picchu. That trip to Machu Picchu, situated on a peak of 7,970 feet, was one of the most memorable of all my travel adventures throughout the world.

After visiting the Inca ruins of Machu Picchu, I wanted to ascend the extra 1,000 feet or so to sleep on Huayna Picchu. On that high peak, I could experience sunrise over Machu Picchu and view the Urubamba River Valley from above. I had learned that it was possible to climb to Huayna Picchu, via steps carved in the mountain by the Quechua natives many years ago. There was a rule that Machu Picchu was to be exited by late afternoon, thereby not allowing visitors to make the extra climb that late. But I intended to make the extra climb just before closing, and there was no gate to stop me.

Of course I wanted company on that mountain overnight, and I had met two law students on the train who also wanted to make the extra climb. They had sleeping bags because they were touring South America and didn't want to spend money on hotels unless it was necessary. I had borrowed a blanket from the generous manager of the hotel located near the Machu Picchu ruins. The climb was exhilarating to say the least. It was a really interesting experience to have birds flying below me while I was climbing up.

That evening we spent a few hours discussing the magnificent views while eating cheese, bread, and apples and drinking a small amount of wine. We had packed for a picnic but had forgotten to bring water, but we knew better than to drink very much alcohol at that altitude. We then slept on a ledge overlooking the Urubamba River Valley. Being a very light sleeper, early the next morning I awoke to the sound of bells from a church and from the bells on goats in the valley. The sun was just about to rise.

I awakened my friends and then wandered off to be alone on another ledge that overlooked Machu Picchu. I had as close to an epiphanic experience as I've ever had. As I sat on the edge of the ledge, the sun rose over the mountain, and the mist from the river valley that encompassed Machu Picchu began to lift, effecting the illusion that the ancient ruins were rising. I felt like I was flying, and at that moment I fully felt the true meaning of life, which I simply cannot explain in words. However, that profound memory served me well later when I had life-threatening experiences.

BOSTON
ROXBURY CLINIC

After all the adventures in Peru, it was time to return to Boston and begin my studies. I also chose to seek part-time employment at the Roxbury health clinic, where I had been advised I could learn how Harvard had organized neighborhood clinics. The clinic was in a very poor neighborhood, but I knew I could not tolerate being unable to practice pediatrics and only spend my time attending classes.

I was greeted with open arms by the staff at the Roxbury Clinic, especially when I agreed to work two evenings a week. I was a little surprised, however, when I was told that it was fortunate that I had an old car (read "jalopy"), because I had to park on the street in front of the clinic. Also, I was instructed to wait in my jalopy car, with the doors locked, until the guard from the clinic came to accompany me to the clinic door. He also escorted me from the clinic to the car when I finished the evening's work. A few years after I left Boston and the Roxbury Clinic, I read that a woman had been doused with gasoline and set on fire near the clinic. I understood more clearly why the precautions had been required.

Despite the street danger, the patients, their families, and the people who worked at the clinic, all of whom were from the neighborhood, were wonderful. Like most such clinics, we dispensed what medicines we had and prescribed over-the-counter medicines whenever possible. Anyone requiring further evaluation by a specialist or laboratory tests, other than the simple blood or urine tests we could perform in the clinic, had to be referred to the hospital clinics. This practice reminded me very much of how we operated in Liberia, both being very effective.

The Book for Pediatric Nurse Practitioners (PNPs)
The formal classes I took for credit at the HSPH were one taught by Professor Rashi Fein, the health economist who later became my friend; two classes and a laboratory experience in curriculum design, which I used to formulate the course I was to use later for training nurse practitioners; a course in health systems in developing countries; and a few others necessary to make up the total credits I needed for the degree. The rest were ad-hoc classes I needed to prepare for my planned program in academic primary care.

I knew that with some specific additional training, nurses could manage many infants and children, who required routine care for checking their general health, growth, and development, and those who had relatively nonsevere illnesses. I wanted to develop a course for them that could be implemented at my first academic position, where I planned to teach PNPs and doctors to work together.

While taking the course in curriculum design, I not only outlined the course to train PNPs, but I wrote what turned out to be the text I would use in the course. I wrote the text because I couldn't find any single book that contained all the basic material necessary to teach PNPs. The hardest part of putting the book together was typing the material, because I had never typed anything since taking a typing course in high school. Computers were to be a thing of the future as far as I was concerned, but electric typewriters were available. So I used my meager savings to buy a used electric typewriter and plowed my way through.

After completing the first draft, I knew it needed to be field tested. I met with Priscilla Andrews, the director of one of the first PNP programs in the United States, at Northeastern University in Boston. She was very happy to have the material, especially since I volunteered to teach in her course, and would be responsible for obtaining reviews on the material from the students. I used the comments of the students and Pricilla to augment what I had written originally. She and they liked what I put together, and she told one of her friends who worked at Little Brown and Company Publishers about it. The publishers subsequently contacted me, and the book was published in 1975. That was just in time to be used in the PNP course I was to teach at my first academic position at Columbia Babies and Children's Hospital.

COURSE ON GLOBAL HEALTH SYSTEMS

In the course I took on health systems in developing countries, otherwise known as global health, we were required to describe a health system that could work in a developing country. I described the system that worked so well in Liberia and was amused when my paper was returned with a C grade. I could not have cared less about the grade, but out of curiosity, I asked the instructor what was wrong with what I described. He told me that such a system would never work in a developing country.

I asked him if he'd had any personal experience working in developing countries. He replied that, although he had never worked in a developing country, he had visited many and had read a great deal about the various systems. I smiled and told him that what I described in my paper was a system that worked splendidly in Liberia, where I had worked for three months. I also told him that a variation on that system was being used successfully in Roxbury. He looked like I had just punched him, so I told him that I really liked his course (which I did), because it augmented my experiences in Africa, Nicaragua, and Peru. He then invited me to join him for coffee, and we spent several hours discussing health care in developing countries. Such is the nature of graduate education with dedicated teachers. Incidentally, in answer to those who have asked me, I can't remember if he changed my grade or not, because it made no difference to me.

NONCLASSROOM LEARNING

One of my best and most lasting experiences involved no specific classroom. Professor William Curran was a lawyer who taught at the Harvard School of Public Health. He also wrote a monthly column on medicine and law for the *New England Journal of Medicine*, the journal that I, like many physicians, had been reading since medical school. I wanted very much to learn from him, but he was not teaching any formal class at that time. I asked to see him, to which he agreed, but it was very obvious that he was a very busy person. I told him of my interest in setting up a health program that would involve outpatient and hospital care, in which doctors and nurse practitioners would provide the care as a clinical team.

He was interested in my idea and the legal questions I had related to that issue, but he had no time to work with me. I asked him if he ate lunch, to which he responded, "Sometimes, and usually on Fridays, but always at my desk." So I asked if he liked Italian food, to which he replied with an enthusiastic yes. I then asked if I could prepare for him on Fridays whatever Italian food he wanted for lunch, and while he ate we could discuss my questions and answers. I suggested that he could tell me where to find the answers. I would then report back to him the following Friday, with the answers and any new questions that I knew would ensue, in addition to the Italian food.

He told me my proposition was tough to decline, so we agreed to try it for a while. We continued that practice, and by the end of the academic year he had eaten every Italian dish I could think of, and I had gained a great deal of knowledge. That knowledge included some legal and ethical implications of expanding the role of nurse practitioners and the laws that had to be changed in order for the PNPs to be able to practice. We even coauthored a paper on the legal implications of extended roles of professional nurses, which was published the year after I graduated.

I was grateful to have been so fortunate to have spent an academic year preparing further for my first academic position, which was about to commence at Columbia University School of Medicine and the Columbia School of Public Health.

CHAPTER 9

Medicine New York Style: The Columbia College of Physicians and Surgeons

DURING MY ACADEMIC YEAR AT the Harvard School of Public Health, one issue that had to be resolved was the place where I would subsequently go for my first academic position. I knew I might be expected to have another period of training or experience in order to be accepted professionally. That had happened so many times in the past, I worried that I'd receive a similar response at this stage of my career. Most frequently, these expectations and requirements were that I was the wrong sex (I could not do anything about that, and I certainly did not want to) or that I had no (or the wrong) fellowship training. The opposite of acceptance is rejection, and no one wants to be rejected. Perhaps that's why I've always resisted using the term "rejected," no matter the situation, including the decisions I made as an editor. But I thought I might have a difficult time finding the position I wanted. At that time, there was no specialty training for that kind of position. So I decided to put together my own special training and hoped it would do.

About midyear at Harvard, I sent out letters to three academic medical centers that I knew had open positions. Each of those positions offered the possibility for me to develop the program I planned. That would include pediatricians and PNPs working as a team, together with others, to provide good outpatient and inpatient care to infants, children, and adolescents. The letters I had sent also included my curriculum vitae and crossed fingers. (The crossed fingers were virtual, of course).

I happily accepted invitations for interviews from all three places and was offered positions from all. I decided to call Dr. Cooke, my former pediatric department chairman at Hopkins, to seek his advice about which position I should choose. With no hesitation, he told me to accept the position in the Pediatrics Department at Columbia College of Physicians and Surgeons. I asked him why he had chosen that one. He replied that he knew that, while I'd learn and do a lot at Columbia, I would want to move on after two years or so because I wouldn't be able to develop fully the program I wanted. He laughed and told me that when I was ready to move, he would offer me a better position at the University of Wisconsin, where he was now the vice chancellor of Health Affairs.

I took his advice because I trusted his judgment and because it verified what already had been my first choice. I didn't believe that I'd leave Columbia after two years, but I also knew that no one really could plan too far ahead, except conceptually. The old adage that humans plan and God, the Great Comedian, laughs, had been so true for me. That's why, early on in life, I had decided to plan carefully but to go wherever the wind would take me and make the best of whatever came along. That philosophy is responsible for the many inspiring and delightful adventures I've had.

In July 1974 I began my academic career as a faculty member in the Department of Pediatrics at the Columbia College of Physicians and Surgeons. I also had a joint appointment in the Columbia University School of Public Health. The move to New York City was great for me, because it was an easy drive to my family's home in northeastern Pennsylvania. I was lucky to have a friend who was a professor on sabbatical from Queens College in New York City. He rented me his apartment, near the Columbia Babies and Children's Hospital, where my office would be. I could park my car on the street in front of the apartment building and easily walk to work. All I had to do was move it across the street every morning, because of the crazy rule for street cleaning called "alternate side parking." Other advantages to that site were that the apartment building was across the street from a cemetery with greenery and trees, and also I could see a bit of the Hudson River from my window. That was almost country living in the big city. I didn't worry too much about my jalopy car, which was old and really not worth stealing. Every cloud has a silver lining.

THE PEDIATRIC NURSE PRACTITIONER PROGRAM

As soon as I started working, I knew I had to acquire some grant money to start the pediatric nurse practitioner (PNP) program that I had planned while I was in Boston. I needed money to pay a very small stipend for the PNP students, who might not be gainfully employed; possibly for the nursing faculty; and for office supplies. Because grant money was and continues to be so difficult to find, I knew that was going to be a big hurdle. I'd heard that the Robert Wood Johnson Foundation (RWJF) might be interested in such a program. I sent them a two-page proposal including a budget. A week or so after I sent it, I received a phone call from Maggie Mahoney, who was then a vice president at the RWJF. She asked me if I was a nun, to which I laughed and replied "hardly" and asked why she thought so. She told me that I wrote a budget just like a nun, such as requesting a total sum of $32,257. That included $27.46, or some such ridiculous amount, for pens, paper and other office supplies. I had indicated the price of each pen, etc. Knowing what I know now about grant budgets, I laugh at my naïveté.

Ms. Mahoney told me that she thought my proposal was very interesting, but unfortunately the foundation didn't fund such programs. However, she also told me to call the New York Community Trust, and tell them about my proposal. I was to ask for $50,000, because that's what she thought I'd need. She had already spoken with someone at the trust but didn't tell me that she had done so. So I called as instructed, not knowing what would happen, but the person who answered apparently was anticipating my call. He asked me to come to the trust's office, located in downtown Manhattan, the next day to present my proposal.

When I arrived with a rewritten budget requesting $50,000, a half dozen or so officials of the trust met with me. They asked me a few questions after I explained what I wanted to do. They then asked me to wait in an outer office while they discussed my proposal. About a half hour later, I was met by one of the gentlemen from the trust. He handed me a check for $50,000, made out to Columbia Babies and Children's Hospital, with my name in parentheses, and told me that in return I was to provide them with a written report in a year.

Of course I happily accepted the money with that easy requirement and thanked him. Later that day I called Ms. Mahoney and told her how grateful I was for her help. That began what was to be a long-standing friendship between us. She was special in so many ways. One was that, although she had only a bachelor's degree, she held many high administrative positions almost always filled by individuals with doctoral degrees. This provided more evidence for my suspicion about degrees.

When I returned to the hospital I went immediately to the Pediatric chairman's office to give him the check. When I handed him the check, he asked me if I'd gone through the grants office. I looked at him blankly and asked what a grants office was. He almost had an apoplectic attack at my faux pas of by-passing the grants office, which handled all grants. Needless to say, my understanding regarding how grants were handled was sorely lacking. The role of a grant's office is to manage all the red tape, paper work, and overall finances of every grant. However, he personally walked me to the grants office and explained what had happened. The person in the office looked at me in disbelief at what I'd done without the aid of that office. She could hardly believe I was that naïve of the process, but she laughed and happily accepted the check. I then used the money for the program.

A year later I sent the New York Community Trust a full report, and they were delighted with the results of their investment. Sometimes ignorance is a blessing. I believe that when the results of ignorance are good, it is known as innocence.

The First Year of the PNP Program

I had intended to have the School of Nursing take the lead for the PNP program, with it managing the funding. You might imagine my shock when I met with the woman who was then dean of the School of Nursing and director of Nursing for the hospital. She essentially threw me out of her office when I explained the program, for which I had received a grant. I erroneously assumed that she would want the PNP program to be sponsored by the School of Nursing. I was shocked by her very negative response, having expected something much different. She told me I was a traitor to nursing because I had gone on to medical school. Further, doctors should not teach nurses, she said, even advanced nursing that included things traditionally done by physicians. I found this peculiar, because she was a trained nurse midwife, but I decided not to argue with her. I kept the grant and planned the program instead through the Department of Pediatrics. This was done with the blessing of the department chair, who was still laughing at how I received the grant for the program.

The next step was to find graduate nurses to be students in the first class. With the help of several individuals, I was able to enroll nurses who were working at Columbia Babies and Children's Hospital, Lincoln Hospital, Roosevelt Hospital, Harlem Hospital, and a nurse who worked in a Harlem grade school. At that time, all these hospitals were in some way affiliated with Columbia. Several physicians agreed to help teach, without reimbursement, in the nine-month certificate program I developed. Fortunately, I had financial support from the grant to pay the nurses who would be involved in teaching in the program, because they required reimbursement for their time by the School of Nursing.

So the program was taught out of the Department of Pediatrics and the School of Public Health, the dean of which offered to permit one year of credit to one nurse who wanted to work for a public health degree. That nurse was my friend Phyllis, a.k.a. Madre Phillips, who by then had left the Maryknoll Sisters. She had agreed to be involved in the PNP program after I talked her out of going to Johns Hopkins to become a nurse midwife. That first-year class was composed of truly magnificent nurses, who had risked comfortable positions to pioneer a new program. Of course, they each maintained a full-time job but had permission to take time for classes.

It was great fun teaching nurses and physicians together and getting them to understand what a nurse practitioner is. In those early years of such programs we had to describe the expanded functions of nurse practitioners, which included routine physical examinations, evaluating growth and development, giving appropriate vaccines, and treating common illnesses of childhood such as upper respiratory infections and rashes. In the classroom, the curriculum for the nurses was based primarily on the book I had written while in Boston, which turned out to be the first textbook written for nurse practitioners. In the clinic setting at Columbia, where the PNPs worked with pediatric residents, I was at first the only attending physician who oversaw the work of the PNP students at Columbia. Pediatric faculty members from the other hospitals did the same in their institutions, including overseeing the PNP student in the Harlem school. However, after several months, other pediatric faculty at Columbia also participated in the training, and the same occurred at the other involved hospitals.

The physicians at the other hospitals agreed with my assessment and reported that the nurses were excellent at caring for routine illnesses, and for well-baby and child health-maintenance visits. These nurses also were careful to ask for assistance with problems they felt were beyond their knowledge and training.

At the end of the academic year, we held a graduation exercise at Columbia, attended by the graduates, by many of the faculty from all involved hospitals, and by some family members. At the ceremony, the chair of the Department of Pediatrics and I handed each new PNP her certificate, which we both had signed. This was followed by a reception that culminated a great day.

The Following Years of the PNP Program

One funny experience occurred in the second year of the program, which involved the next group of PNP students who worked in the Columbia clinic. I had arranged for the hospital pharmacy, located right next to the clinic, to fill prescriptions, written on specific prescription pads and signed by the PNPs. These prescriptions were only for a few specified medications, such as medicines for upper respiratory problems and certain antibiotics. I would then cosign the prescriptions later in the day. By doing so I displayed my trust in the PNPs and could oversee what was being prescribed and by whom.

A few days after that program started, I cared for a patient myself to help with the crowded clinic. I wrote a prescription, for an antibiotic, on one of the special pads. The parent of the patient came back to the clinic, and she told me that the pharmacist refused to fill the prescription because it hadn't been signed by a PNP. Apparently, that pharmacist had been on vacation when I explained the program to the pharmacists and had misunderstood the directive. After I straightened out that situation, we all had a good laugh. For many weeks, several of my colleagues kidded me about needing permission from a PNP to write prescriptions.

When the worth of the program was established with the graduation of the first class, the dean of the School of Nursing changed her mind. She now wanted the program to be cosponsored by the School of Nursing, to which I happily agreed. The first certificates had been signed by the pediatric department chair and me, but the next year the nursing director and I signed them, apparently much to her delight. She even told me that she thought the program was wonderful because of the way I had organized it...go figure.

Because of my respect and admiration for so many people at Columbia, and my desire to have the PNP training program continue, I made sure funding would be available for the program. In addition, it was essential that a very capable nurse director of the program would take over, because I wanted to step down. The nurse director I chose,

Delores Jackson, had a great deal of experience as a faculty member. She had taken the PNP course in the second year, seeking something new and challenging. What she subsequently did with the program was analogous to taking a fertile acorn and nurturing it into a magnificent oak tree. In fact, almost everyone from the first PNP groups advanced to higher education or directorship positions. That single PNP program has now grown to a five-track master's program at the Columbia College of Nursing.

In 2000, many years after I'd left Columbia, I received a call from the then dean of the Columbia School of Nursing, who had published a study in the first issue of *JAMA*, in which I was listed as the editor in chief. Because the article had been accepted for publication before I became the editor, I was unaware of it until it was published. The study showed the efficacy of nurse practitioners, and the dean wanted to know what I thought of it, knowing of my long support of nurse practitioners.

She told me of how proud she was of the nurse practitioner programs at Columbia. I asked her if she knew who had started the first program there, and she said she didn't know. I then faxed her a copy of the first certificate, which had been signed by the chair of Pediatrics and me. She called me stating that she was at once shocked, embarrassed, and delighted with the fax. I then reiterated the story of how the program had started, and we had a good laugh.

CLINICAL RESPONSIBILITIES

While teaching PNPs in the classroom took a great deal of my time, I also had the responsibility of caring for a number of private patients; attending in the outpatient clinic teaching pediatric residents, medical students, and PNP students; and attending for several months in the inpatient units. All these experiences were interesting, but as I've done with other clinical encounters, I'll relate the story of one hospitalized patient, which will provide a glimpse of my time at Columbia.

I was on call for inpatients one evening when I was asked to see a newborn infant who had been transferred from another hospital. The infant had a problem that involved her lower trunk, including primarily her genital tract. It was clear, even from a general physical examination, that she was going to require a great deal of surgical and medical care over the following years. I called for several consultants, ordered a variety of diagnostic tests, and then went to the family room to speak with the infant's father. The mother was still in the hospital, where she had just delivered the infant.

You can imagine my surprise, and greatly increased heart rate, when I was met by the father and four grandparents, all of Italian descent. Bambinos (babies) are the heart and soul of Italian families, and this was not going to be easy. The difficulty was especially true in this case, because the parents had been trying to have a baby for a number of years. Further, the grandparents were an intricate part of the extended family.

So how in the world was I going to explain the complex situation to five very worried and emotional individuals? They seemed to have relaxed somewhat when they realized that I also was of Italian descent, but that made the pressure greater for me. It actually took a lot of time and effort, over the next two years, to coordinate the care of the little girl. Her care required a number of physicians and procedures, but working with these dedicated and loving parents was a joy. The same level of effort was required from the carefully chosen pediatrician who took over the child's care when I left Columbia almost two years later.

I kept in close touch with that pediatrician and the family over the next thirty years or so. I had the privilege of watching (sometimes from a distance) the infant grow into a beautiful woman, who is now married. Her mother was so inspired by this experience that she became a nurse and has used her life's experience to provide excellent, compassionate care to other patients and their families.

There were so many memorable people I worked with at Columbia, but one who stands out is a woman pediatrician, Dr. Susan Gordon, who became a role model for me. I was in awe of her compassion and understanding of the human condition. She was white and was married to a black man at a time when that was hardly well accepted. Both she and he were accomplished in their respective fields. He was a professor and department head at Columbia University and commanded the respect and admiration of so many. In fact, their story formed the basis of the film, *Guess Who's Coming to Dinner*.

Susan and I became close friends, and I could speak to her about anything, knowing she would understand and would provide excellent advice. We became so close that, a number of years later and after I had left Columbia, she and her husband, Ed, hosted a reception at her home, after Jim and my wedding. In fact, her husband, also an ordained minister, helped officiate our wedding.

TIME TO MOVE ON

In the middle of my second year at Columbia, I received a call from Dr. Cooke, who told me he thought it was time for me to move on (as he had foretold) and work with him at the University of Wisconsin (UW). He wanted me to be the dean of their new School of Allied Health Services. I laughed, because I was barely out of my residency training, and I definitely had other ideas of how I wanted to spend my career. When I politely turned down his offer, he and the chair of Pediatrics at UW asked if I would come for a visit. They wanted me to look at the directorship of their outpatient pediatric clinic. That was not necessarily in my plan for a next step, but at their request for a consultation, not a job interview, I spent two days with them and a number of faculty members. I outlined a plan on how to upgrade their pediatric outpatient clinic and build it into a real academic, general-pediatric unit.

They told me my plan would be impossible to implement there, and I responded that it was absolutely possible but it necessitated the complete support of the department, the hospital, and the medical school. At that time, general pediatrics, and especially the pediatrics outpatient clinic, was treated like a second-class program. We went back and forth, arguing about the supposedly impossible issues to overcome. I finally accepted their challenge to go there, and "prove that it could happen" with their promised support.

I'm not sure who outsmarted whom (probably all of us), but they had called my supposed bluff (although I was not bluffing), and I negotiated a contract that provided me with what I thought was needed to succeed. This decision was another turning point in my career. I'd say all of us won, as I hope will become evident in the next chapter.

CHAPTER 10

Much More Than Cheese and Brats: The University of Wisconsin School of Medicine

SO IT WAS "ON WISCONSIN," indeed. In the last week of June 1975, I packed my broken-down jalopy Pontiac GTO and set out very early in the morning, accompanied by Phyllis, who had secured a position on the faculty of the University of Wisconsin School of Nursing. We car toddled across the United States, stopping every 150 miles or so to pour water and a can of oil into the leaking parts of the car. The Great Comedian helped us.

We arrived safely in Madison and unpacked our relatively few but precious belongings. We settled into our prearranged rented, furnished apartments located in the same building. Within a few weeks, we found a beautiful two-bedroom apartment in the home of someone who had moved east, and we moved in together. There were actually two large and two small apartments in that house, situated right on Lake Mendota. It was pure heaven, and a year or so later, when the owner decided to sell the house, I purchased it.

Soon after our arrival, I bought a new BMW 2002, which was well suited to the Wisconsin winters. The day after I picked up my new car, I drove the old one to the local garage. A young man at that garage had helped me keep the old jalopy running until my new car arrived. With no preamble, I asked him if he had a dollar. He looked at me and handed a dollar bill to me without question (what a generous heart). I handed him the keys and the title to my old car and wished him luck with it. He was shocked, but he beamed and told me he was sure he could get it into reasonable working condition. We both showed equity toward each other in that exchange with a wonderful result.

A few weeks later, he drove the completely refurbished car to my home to show me what he'd been able to do with it. God certainly is a comedian when you consider how he created some of us (the young man) to have skills that amaze others (me), who would have junked something that had great potential. Beauty is indeed in the eyes of the beholder. I have tried to keep that lesson in mind when I remember the power of hope and faith when caring for patients.

The Academic Pediatrics Program
The next three years at Wisconsin were an adventure, and then some. I had had the most generous and caring colleagues everywhere, but this was especially true at Wisconsin. I was going to develop and implement the General Academic Pediatric and Adolescence Medicine Program (GAPAMP), using the pediatric outpatient clinic as the foundation. Dr. Meme Chun, who had been directing the clinic, welcomed me literally with open arms and specifically made it clear that she had no desire to continue as the director. She unselfishly proceeded to guide me through the politics and history of pediatrics in Madison. The major problem was that there were many pediatricians and group practices in town who had no desire to have yet another competitor for patients.

However, when I met with all the pediatricians in town as a group, they agreed that if they wanted the University of Wisconsin (UW) pediatric residency program to continue, we had to have sufficient pediatric patients. Most of the practicing pediatricians had been trained in the UW program. All of them admitted patients to hospitals, where they depended on the UW residents to assist in taking care of their patients. Therefore, they wanted the training program to continue and succeed.

I informed them that I had no desire to "steal" patients from them and would take any patients they might prefer not to see. I told them that I intended to have a continuity clinic for residents, where they would care for a panel of patients. The residents would follow their patients much like private pediatricians. This would include inpatient responsibilities for their patients, with the GAPAMP faculty serving as the official attending physicians and overseeing care. They all agreed to cooperate and assure continuance of the UW residency, and I reiterated my promise not to "steal" patients from them. That is, I would not accept a patient into our clinic who already had a private pediatrician who was providing good care. I hoped to find sufficient new patients, so the residents could care for them, always being backed up by our faculty.

THE EAGLE HEIGHTS CLINIC

As the Great Comedian would have it, a few days after meeting with the Madison pediatricians, I was driving home and saw a half dozen black women and children standing on a corner waiting for a shuttle bus. At that time, Madison's population consisted of very few black persons, and I was feeling very lonely for so many of my usual patients. I pulled over to the curb, parked the car, and engaged in conversation with them. As it turned out, they all were wives of African graduate students at UW who lived in a place called Eagle Heights. This was a complex of apartments about a mile or so from the UW campus, where graduate students and their families, primarily from outside the United States, lived. There were about a thousand families who lived there, and they received their health care from a variety of places, including the emergency rooms in the hospitals, which acted as walk-in clinics.

To the delight of the families, the private pediatricians, and the UW faculty, I set up a tri-weekly clinic in a few rooms of a gymnasium located in the Eagle Heights apartment complex. That gymnasium also housed a cooperative collective (co-op) grocery, which sold fresh produce and spices native to the countries from which the families came. I'll never forget the incredible aromas that emanated from that place, which were completely different from the usual alcohol (or worse) aroma of health clinics. The residents and I would care for the children in that clinic and enroll them into the residents' practices. The children could also be seen in the GAPAMP clinic and, when hospitalized, they would have the resident care for them backed up by one of the faculty attending physicians, from GAPAMP. In very short time, we were able to enroll many children, and there was no longer a problem with having an insufficient number of patients for the residents. Additionally, the private pediatricians voiced no objection and were actually quite happy with the new arrangements to provide care for these children.

One added teaching advantage of having so many patients from foreign cultures was the variety of illnesses many children had. One specific patient experience provides an excellent example. Soon after starting the Eagle Heights clinic, I saw a young child from East Africa, who presented with a swollen left elbow, pain, and a high fever. Having cared for so many similar patients in Africa, East Baltimore, and New York City, I immediately recognized the problem as sickle cell crisis, which is a problem that can occur in people who have sickle cell disease. Their red blood cells are not normally shaped (like doughnuts) but are sickle –shaped and can be rigid and sticky blocking the flow of blood in small blood vessels especially when they are dehydrated. This can cause pain and swelling in joints. After instructing the resident at the clinic, I called the UW Hospital pediatric ER. I told the resident in the ER that I was bringing in a child with a sickle cell crisis. He told me there were no patients with sickle cell disease in Madison. I replied, "Well, now there are, so get ready to see your first child with the problem."

I traveled to the ER with the child and her mother in my car. When we arrived, a half dozen or so residents and a few faculty members were waiting for us. I was delighted that they were curious and wanted to learn something new. We set up an intravenous (IV) drip, and the resident wanted to start heavy doses of antibiotics and to call a surgeon to tap the elbow. I smiled and said we'd hold off on the antibiotics until we saw a sample of the elbow fluid under a microscope. I then showed that resident and the others who were present how to tap (remove fluid from) the child's swollen elbow joint.

All of us then inspected the yellow fluid sample under a microscope, after sending some fluid to the lab for culture (to grow any bacteria present in the fluid) and sensitivity (if any bacteria were present, show which antibiotics should be used), just in case. As I expected, under the microscope there was no indication of infection in the joint fluid sample, so we held off the antibiotics and made sure the child was well hydrated. The next day the child's fever was gone, the culture was negative for bacteria, and she was well on her way to recovery. We sent her home with a no-longer-swollen elbow joint and a very happy mother. Many people, including me, learned a great deal from this child, as I did from all patients. And now I was well on my way to becoming a respected faculty member.

Another initiative I became involved in, along with Phyllis, was working with the School of Nursing to help develop and advance their Nurse Practitioner Program. It was fairly easy to accomplish this initiative, because the spirit of cooperation and desire to help patients permeated the environment, in all of the university's health-related schools. The motto of being able to accomplish almost anything if you didn't care who received the credit seemed to be the general *modus operandi*. Fresh air was not only present in the outdoor environment, but it was ever present all over. Perhaps what is needed to advance anything in the United States are gigantic fans circulating the same kind of fresh air throughout the country. It's a thought, anyway.

ANOTHER BRUSH WITH DEATH

I had another personal brush with death, which occurred a year or so after my arrival in Madison. I awoke very early one morning, nauseated, and just made it to the bathroom, where I vomited blood and then passed out. Phyllis heard me crash to the floor and came running in just as I was coming around. I had flushed the toilet (maternal habit-training never leaves us, no matter what the situation) just before I'd fainted, so we had no idea how much blood I'd lost.

Despite Phyllis's protests, I made her wait for an hour or so until dawn before she called our friends Meme and Ray Chun. They immediately sent an ambulance and met me in the ER. The rest of the story is very complicated, so suffice it to say that I had developed esophageal varices (swollen blood vessels in my esophagus). They were the result of the congenital blood vessel anomaly that had led to the surgery I'd had while in medical school. That surgery involved the removal of my spleen and tying off of many collateral (not normally present) blood vessels surrounding my spleen. The closing off of that circulation forced the blood to find a new path into the vessels in my esophagus, forming varices (engorged blood vessels). The varices had reached the point of bleeding and seriously endangered my life.

After a number of tests, invasive and otherwise, it was evident that surgery was needed to bypass the blood-vessel-blocked area, which was causing blood to be rerouted to the bloated esophageal veins. When that volume of blood had no place to go, the veins had ruptured, and bled into my esophagus. This occurred on a weekend, and Dr. John Pellett, a pediatric surgeon and the only surgeon in Madison who could handle such intricate surgery, had gone on his annual duck-hunting trip to northern Wisconsin. I'm not sure how they reached him (there were no cell phones then), but he soon arrived to find me in a very weakened state despite many blood transfusions. The blood had come from several dozen physicians and nurses, who had learned what had happened to me and responded to a call for blood donors. So I now carry the essence of so many Madison friends, to whom I owe my life.

I wore a baseball catcher's mask attached to a tube inserted into my esophagus. That tube was inflated and pulled under pressure by being attached to the catcher's mask. This tamponed the varices, in order to prevent further bleeding. In addition, nurses periodically passed ice water in and out of the tube, in order to further constrict the veins. Thankfully this form of medieval torture is no longer used. At that time, it was only a temporary maneuver until the bypass surgery could be accomplished. The pressure on my nose, through which the tube had been passed, was so great that my nose was beginning to show signs of necrosis. That is the death of cells in body tissue, in this case caused by pressure from the tube cutting off blood supply. Since no one wanted me to lose part of my nose (especially me), the catcher's mask was used for protection of the tissue. I have always been an avid fan of the New York Yankee's catcher Yogi Berra but never realized how important it would be for me to emulate him for a brief period of time. As I thought about it, I could only imagine what I'd look like with part of my nose missing.

My mother arrived, with rosary in hand, just before I went to surgery and saw me looking like a puffed-up balloon, wearing a catcher's mask. I was out of it, so I can only imagine her reaction. Fortunately, my sister Grace, the nurse, accompanied her. She and Phyllis tried to explain to my mother what was happening. They never left the hospital until I was out of surgery and able to speak, sans mask and with much less edema (swelling). They needed for me to tell them that I was fine, which I was.

I will always be so very grateful to Dr. Pellett, who saved my life and was so kind and comforting to my mother while I was recovering from the delicate surgery he had performed. There had been real doubt that I would survive, but he never left my mother without hope. Many years later I was asked to be a keynote speaker at the American Academy of Surgery's annual meeting, and I dedicated that presentation to him.

I had a very interesting dream experience associated with that surgery. I remember feeling very peaceful and seeing a light (was it the bright operating room light?) to which I was drawn. The closer I got to the light, the more peaceful I felt. However, at one point my dream switched, and I was sitting on the patio outside my parents' house. I heard my family inside, crying because I had died. I thought how sad they were and how much I could do for so many people if I were alive. At that point I fought the light, and the next thing I knew I awoke in the recovery room of the hospital. I guess the Great Comedian had other plans for me.

My mother stayed with me until I was released from the hospital, and she was assured that I was truly going to live and continue to drive her crazy. A mother's love truly knows no bounds.

ALIVE AND KICKING AGAIN

I love college football, so a few weeks after I was discharged from the hospital, I went to the first UW football home game of the season. Since I had lost so much weight, I had no qualms about consuming brats (the food, bratwurst, not disorderly kids) and beer...a tradition known to all Badger fans. The only Wisconsin food better than brats is cheese. Of course, during that time the Badger football team was not in its glory days. The always-sold-out stadium fans cheered for inane things, like when the sun came out, not expecting a score for which to cheer. Football Saturdays in Madison were always holidays, beginning with the morning parade. I have never felt more alive than when I attended that first game after my surgery. I sat with Phyllis, Meme and Ray Chun, and their three children, with the youngest sitting on my lap for much of the game. He's now an astrophysicist in Hawaii.

A PEDIATRIC DIAGNOSTIC CLINIC

I wanted to understand what was happening with pediatric health care in the state. I asked the director of the university's agriculture program, whose child I had cared for, if I could accompany him on some of his trips across the state. It soon became clear to me that, whereas most of the children in the rural areas were well cared for by family physicians, there was a need for someone to provide a pediatrician's perspective for some children. That pediatrician had to be someone the family physicians could trust to provide immediate feedback to them and not try to take patients away from them.

By then I had begun accepting family-medicine residents for training in the GAPAMP clinic. This occurred after a few family-medicine residents had elected to spend a month with us and had reported excellent experiences. When the director of family medicine asked if I'd accept one of their residents each month for training, I readily agreed. I was delighted to offer such training because of several incidences in which children, especially infants, had been admitted to the university hospital having been referred by family physicians. Perhaps if pediatricians had been close by, or readily available by phone, those hospitalizations could have been prevented or, in some cases, would have happened sooner and with better results.

I spoke with many of the family physicians practicing in the rural areas about my seeing their referrals and explained that they could ask the university chair of the Family Medicine Department about me. After my speaking with them, I began encountering a number of children whom I'd been asked to see for a second opinion, so I decided to organize an official diagnostic clinic at the university clinic, which I personally staffed once a week. That clinic allowed the residents to see many children whose parents were from the rural areas. The parents, unlike those from Madison, were farmers and laborers who mostly did not have college degrees and were less academically "sophisticated." Their special gifts lay elsewhere.

I delighted in caring for those children, in many cases using simple remedies. One such example involved a ten-year-old boy whose mother took him to the diagnostic clinic. He had a very bad problem with scaling of his scalp. The youngster always wore a baseball cap; he was embarrassed because he had skin scales all over his clothes. The dermatologist who had seen the boy had suggested shaving his head, which his mother had done. The dermatologist wanted to inject the boy's scalp with steroids, which his mother would not allow without a second opinion. I decided to try an old folk remedy I had learned from my Mother. I asked the child's mother if she had vegetable shortening—not oil but shortening—in her cupboard at home, to which she replied yes. I then explained that I wanted to try something that would cost almost nothing. If it didn't work, I'd see her son again, and there'd be no charge for that visit. She agreed.

I instructed her, each night before bedtime, to wash her son's scalp with a dandruff shampoo. That was to be followed by very gentle fine combing to remove the loose scales. She was then to take a generous amount of the vegetable shortening and rub it into her son's scalp. She could put a shower cap on him in order to protect the pillow-cases and bed sheets. She was to repeat this process every night for a week and then call me. The look on her (and the resident's) face made me smile. I'm certain they assumed I was a quack, or quack pot. However, a week later, instead of calling me, she came to the clinic. She wanted to show me her smiling son, sans baseball cap, whose scalp was essentially free of scales. Some days it's worth getting out of bed!

An interesting occurrence aroused my curiosity for political action. I had noticed that infant circumcisions performed by obstetricians were reimbursed at rates set by the hospitals, which were twice the amount paid to pediatricians. You also might ask why pediatricians were performing such procedures. So who should perform them, physicians trained to care for women, not baby boys? Surgeons? Mohels certainly, but not all boys are Jewish, so whom?

I had discovered that on their first well-baby visits, three or four days after discharge from the nursery, there were many infant boys who had problems with bleeding or rawness around their circumcision sites. So I asked a Jewish mohel (is that redundant?) to teach me how to circumcise with a Gomco clamp, which was sometimes used by physicians and he thought would work well for a non-mohel (and a woman, yet!). I explained why I wanted to learn this procedure. He was amazed at the request but kindly agreed to teach me. I proceeded to circumcise some of the infant boys born in our practice. I also said I'd teach any physician on the staff who wanted to learn how to do it, providing they kept record of the outcomes. Only a few wanted to learn.

I kept careful records of the results of the obstetricians' versus the pediatricians' circumcisions. I discovered that the problems when pediatricians (mostly me) circumcised were rare and mild, and the results were significantly better when compared with the obstetricians' results. With those data in hand, I went to the state agency responsible for reimbursement of physicians. After that visit, I expected that all circumcisions would be reimbursed at the lower rate, only to find that the higher rate was to be used for all circumcisions. The pediatricians (mostly me) were delighted (it meant more income for the clinic), and the obstetricians didn't seem to care. Because the infants fared better, it was a victory for all. Although I never published that study, the incident further whetted my appetite for using data to alter bad situations. And to publish those data whenever possible to share the results with others.

So You Don't Want to Be a Politician?

Another interesting situation involving politics occurred when a group of representatives from the local Democratic Party Committee, invited me to have coffee with a few of them. I assumed they were going to solicit a donation. I was surprised and amused when, instead, they asked me to consider running for state representative in the upcoming election. I had been a resident of Wisconsin for only two years or so at that point, but that didn't seem to matter to them. I asked why they thought I should run for office, and they pointed out that I'd been able to organize a successful medical clinic, had convinced people to change the reimbursement for circumcisions, worked with rural groups, and conducted a pediatric diagnostic clinic that was recognized throughout the state. They said I was respected by many people in the state because they could trust me to do what I said I would.

That was interesting feedback to me, but I told them that I was an academic pediatrician and had no funds for a campaign, assuming that would end the conversation. But they persisted, stating that the Democratic Party would raise the money, and all I had to do was speak at various meetings they would set up. I decided to end what I considered to be a ridiculous request. I told them that I meant no offence, but if I did all that was expected to raise money, make political promises to get elected, and stay in office, I would no longer be someone who could assure the public that my word was golden. Either that or that I'd remain the person who could be trusted.

What I didn't tell them was one of my favorite quotes is from Mark Twain, who said, "Politicians and diapers must be changed often and for the same reason." Clearly, I wanted to remain doing what I was doing and striving to improve the way I was doing it. Considering what is happening in politics today, that was definitely one of the wisest decisions I've ever made.

TIME TO MOVE ON AGAIN

After three years in Madison, I was very happy with my position, with my friends and colleagues, and with the results of the clinical, educational, and research aspects of the GAPAMP program. However, my heart was on the East Coast, specifically back at Hopkins. In truth, what I had been doing professionally up to then was preparing with the hope of returning to Hopkins someday. In addition, I was very lonely because Madison was definitely a college and family town. All the wonderful men whose company I enjoyed were either married or gay, and I had reached an age when I wanted to have a husband and children.

I had continued my special friendship from a distance with my future husband, Jim, with whom I'd been a pediatric resident at Hopkins. He had even visited the University of Wisconsin, interviewing for a possible faculty position in child psychiatry so we might be together. However, his supervisor at Hopkins had had other plans for him and had discussed these plans with the Wisconsin folks. They didn't want to offend Jim's Hopkins colleague and, therefore, did not offer him a position. That decision was fine with Jim and with me, because Jim was very happy at Hopkins, and I wanted to return there some day.

Because I wanted to return to the East Coast, I let it be known to a few people in academic centers there that I was looking to move. I almost immediately received invitations from Hopkins and the University of Rochester to interview for positions. I first went to Rochester to look at the directorship of Ambulatory Pediatrics position, one of the best programs in the United States at that time, whose director was stepping down. The two-day interview with the dean, the chair of Pediatrics, and most of the pediatric division directors was a delightful experience. I left feeling they really wanted me to join them. They soon offered me the position and also invited me for another visit so I could meet with more faculty and administrators. I told them that another visit would not be necessary, but I had another interview for a position and would call them when that was completed within a week.

I then interviewed at Hopkins, another amazing experience, but for opposite reasons. The open position Hopkins folks wanted to fill was in the pediatric outpatient clinic. I met with Dr. John Littlefield, who was the chair of Pediatrics; with the outpatient clinic director; and with a few faculty members. However, most of my time, including dinner, was spent with the outpatient chief resident. He was someone I knew from our Pittsburgh medical school days, when he was a medical student and I, an intern. I had, and continue to have, the utmost respect for him, and I like him a lot. However, despite the good company of a friend, I found the entire interview process demeaning, especially when I compared it with the experience I'd had at Rochester. There I met and dined primarily with many senior faculty members, the department chair, and not primarily with the chief resident as was the case at Hopkins..

So the next day, after I had returned to Madison, I wrote to Dr. Littlefield, informing him that I was not interested in the position. I called the Rochester folks to set up a meeting so we could discuss the details of their position. I had no response from Hopkins, but the Rochester folks were obviously very happy with my decision. However, in the meantime, Jim asked me if I would attend a reception with him at

Hopkins, the week before the scheduled next Rochester visit. I accepted his invitation because it was always a joy to be with him.

At the Hopkins reception, Dr. Littlefield came up to me and, in his always gentlemanly manner, told me that he couldn't understand how I could turn down a Hopkins position for Rochester. At that point, I'd had a glass of wine, and any semblance of décor vaporized. I truly respected Dr. Littlefield, but I told him that I found the Hopkins interview process insulting, especially compared with my interview at Rochester. I also politely told him that I thought he had no real understanding of what was needed at Hopkins in general pediatrics. He asked if that meant that I might be willing to reconsider. If so, could we meet at his home for breakfast, with the outpatient clinic director, the next morning to discuss the matter?

When Jim and I drove into Dr. Littlefield's driveway the next morning, I told him there was hardly any chance that I would be coming to Hopkins. However, after a long, warm, and cordial meeting (all meetings with Dr. Littlefield were like that), Dr. Littlefield and the outpatient clinic director agreed that I could come to Hopkins as the director of a *new* clinic. They would provide resources for a small clinic area, support staff, one faculty member, and one Pediatric Level 1 resident per month assigned to the program. I won't belabor the negotiation process, but in essence I had pulled no punches and outlined exactly what I thought was needed for general pediatrics at Hopkins and told them how I would try to accomplish it.

The next, very difficult part was twofold. First, to inform the Rochester folks about my decision not to accept their very kind offer. Second, to inform my Wisconsin colleagues about my decision to leave, at the end of the academic year, on June 30, 1978, only three months hence. One important thing I had to do before alerting the Wisconsin chair of Pediatrics was to discuss my decision with Meme. In her ever-present, gracious, and generous manner, she told me that she was not surprised. She would take over the directorship until a new director was found.

I also had to alert two residents, Modena Wilson and Alain Joffe, with whom I had discussed their joining me as Wisconsin fellows in the coming years. After discussing my intent to leave Madison, Alain decided to obtain his MPH at Harvard the coming year, during which Modena would complete her third year of residency at Wisconsin. I told them I would work very hard to find a way for both to join me at Hopkins the next year, so we could build the program there together.

The good-byes with my Wisconsin colleagues were tearful, but all wished me good luck. I remain friends with most of them to this day. I sold the house on Lake Mendota to the two nurses. They had lived in one of the apartments even before I arrived in Madison. I was delighted to sell it to individuals who appreciated the beauty of the house and the environment on the lake as much as I did. With Phyllis's help, I packed my car the night before I was to leave for Baltimore. She would remain in the house for a few more weeks before going to her next job with the Pan American Health Organization (PAHO), which she had secured months before.

When I closed the door to my Madison home for the last time, I almost tripped over a package of croissants from my favorite bakery and fresh strawberries. They were a gift from Alain, along with a simple note wishing me bon voyage. I was to remember that beautiful act frequently over the coming years when he, Modena, and I worked on building a new program at Hopkins.

CHAPTER 11

A Hopkins Faculty Member

DRIVING FROM MADISON TO BALTIMORE provided time for me to reflect on what I had learned so far, what I planned to do at Hopkins, and to sense the gut-wrenching feeling that can permeate someone about to start something big and new. That kind of feeling has always stimulated a profound stubbornness that "assured" me that I could not, and would not, fail. I knew that what I wanted to develop at Hopkins was important; that I would have family, friends, and colleagues to help me overcome unavoidable barriers; and that the excitement I felt would get me through the rough parts. So, I thought, *OK, Great Comedian, here we go.*

My first day back at Hopkins, this time as a faculty member, brought back so many memories. Those memories began with the dream engendered by the pictures about Hopkins Medicine in the windows of the corner pharmacy when I was a child. It is amazing how something seemingly so simple can profoundly affect one's life.

It took four hours for me to walk through the buildings that are in one way or another related to pediatrics, in an effort to regain the feel of the place. During that tour, I traveled from the inpatient units in the Children's Medical and Surgical Center, or CMSC as it was then known, through the basement tunnel connecting some of the buildings. I remembered that during my residency it was in that tunnel that I discovered a mattress being used by some adolescent patients for extracurricular activities. Needless to say that particular mattress was removed immediately, and the security guards were instructed to make regular rounds in the basement tunnels. On this tour I met so many of my former colleagues, who greeted me like a long lost friend. The walk down "memory lane" (Harriet Lane) was worth every minute of my time.

I had arrived a week before the day I was to start officially, in order for me to have some time to get reacclimated to the Hopkins environment. I wanted the vast majority of my time and efforts to be devoted to work, so I had already arranged to rent a furnished apartment a few miles from the hospital. I was told that it was too dangerous to live much closer to the neighborhood where the medical center was located, even though most of the patients that I'd care for lived there. I knew I'd be working long hours, and it was important to know that I could return home from work each day, no matter what the hour, and not be concerned about safety. I had brought only a few precious possessions from Madison, so it was easy to settle in to my new apartment The apartment building was especially agreeable for me, because several other Hopkins faculty members lived there.

The New General-Pediatric and Adolescent Clinic

Some of you might read this section and wonder what is so special about a clinic such as the one I am about to describe. Further, why would I bother to describe it in such detail? What is now a common program essentially did not exist, anywhere as such, when I returned to Hopkins. Anyone interested in building something should be interested in process, not only outcomes.

I was about to organize and implement a new kind of outpatient clinic for Hopkins, which would be suitable for most other medical schools. The goal for this program was to provide a program for poor patients who used Hopkins clinics as their source of medical care, one that was equitable to what better-off patients had. My hope was that, if we were successful, we could convince Hopkins resident graduates and other medical-center programs to do the same.

Teaching residents in a setting that emulated primary care as it was practiced in the community had not commonly been part of pediatric training. Like Hopkins, most programs emphasized subspecialties and research. Academic centers at that time greatly emphasized serious diseases, with little thought to common problems and health maintenance. It was certainly essential for physicians to be educated and trained to care for the seriously ill. However, we also had a responsibility to keep patients healthy and to care for illnesses before they became serious.

My plan was to establish a clinic patterned after a private pediatrician's office and to incorporate research on common problems and best ways to deliver care. This was going to be a difficult undertaking academically, because not much of that sort of research was being performed or published anywhere. My academic career and that of the faculty I would hire would depend on successfully performing research and publishing results. The academic rule of "publish or perish" did not concern me because I was certain we could succeed academically while providing excellent primary care for children and adolescents.

My first chore in organizing the new clinic, General Pediatrics and Adolescent Medicine (GPAM), was to find support staff who would help set up the clinic. We needed to emulate the atmosphere of a private pediatrician's office, even though it was located on the second floor of the pediatric outpatient clinic building, which was attached to the hospital.

I was so pleased that three staff persons, whom I remembered as being especially helpful to the patients and physicians when I was a resident, were willing to join me in the new venture. These three essential people consisted of the registrar, the first person that patients and parents would encounter, and who entered the patients into the system; a licensed practical nurse, to set the stage for the clinicians who would care for the patients; and a nurse's aide, essential to assuring the clinic would work efficiently.

All three individuals were very familiar with the Hopkins pediatric culture and environment. They had a wonderful way with parents and children, making them feel welcome and comfortable. Because they were members of the community from which most of our patients came, they also set rules for behavior in the clinic by parents and children and made sure they were followed. Many administrators fail to recognize the importance of such support staff. They hire the least expensive persons or simply pay no special attention to these positions. That is a big mistake. As the clinic became busier, more support staff was hired, but these three individuals had already worked with the clinicians, parents, and patients to create the necessary atmosphere.

I also hired a pediatrician, who worked two days a week for the first year, to fill in when I could not be in the clinic. She stayed on until my two colleagues from Wisconsin, Modena Wilson and Alain Joffe, joined me.

Very soon after my arrival, I wrote one grant and one contract proposal, which were funded. They allowed me to hire both of my Wisconsin colleagues and some other staff the following year. The final staff members who joined us were two pediatric nurse practitioners (PNPs). One of them grew up in the neighborhood and had received all her medical care at Hopkins. The other PNP grew up in a middle-class family, was married to an attorney, and could have worked in almost any office or clinic she wanted. However, she chose the Hopkins GPAM clinic because she wanted to work with the poor children of East Baltimore. All the staff, in one way or another, signified their belief in equity.

My budget contained a salary for myself and one other faculty member, as part of my agreement with Dr. Littlefield. I also had one fellow position from the grant. It was a matter of which position would be taken by Alain, and which by Modena. It would have been logical to give the faculty position to Alain, because he would have completed his MPH degree. Modena would be the fellow, because she would have just finished her residency and wanted to work toward her MPH degree while working full-time in the GPAM clinic. However, because Alain was a bachelor and Modena was married to a professional writer and planning soon to have a child, Alain kindly offered to accept the lesser paying fellowship position. Alain's unselfishness and generosity were also characteristic of Modena, making it relatively easy for us to work out any problems that arose as we developed the clinic.

During the first year of the GPAM clinic, before the arrival of Alain and Modena, I was mostly in the clinic three full days a week and used the other two for administrative issues and writing grants and papers. I was also on call, virtually all the time, for GPAM patients admitted to the hospital. This was essential, because our rule was that I was the attending of record for any GPAM clinic patient who was hospitalized.

This attending arrangement was new to the culture, because up to then, no one was accustomed to general-clinic patients having a private Hopkins physician on the inpatient units. The arrangement included our residents being backed up by an attending faculty physician from the clinic, with the faculty member being the attending of record. Because I was not always called when one of our patients was admitted by another service such as surgery, I had to set the record straight by coming into the hospital, sometimes in the middle of the night. I wanted to make sure our patients received what we wanted, especially from the pediatric-surgical and other subspecialty staffs.

An interesting incident occurred when Dr. Littlefield asked me if I would be willing to give up the twelve first-year residents rotating on the service each year in exchange for a 10 percent raise in my salary. Several faculty members, who wanted the residents for their services, complained that it was more important that these residents learn how to care for "really sick" (as opposed to "un-really sick"?) patients. I told him that the whole idea of what I was organizing was to teach the residents to "really" care for infants, children, and adolescents as in the "real" world, where most pediatricians work. He did not try to force me to change my mind. I think he was merely doing what he had promised the other faculty members he would do, by discussing their concerns with me.

I was delighted when the six residents who had not rotated on our service the first year (the pediatric program trained eighteen new residents annually, and we were assigned only one a month), went to Dr. Littlefield toward the end of the year. They requested that they be allowed to rotate with us in their second year, to gain what they, and others, described as a great educational experience. Arrangements were then made for all eighteen incoming first-year residents, plus the six now-second-year residents, to rotate with us (for a total of twenty-four residents that year). Fortunately, by then we had many patients, and Modena, Alain, two PNPs, and more support staff would be present to teach.

TIME TO GET MARRIED

During that first year, before the arrival of Modena and Alain, the only time I took off was two weeks at the end of May for my wedding and honeymoon. The part-time pediatrician covered me during that time. I guess I should back up a bit.

Within a few weeks of my arriving in Baltimore in July, Jim wanted us to date only each other. I agreed with the stipulation that if, by the end of the calendar year, we decided not to marry, we would remain friends but once again date others. I thought we were both getting too old not to marry soon. I knew Jim, who is a great procrastinator, did not like the idea, but he agreed to go along with the proposed plan. The result was that, at just past midnight on January 2, 1979 (my birthday), he proposed with three roses. Each rose has a small tag: one read, "Will," the second "you" and the third "marry me?" Such a romantic! I still have the "marry me?" rose, which I pressed in a storybook. The book is *The Wily Witch* by Godfried Bowmans, from which Jim reads to me periodically. It is a wonderful storybook for children and adults.

Naturally I accepted, and we were married on May 26, 1979. I wanted us to exchange our vows in the outdoors. Jim is Protestant, and I am Roman Catholic, and although it didn't seem to matter to him if we married in a Catholic church, I did not want to chance offending his mother, whom I really liked a lot. After discussing where an outdoor wedding might occur, Jim had the brilliant idea that we get married at the Maryknoll Missions headquarters in Ossining, New York. By doing this, I would be taking vows at Maryknoll, as I had intended before deciding that a missionary life was not going to work for me. The difference would be that the vows would be for marriage, and not for the nunnery. The nunnery as a life for me is hardly thinkable as I write this now.

We arranged the ceremony with Father Alan Goebl, a Maryknoll priest friend of ours (who left Maryknoll a few years later), and Phyllis (whom you'll remember was another former Maryknoller) was my maid of honor. For the only time in our life together, Jim arrived early and I arrived late. My family and I were lost, trying to find Maryknoll on unfamiliar roads, in upstate New York. I had been rushing to get the page proofs for the second edition of my textbook mailed to the publisher before my wedding. Therefore, I had not made sure I had a proper map in my car. This was way before the GPS era. Fortunately, we all arrived in time for our outdoor ceremony. This ceremony had to be completed before a planned picnic for Korean missionaries, which was to be held on the grounds.

We exchanged vows at the Pagoda of Our Lady of Maryknoll and exchanged rings near the bell, which was routinely rung when the Maryknoll missionaries left for the missions. The little boy , Peter, who was our ring bearer rang the bell (quietly, of course). His sister, Julia< was our flower girl. Both were children of Nancy and Bob Charles, the latter of whom had been the director of the Peace Corps in Thailand when Jim served there. Our dear friend, Terri Menke, sang several songs of joy during the ceremony. Jim and I had choreographed and written our own outside ceremony. Allie (as we called Father Goebl) served as witness for the ceremony. We all then went into the chapel for a nuptial mass.

Three religions were represented at the mass, with Father Allie (Catholic), Reverend Ed Gordon (Protestant), and Jack Kornfield (Buddhist). Ed is married to Susan Gordon, the terrific pediatrician with whom I worked at Columbia, and Jack was a friend of Jim's, whom he met while serving in the National Health Service as a Peace Corps physician in Thailand. The presence of three religions at mass and a ceremony that occurred outside really confused many people. In fact, Jim's mother asked Nate, my sister's husband, if it was a traditional Catholic ceremony. He responded that he thought it was a traditional Protestant ceremony. Clearly, it was a traditional Jim and Cathy ceremony, as produced by the Great Comedian.

THE HONEYMOON

Our honeymoon was a continuation of what had been and was to be our life together. We went to Bali, via Thailand, where I met the Buddhist monk who had mentored Jim in meditation. Jim had lived in the monk's village for several months. Jim did this after completing his time in the US Public Health Service in Thailand. The monk was a jolly person, who—when he saw Jim's beard, which I loved—asked me if it tickled. He laughed when I said, "Yes, but I like it."

While we were in Thailand, Jim also introduced me to Josie Stanton, who had been a "mother hen" to many Peace Corps people, including Jim. Her husband had been the US ambassador to Thailand during World War II. She introduced us to the head of the Buddhist Order in Thailand, who blessed our marriage. The blessings of all those religions must have worked, because Jim and I have lived happily ever after. At this point in our lives, thirty seven years later, we are like two old shoes; we might not look so good anymore, but we sure feel very comfortable together.

Our honeymoon trip continued to our final destination of Bali, with a stop to visit the Buddhist Borobudur Temple in central Java, Indonesia. A friendly Dutch tourist took what was to become our "official" honeymoon picture of us sitting at the top of the temple. Because it was a double exposure, we appear to be sitting in the sky looking down at the temple and garden. That is probably a clear depiction of how we were feeling at the time.

OUR SPECIAL HOUSE

I did not want us to continue living in a rented apartment where Jim had lived. So we sold our house in Madison, which we had been renting to two nurses and a teacher, and purchased a very large house on an acre of land. The house was in a lovely neighborhood of Baltimore, just four miles from Hopkins Hospital. The house and grounds needed a great deal of cosmetic work, including trimming a heavily overgrown garden, which concealed a double pond, fed by an underground spring. The requirement for so much cosmetic work made the price of the house within our budget, providing we were very careful and did most of the work ourselves.

My family helped in clearing the pond area one weekend. It was fun getting wet and dirty, so it didn't seem like hard work. It took about a year or so to get the place into good shape. We continued to work on it for many years thereafter, until it became the beautiful property that we wanted to share.

Jim labeled the house "Castalia," to honor the original owner, Virgil Hillyer, who had labeled the pond as such. He was a classics scholar and had had the house built when he was the first headmaster at the Calvert School. The school was located across the street and also had an athletic field next to our house. The twenty-seven years we lived there, and especially the twenty-one when we worked at Hopkins, are filled with fond memories. We rented the two apartments in the house, each with separate entrances, to Hopkins-based people. Modena and her husband, Gary, lived in the larger apartment. Their two boys, Christopher and Nicholas, became our "surrogate sons."

We also hosted many picnics and dinner parties as well as three weddings, mostly attended by Hopkins-associated folks. The three weddings were planned for the first week of May, when the pink dogwood trees that shaded the ponds were in full bloom. We would clean and stock the ponds with koi fish just before the celebrations. The weddings were very memorable because they involved Hopkins resident couples whose religions were different.

The first wedding ceremony, involving a Jewish-Methodist couple, required having only nonalcoholic beverages served to please the bride's family. However, to also accommodate the groom's family, we quietly provided alcoholic beverages behind the house.

Because that wedding had been planned for the first week in May, and it had been a cold winter, the dogwood was not in bloom. The night before the ceremony, Jim purchased three hundred pink carnations and wired them to the dogwood tree, so it appeared to be in full bloom for the ceremony. We joked that the wedding was indeed blessed, as evidenced by the miracle of pink carnations growing on a dogwood tree. The Great Comedian is not alone in having a good sense of humor.

The next wedding involved an Irish-Jewish couple, for whom no problem existed regarding serving alcohol. In fact, the joy and enthusiasm of some of the cousins when the Irish jig met the Jewish horah was such that a bookcase was tipped over. The result was our purchasing a new bookcase, which had been in dire need of replacement, after all. The bride's cousin (a priest) and a cantor conducted the ceremony. Jim learned about the Jewish custom of replacing the required glass for the groom to break (the symbolism of this custom should be self-evident) with a light bulb, wrapped in a cloth napkin. This is to make the glass easier to break. Male ingenuity at its best!

That couple planted another dogwood tree in our garden, which showed great foresight, because many years later our original dogwood died. When we sold the house, also many years later, we made sure the deed stated that the tree was to be preserved. The deed also stated that when she was married, the couple's daughter could have the ceremony, or take pictures, under that tree. She and her groom did take pictures under the tree when that time came many years later.

The third wedding involved a Korean-American couple. Because of the Korean custom that required many hours of preparation, the bride did not show up until several hours later than planned. The groom did arrive on time but seemed to know that his bride would arrive later.

During the time awaiting the bride, many Korean women, dressed in lovely pink gowns, and their husbands, none of whom spoke English, mingled with the Hopkins folks, who spoke no Korean. That seemed to be of minor importance because, while waiting, all were entertained by a Peabody string quartet that played under our giant elm tree. When the bride arrived, the ceremony was lovely, and the food, prepared by the bride's sisters, was delicious.

Jim, quite the photographer, took videos of every wedding ceremony, which we showed the families after the couples had left. Jim then sent a copy of the video to each family and to the couple. Because we knew how fortunate we were to have such a beautiful place to live, this was one way to share it.

BACK TO WORK

By the second year, Modena and Alain had arrived; we had two fellows, who were paid for by a grant; the three original support staff had settled into their routines; and the two nurse practitioners had been hired. In addition, we now had twenty-four residents, rotating one month each in the clinic. Also, all first- and second-year residents had their one-half-day-per-week clinics, in which they saw their private patients. Clearly, the GPAM clinic went into full gear, functioning like a Swiss clock.

While Alain was officially a fellow that year, he really functioned as a faculty member and carried out his research project. We had to make a decision about who would take primary responsibility for the infants and younger children and who would assume primary responsibility for the adolescents. It took about a nanosecond for Modena to volunteer for the younger patients and for Alain to volunteer for the adolescents. That spirit made progress so relatively easy when it involved them. Equity was never in question with them, no matter the situation.

Each year we were responsible for training two fellows, eighteen first-year residents, and some medical students in our clinic. We also had to oversee the afternoon clinics, where the second- and third-year residents saw their "private" patients. It was clear that we once again had to expand the number of patients enrolled. Almost all of our patients came to us having been enrolled by the residents, from the ER or the inpatient services, to their clinics. When a resident cared for a child in the ER or in hospital, the resident could enroll the child in his or her panel of private patients, for whom he or she assumed primary care.

During the second and third years of residency, each resident was assigned to a half-day session each week in the GPAM clinic, where he or she would care for those private patients. If a child needed to be seen in our clinic, at a time his or her private resident was not available, one of the other residents assigned to the clinic that day would see the child. That resident made sure the private resident knew what happened. Sometimes a resident could only come to the clinic for a moment, to assure the parent and child that the resident seeing the child would take good care of them. It really didn't take much time for the residents to assume the role of private pediatricians and to work out how their patients would be taken care of in their absence. A clinic faculty member mentored the residents at all times.

Expanding our panel of patients made our clinic a very hectic place, so I would take muffins into the clinic on the mornings after especially busy days. I am amazed how much the staff appreciated that simple gesture, and it taught me the importance of paying attention to people.

Space Needs and the ER

It soon became clear that we needed more space to care for so many patients. Because space remains the final frontier for so many institutions like Hopkins, that seemed to be an impossible problem to solve. Well, not quite. The first floor of the outpatient building held the pediatric ER, which was very busy during the evenings and nights. But it was not very busy during the day, especially because our clinic had been enrolling the patients who had been using the ER as a primary-care facility.

I was able to arrange for our clinic to move into one side of the much roomier first floor while keeping the other side for the ER during the daytime. Therefore, the GPAM clinic occupied half the first floor from 8:00 a.m. to 5:00 p.m., and the ER occupied all of it after 5:00 p.m.

Because we were now in close proximity to the pediatric ER, the GPAM clinic attending physician was frequently asked about a child who was in the ER. At that time, the senior residents and the outpatient chief resident supervised the younger residents in the ER. There was no assigned attending. After several months of our sharing the first floor space, I volunteered to take over directing the pediatric ER. This was gratefully accepted and the pediatricians on our staff took turns attending there. In addition, I negotiated funds for the hiring of more staff so we could better manage the clinical and teaching needs of the ER.

We also moved the pediatric ER patients who were being seen at night in the adult ER to our own pediatric ER. How that happened is worth revealing. I knew the adult ER was not a good place for children. Many violent episodes and drug-related illnesses of adult patients were seen in the adult ER, especially at night. I thought that, except for acute trauma, all children should be seen in the pediatric ER. I tried to convince the hospital administrator in charge that we needed to make the move. He refused politely, believing things were proper the way they "always had been."

So I invited him and his wife to have dinner at our home one Saturday night. When they decided it was time to go home, I asked him if I could show him something at the hospital while Jim took his wife home. He and his wife agreed, and he and I went to the adult ER, which was, as usual, especially on a weekend night, a very scary place for anyone.

Several inebriated (or worse) patients carried on terribly. Two patients with gunshot wounds were being treated in the ER when we arrived and their family members were sobbing uncontrollably. I asked the administrator how he would like his young grandson to be present. The look on his face gave the answer immediately. The following Monday, plans were set in motion for all children to be seen in the pediatric ER except for those with acute trauma. Ah, yes, sometimes it takes imagination, and a home-cooked Italian dinner, to solve a problem. This was a variation of Harvard and Professor Curran, as described in a former chapter. Truly, the way to a man's heart (and mind?), is through his stomach.

A few months after we assumed attending responsibility in the pediatric ER, the chair of Emergency Medicine (who was very happy with the new arrangement) asked if the adult ER residents could also rotate with us for a month each. I readily agreed, knowing that we all would gain from interchanging knowledge and skills, and that's exactly what happened.

THE INPATIENT EXPERIENCE

Educating the inpatient staff took a bit more effort and time. An example occurred one night when I was called by a pediatric resident who asked if I would come to the hospital. The resident was admitting one of our GPAM clinic patients who had acute abdominal pain. I went to the hospital after he and I discussed the child on the phone, before the decision for admission had been made. When I arrived at the hospital inpatient unit, where the child had been admitted, I was told that the pediatric surgical resident was going to wait until morning to call his attending. As was the custom, he didn't think it was necessary to awaken an attending in the middle of the night for this particular clinic patient. I pointed out to him that, like his surgical attending, I was also member of the Hopkins faculty and the child's attending physician, and I was not only awake but also present.

I then examined the child with him, pointing out a few tricks of how to deal with a screaming toddler, who apparently had an acute abdomen. That is, sudden, severe abdominal pain of unclear etiology (cause) often requiring surgical intervention.

The toddler had been crying inconsolably and pointing to his "belly." The resident immediately called his surgical attending physician, and the child was taken to the operating room. Within the next half hour, an inflamed appendix was removed, and the child did very well thereafter.

The next morning, I took the surgical resident to breakfast; surgical residents are always hungry. I explained to him that our clinic was no different than any private practice. He understood and seemed impressed with this "new" arrangement for our clinic patients. It took a number of these direct incidents, and breakfasts or lunches, to convince the entire pediatric community that we were serious about being the private pediatricians for our clinic patients.

By the end of the second year, there was no question about our purpose and legitimacy. By that time, two years of residents had completed the process, and a new set of residents was beginning. The new residents would be introduced to a well-established program. By the time all three years of residents are familiar with the setting, it's not new anymore. I guess you just have to live long enough to get some things established. (That's probably why women live two to three years on average longer than men; we need the extra time to overcome the biases and lack of equity. The other reason we live longer might be to make up for all the time women wait in line in the ladies' room.)

Having Modena, Alain, or me serving as the attending pediatrician for most of the pediatric residents and mentoring some young faculty from all pediatric specialties helped secure the success of our clinic. After all, familiarity breeds content.

One thing I insisted on for every child for whom I was the private pediatrician (mostly children of residents and faculty), was that the father would attend the child's visit to me with the mother, as much as possible. Also, because the vast majority of mothers breastfed, I expected each father to feed his infant the mother's bottled milk or formula once a day, if possible. I wanted him to do so, while bare chested, and with the child also bare chested. That way both parents could have a similar bonding experience, feeding the infant skin to skin.

A few surgical residents balked at first but relented when I promised to not reveal this to anyone. As if I ever would do that! Many of these fathers have told me how wonderful the experience proved to be. Many of them have passed that advice on to their sons. If you teach something good, it will be passed on.

Beyond the GPAM Clinic

How the clinic progressed into a pediatric division is an interesting story. As we saw a need for some special service, we simply established the special program or project that would meet the need. Nothing fancy, we just did it.

Adolescent Medicine

Dr. Janet Hardy had a clinic for adolescent mothers; it was located across the street from the hospital clinic area and near a high school. With her blessing, her clinic was combined with our adolescent clinic, and we were then able to provide full coverage for adolescent patients in the Hopkins area.

We later expanded the adolescent program to include a mother-and-infant clinic, where the first postpartum visit for teenage mothers was merged with the first infant visit and was held in the same area. We made an arrangement with a very cooperative and interested faculty obstetrician who worked in that clinic with one of us. After that first postpartum visit, both mother and infant were seen by a pediatrician. Much to the obstetricians' and our delight, this arrangement resulted in significantly decreasing the number of repeat adolescent pregnancies. Teenage mothers were quite reliable in taking their infants for immunizations and other well-baby visits, but much less so in taking care of themselves, for their own checkups. So by combining both, the mothers' compliance with visits, which included birth control, was enhanced.

COLLEGE HEALTH SERVICE

Because Jim is a psychiatrist, I frequently attended parties where most of the guests were psychiatrists. At one such gathering, I met the director of the Hopkins College Health Service, who was a psychiatrist. She described the frustration she was having in finding physicians who were interested in college-age students. I told her about our adolescent medicine program, and we made an agreement for us to assume the responsibility for the medical portion of the College Health Service. Alain took responsibility for that service and became the director of the entire College Health Service when the original director retired several years later.

THE HIV CLINIC

Another example of adding something needed was the result of our seeing many infants whose mothers were infected with HIV. Dr. Nancy Hutton, one of our former fellows and now on our faculty, became the director of the Intensive Primary Care Clinic, an oxymoron if ever there was one. However, under Nancy's directorship, this clinic for HIV-positive infants and children has thrived and is now bigger and better than ever.

THE DIVISION OF GENERAL PEDIATRICS AND ADOLESCENT MEDICINE

By 1984, six years after starting the GPAM clinic, and having added the pediatric emergency room, the adolescent-mother-and-child clinic, the intensive-primary-care clinic for infants and children with HIV infections, the college-health service, and a fellowship program and garnering a number of grants and publications in peer-review journals, I thought we had all the ingredients for a new division. Everyone agreed, and we now became the new Division of General Pediatrics and Adolescent Medicine. While we were still referred to as GPAM, now we were a division, actually a big deal.

Medical departments are made up of several divisions, each of which has one or several clinics. The hierarchy goes from the department chair to division chiefs, to clinic directors, to other members of the faculty who serve in one of the clinics that make up a division that make up the department. It is amazing what can be accomplished with teamwork involving so many accomplished and generous individuals working in this rather complex environment.

One of the saddest experiences of our group involved one of our fellows, Dr. Maggie (as she wanted to be called) Walsh. Like so many of our fellows, Maggie was very bright, industrious, and a joy to be with. It was soon obvious that she was headed for a successful career in academic pediatrics. Unfortunately, that was not to happen. Not long after starting her fellowship with us, she was diagnosed as having a very lethal form of leukemia. Experiencing her reaction, and that of her husband, parents, and brothers, to this harrowing illness was heartrending, to say the least.

I vividly remember visiting her every day while she was hospitalized and seeing her decline slowly as her beautiful body was ravaged by disease and almost pain despite the medications. She tried to maintain her dignity and protect all of us by her brave reaction to what every day brought.

At the end, she died surrounded by her family and a few of us who had grown to love her so deeply. After her funeral, her parents gave me one of Maggie's dolls, which looks so much like her. I keep it in a special cabinet with glass doors and take it out periodically to remind me of just how precious and precarious life is. We can do nothing to change yesterday, and tomorrow might never come, so today is the only real life there is.

The Department of Pediatrics

In 1983 Dr. Littlefield asked me to be the deputy chair of Pediatrics and director of the Pediatric Residency Program. I agreed to do so, providing my salary would be the same as the pediatrician who had stepped down from that position. He he had accepted a pediatric chairmanship at another medical center. He and I were essentially the same age, and both of us were division directors and had generated the same divisional income from research and contracts. I knew that he was neonatologist, whose salary was higher than a general pediatrician. However, because the position was what I negotiated, I wanted an equitable salary. Dr. Littlefield readily agreed to the salary, and I was shocked to learn that my current salary would be increased by almost 40 percent. That confirmed my belief, which has held firmly over the years, that women especially must be firm negotiators for positions and salaries. That is the only way to assure equitability.

My new administrative and educational responsibilities were added to those involved as director of the GPAM Division. This was only possible because of the strong leadership and generosity of Modena and Alain. Fortunately, the new responsibilities supposedly were to take only 30 percent of my time. The new responsibilities did take about 30 percent of my time, but based on an eighty-hour week. That was pretty much par for any academic position at that time.

No matter how much time they took, the new responsibilities were great fun, and I learned a great deal. Conducting morning rounds with the residents was educating and enjoyable. In those rounds we discussed new patients, who had been admitted the previous day. We followed up on issues and assured that the residents were working well and progressing. The residents were very smart, and the chief residents and senior residents took responsibility for much of the routine needs. Most of my time was spent teaching and learning.

The role as deputy chair somewhat overlapped with the residency directorship and provided me with more ability to "negotiate" for the residents. For example, I kept close watch on the various rotations, trying to assure that the experiences on each rotation were educational and reasonable for the residents. A few of the rotation experiences were not required for accreditation but were scheduled for the good experiences they offered. These were the activities I watched especially closely, because some were not directed by pediatric faculty.

One such rotation, in pediatric neurosurgery, was the source of many complaints from pediatric residents. They felt they were being used primarily as "gofers." That is, they were responsible for chores that the residents from the pediatric neurosurgery service preferred not to do or were too busy to take care of themselves. The learning experience for our residents reportedly was sparse, at best. I discussed this with several pediatric faculty members, who thought the residents were correct. The director of the service in question apparently had little respect for pediatricians. One resident reported that the director had stated openly that all pediatricians needed was "a pat on the head and a smile, and they would do anything you asked, like magic." He soon learned that if he tried that trick on me, or on any of our residents, all that would happen was we would disappear like magic.

After discussing this disturbing issue with the smiling and charming director of that service, I was convinced that the residents were correct. I told him that beginning with the new academic year in July, which was only a few months away, there would be no pediatric resident coverage on his service. He could certainly request consultation from our attending pediatric faculty if needed, but that would be it.

He was not happy and declared that I could not do that and that he was going to the president of the hospital to complain. I wished him well, knowing that the only person who could change my decision was Dr. Littlefield, to whom I had explained the problem, and who had approved my plan. The final outcome was that, after two months with no pediatric resident coverage, the director asked me to please reinstate them on his service. He promised that the residents would have a good educational experience.

As I had requested, he showed me a schedule, which he promised to have the residents follow. He and his chief resident had written it after discussing it with the pediatric residents who would be involved. Consequently, the residents had a good educational experience while providing good care to the patients. Stick to what you know is right, and depend on good people to act appropriately. They almost always do, and when they don't, just stay with what you know is right. That's one way to assure equity.

I was very lucky, because there was no resident who didn't work hard. Some were real characters, like the young man who refused to wear socks, despite my warning him that the hospital germs could be vicious. I suggested that if he insisted on not wearing socks, he should wash his feet with the same frequency that he washed his hands, obviously to no avail. I chose not to fight that battle. You win some and lose some.

Another resident was the tall, thin father of two young boys. I noticed that he was losing weight and seemed sad. These were some signs I watched for in the residents. They worked so hard, and I wanted to be sure they remained healthy. I began paying attention to what he ate and discovered that his lunch always consisted of one peanut butter sandwich and an apple. When I spoke to him about my concern for his weight loss, he began to cry. He told me that his sons needed shoes, and he and his wife were trying to save for their purchase. I went to the bank across the street (no ATMs back then), and when I came back I gave him one hundred dollars to buy the shoes. He refused to take the money until I insisted that it was only a loan that he could pay back once he was working for a real salary.

I then applied to the American Academy of Pediatrics (AAP) special "scholarship" program that had been set up for pediatric residents in need of funds. When the resident received the AAP check, for which he and I were very grateful, he came directly to my office and returned the one hundred dollars. I told him that he was to give it to someone else who needed it more than he did, and I doubted that would happen, until he was really gainfully employed. I have every confidence that he has passed on that amount, and much more, since then.

The residents made my life so fulfilling and joyful. I refer to them as my "kids," and to this day I receive cards, e-mails, and visits from many of them. Who could ask for more?

I'm a Professor!

In 1984, a few days before Christmas, I received a phone call while on vacation at my parents' home. The callers were the dean and Dr. Littlefield, who told me I had just been promoted to full professor. That call, combined with the dozen chocolate roses Jim gave to me, was absolutely the best Christmas present I've ever received. They were even better than the chemistry set I received when I was nine years old. So in January 1985, I became only the twelfth woman professor, in the then ninety-two-year history of the Johns Hopkins School of Medicine. That was not a great record for women, so I made a promise that I would do whatever I could to remedy that situation.

Changing Chairs

In 1985 Dr. Littlefield stepped aside as chair of the Pediatric Department, and Dr. Frank Oski became the chair. Thus began a whirlwind experience with one of the brightest (a better word than intelligent in this case because of the light he shed), most interesting, and enjoyable people I've ever met. Of course, I offered to step down as deputy chair so he might name his own person, but to my delight he laughed at my suggestion.

The difference between the two chairs was like night and day, except for the great integrity and intellect of both men. John Littlefield was a quiet, soft-spoken New Englander who had been trained as an internist, whereas Frank (he made it clear from the outset that he wanted me to call him by his first name) was an outspoken, adamant, pediatric fighter.

Frank was very much a hands-on chair, who attended morning rounds and was ever-present on the inpatient units. His sense of humor was such that he could make it clear he disagreed with someone while not offending. The operant word here is "could," because he sometimes deliberately chose to offend those in power or others who did something Frank felt was harmful to children or the residents and faculty. Every day was an adventure with him; he was so full of life.

I remember one incident that epitomized his personality. He and I were in Philadelphia for a meeting, and we met one of his close friends, who was also a pediatric chairman, for dinner. Afterward, as we were walking back to the hotel, we passed an auction house, which was obviously in full swing. Frank told us to follow him inside "for a little fun." We entered the hall, where the auctioning of a warehouse was just beginning.

The bids began with one million dollars, and Frank bid that amount, much to my chagrin. I almost fainted when Frank bid twice more, to the tune of more than two million dollars. Clearly, Frank did not have that much money, at least not to spend on a warehouse. He stopped bidding, and we left. Outside the building, he and his friend laughed, and his friend told me that Frank did that all the time. He knew the value of the auction item, and stopped bidding way below that amount, just for the fun of it.

I learned so much about human nature and how to get things done from each of the two chairs. Each of them used completely different approaches to accomplish what they wanted.

At that time, all department chairs at Hopkins served on the Dean's Advisory Council, which met monthly. The two largest departments, Internal Medicine and Pediatrics, were allowed two members each on the committee. Frank asked me to serve with him. This was my introduction to academia from the top. Because Frank was new to Hopkins, at the Dean's Advisory Committee meetings, I often slipped him a note about the underlying issue or the person being discussed. The only women at those meetings, besides myself, were the nonphysician administrative director of the dean's office and a secretary. I learned a great deal about how academic leaders (all men) thought about various issues, but from a woman's (my) perspective.

Almost a Mother

The year 1986 was a year that Dickens would recognize immediately as the best and worst of times. The best was almost everything that occurred at work and home, and the fact that I, finally, was pregnant. At forty-three years old, I knew there was not much time left for me to become pregnant, and I can never fully describe the joy the news of my pregnancy brought to Jim and me. We had been trying to conceive since the day we were married.

Some people thought we were crazy for trying to get pregnant because of my mesocaval shunt performed in Wisconsin. Others thought I should have an amniocentesis because of my age and the likelihood for a developmentally disabled child. However, all shared our happiness. Because of our spiritual beliefs, Jim and I refused to even consider an amniocentesis, and certainly not anything more drastic. On the other hand, we also recognize the right of others to make such decisions based on their beliefs. The discussions we had on this subject with many individuals were indeed interesting and educational.

However, our joy was shattered when I had a miscarriage ten weeks into my pregnancy. I'll always be grateful for those weeks of pregnancy, but anyone who thinks a woman or man (father) doesn't mourn such a loss knows nothing about parenthood. I still keep the tiny infant's shirt from Peru, given to us by Phyllis, in a drawer, and I hold it periodically and did especially when I was taking care of very sick children.

Advancing Women Nationally

I became active in pediatric national academic committees and societies as soon as I finished my residency in 1974. After years of attending the annual meetings, presenting papers, and serving on committees, I became the president of the Ambulatory Pediatric Association (APA) in 1985. That organization dealt with issues related primarily to general pediatrics. It was clear to me that, while there were many women pediatricians who belonged to this and the other pediatric academic societies, very few were officers. Therefore, I worked to advance women to leadership positions in the APA; the American Pediatric Society (which dealt with all areas of pediatrics), where I served as secretary treasurer from 1989 to 1994; and the American Board of Pediatrics (which was responsible for certifying pediatricians), where I served on the board from 1990 to 2005 and became the chair of the board in 1990. I also served on the executive committees of various accrediting bodies of medical programs.

Often in these societies, it was necessary to be forceful in a nonconfrontational manner. It helped that most of the other members (mostly men) were friends, who appreciated my humor but recognized when I was serious about an issue. I found that almost all of the men simply did not recognize the paucity of women on the committees and in leadership positions. I often thought there just might be an inborn bias in many or perhaps most men about women that was augmented by experience. However, success came slowly but surely, especially with the pediatricians.

PATIENTS AND RELIGION

It was no surprise to me that religion played a significant role with patients and their families. It is natural to seek solace when we find ourselves in dangerous or stressful situations. Religion, however practiced, can provide great comfort. As a Eucharistic minister, I attended mass every morning in the hospital chapel, assisted the Catholic chaplain with services, and sometimes delivered the Holy Eucharist to patients. The morning mass was always attended by a number of patients, family members, and clinicians.

On occasion, religion played a direct role in my interactions with patients and their families. Two examples of those situations stand out in my mind. The first involved a little five-year-old boy, "Noah," whose parents were of the Jehovah's Witnesses faith. That faith urges members to refuse blood transfusions and not allow them to be given to their children. Ordinarily, this doesn't present a problem, but on occasion it can greatly impede the delivery of sound medical care, as it did with this child.

I was supervising residents in the pediatric ER when Noah was brought in with a substantial loss of blood from a deep hemangioma of his scalp that had ulcerated. A hemangioma is a swelling or growth of the cells that line blood vessels and is characterized by increased numbers of normal and abnormal blood vessels. Noah had a rare problem, because the vast majority of hemangiomas resolve spontaneously or respond to medical treatment. In his case, the lesion was fed by sufficient blood vessels so that any trauma to the site caused much bleeding.

Because the parents, who had recently moved to Baltimore, wouldn't allow blood transfusions, I agreed to allow Noah to be followed in our clinic by a resident who cared for him under my supervision. We prescribed iron, to replace the iron lost with the bleeding, and made a follow-up appointment a few days out. At that visit, he appeared to be doing well, and his blood count was on the rise. However, a few weeks later, Noah was once again in the ER with another substantial bleed. This time he had to be admitted to the hospital. He was very weak, and his red-blood-cell count was very low. I was concerned that he might go into shock, despite the intravenous fluids we were allowed to give him.

I met with the parents, along with the resident who was caring for him, and told them that he badly needed a blood transfusion. Even more importantly, his deep hemangioma needed to be fixed surgically. We had performed an angiogram (an X-ray test in which special dyes and a fluoroscopic camera displays blood flow in blood vessels), discussed the problem with our pediatric surgeon, and knew that the lesion could be fixed. However, Noah's blood count had to be higher in order for surgery to be performed, and more blood might well be needed during surgery. This information was not received well by his parents who cringed.

I further explained that if his scalp was not fixed, he would continue to have bleeds. After all, he was a playful child, and any trauma to his scalp would have the same result he had just experienced. There was a danger that he might not survive the next bleed. The young parents (they were in their mid-twenties, and Noah was their first and only child) began to cry. They said they loved Noah very much and knew he needed blood. If they allowed him to receive blood, they would be excommunicated from their church, and their parents might disown them.

I then discussed the problem with the hospital's lawyer and asked if I could, for medical reasons, take temporary legal responsibility for Noah. That would relieve his parents from their responsibility to the church while allowing Noah to receive the necessary treatment. I could not ask Noah's parents for permission to do this because it would make them responsible for the surgery and alienate them from their parents and their church. It was arranged for me to take legal responsibility, Noah received a blood transfusion, and the surgical repair was a great success. I spent a great deal of time with his parents in the hospital chapel during the surgery. I'm not sure who was more relieved when we saw Noah in the postoperative recovery room. Of course, I immediately signed the papers, that I had in my white coat pocket, transferring Noah back to his parents.

I had expected that I might receive some hate mail, or worse, from Noah's grandparents, but none was received. The Great Comedian works in strange ways, indeed.

The second religion-related episode was quite different. This episode involved a seven-year-old girl, "Emily," who was brought into the emergency room late one evening. Once again I was there supervising the residents. Emily had been transferred from a community hospital because she had a very serious infection that could not be controlled. She required care that only could be provided in a hospital that specialized in the care of children. The seriousness of her condition was evident immediately, and she was admitted to the hospital within a very short time after her arrival. I would serve as her attending physician; that meant I was professionally and legally her primary physician.

I spoke with her parents, who obviously were extremely worried about their little girl. I tried to assure them that we would do everything possible for Emily and that the team of physicians, nurses, and others at the Hopkins Children's Hospital was among the best in the world. The mother sat with a rosary in her hand throughout our conversation, and she asked me if I was Catholic. I told her I was but that there were team members of many religions, so she had a full range of beliefs, hoping to give her some comfort. She smiled at me and said that was good, but she was happy that I was Catholic.

In the hospital I ordered more tests, maintained strong intravenous antibiotics, and immediately sought the consultation of an infectious-disease expert. Over the ensuing hours, Emily began to bleed from her nose and showed signs of internal bleeding. A hematologist, an expert in blood and clotting factors, agreed with the diagnosis of disseminating intravascular coagulopathy (DIC). That is a problem in which blood clots form throughout the body's small blood vessels, damaging organs and causing internal and external bleeding. One cause of DIC is sepsis, a life-threatening complication whereby chemicals released into the bloodstream to fight the infection trigger an inflammatory response throughout the body. We (the subspecialists, residents, and I) all worked throughout the night to get little Emily through the crisis.

I went home at five in the morning to shower and change my clothing and then immediately drove back to the hospital to check on Emily. She was still seriously ill but seemed to be holding on. I then went to the chapel, where I was to serve as a Eucharistic minister that morning. Emily's mother was in the chapel, and we hugged before mass began. We then went to Emily's bedside together, and I tried to assure her mother that we were doing everything possible. She told me she was very happy that I was a Eucharistic minister, because that meant Emily had "a special connection to God." I told her that was not especially true, but that I would continue to pray while caring for Emily. That is exactly what I did.

I checked on Emily every hour or so throughout the day, but I was concerned because she seemed to be failing. Late that afternoon, I heard a code called for Emily's unit, and with trepidation I raced to her bedside. As I feared, the team was attempting to resuscitate Emily. After a while, it was obvious that we had lost her. I went with the resident to speak with Emily's parents, who were in a special conference room in the unit.

As we walked in the room, Emily's mother looked at me with great fear on her face. I whispered to both parents that I was very sorry but Emily had not made it. Her mother stood back, threw her rosary at me, and screamed that I was a fraud. I felt like someone had punched me in the stomach, but I knew how devastating the loss of a child could be to a parent. So I reached down, picked up the rosary, kissed it, and folded it into Emily's mother's hand, again whispering that I was very sorry. Emily's father was holding his sobbing wife, and we all had tears in our eyes. There is simply no way to describe how I felt on that occasion and every time I think of Emily and other children who I couldn't save.

More Adventures in the Department

Another life-enhancing event happened to me in 1987, when I replaced my retiring administrative assistant. My new assistant was an amazingly organized woman who had a great sense of humor. Both were essential traits for what was happening in my professional life and what was about to happen, or perhaps *explode* is a more accurate term. Her name, Roni Green, in no way described her expertise and experience. It took about an hour for her to understand me, but I'm not sure I've ever figured out what makes her tick. All I knew was that the Great Comedian was taking good care of me.

Beginning about 1985, I continued to received invitations to interview for pediatric chairmanships (chairwomanships?) at a number of medical schools, and I actually looked at a few. Frank was very supportive of my accepting one if I wanted to, but I chose not to do so at that time. I was so happy working with Frank for many reasons. One big plus was that he allowed me to continue directing the GPAM Division and to have a great deal of independence in making decisions. He was so active and respected internationally that he had no problem delegating responsibility and giving credit freely. He epitomized equity in all he did and truly loved life.

It was therefore so surprising and sad, several years later, when he disclosed that he had a very serious form of prostatic cancer. Even through his illness, his sense of humor was present. For example, he had been admitted twice to the hospital the year prior to his diagnosis of prostate cancer, for some minor cardiac issues. During those hospitalizations, no one had performed a rectal exam that might well have led to earlier discovery of the prostatic cancer. He therefore published an editorial entitled "Don't Get Caught with Your Pants Up." I saw that editorial tacked on bulletin boards of many faculty members, especially men, in several medical centers.

He was having a great deal of gastrointestinal (GI) problems, mostly diarrhea, from radiation therapy. My mother sent him two jars of blueberries she had canned and a small bottle of holy water she had kept from our trip to Israel, or as she called it, "The Holy Land." The blueberries were a favorite treatment of hers for such GI problems, and the holy water was a heavy armament in her war chest for helping people with all sorts of problems. I think she would have liked to have taken back several gallons of holy water from our trip. She distributed a few quarts to carry on the plane among all of us who were traveling with her. I am grateful that the current law against carryin fluids on planes was not in force back then.

In any case, a few days after I had given Frank my Mother's gifts, he told me that he had eaten the blueberries, drunk the holy water, and was feeling much better. I laughed and told him that he wasn't supposed to drink the holy water, but that it was to be used to bless himself—that is, to put some on his finger and place it on his skin. He said his problem was not his skin, but his prostate, and drinking the holy water was as close as he could get it to the problem site. What could I say?

CHAPTER 12

The Hopkins Dean's Office

In 1990, with Frank Oski's blessing, I made the decision that I would probably accept the chair of the Department of Pediatrics at a California institution. I wanted to notify the very recently appointed Hopkins dean, Dr. Michael Johns, in person about my decision. Because I had continued to serve on the Faculty Advisory Committee since 1985, and Dr. Johns had been the chair of Otolaryngology and therefore also served on the Faculty Advisory Committee, I knew him very well. I thought he deserved the courtesy of a personal visit before I left.

When I sat down in his office on a Friday afternoon, he told me he had requested the meeting because he had something important to ask me. I was puzzled and told him I had requested the meeting, so he asked his administrative assistant what happened. She, like all great organizers, replied that, because we both wanted to meet, she simply had scheduled one meeting, assuming we thereby could both accomplish our goals. Smart woman.

When I told him I was planning to leave, he said "no way." He wanted me to be his senior associate dean of Academic Affairs. I was flabbergasted and told him I would have to think about it over the weekend, because I had essentially accepted the other position in California. I was really ambiguous about which decision would be better. On the one hand, the pediatric chair in California would involve continuing on a very familiar path, but the deanship felt like an exciting opportunity, especially at Hopkins, working with someone I greatly respected.

That evening I discussed the decision that had to be made with Jim, and he told me to think about it over the weekend. Because we both had made preliminary plans for California, I was tending toward that position. On Saturday afternoon, Jim told me I was wanted on the phone— by the new president of Johns Hopkins University (JHU). I told him that was bizarre, because I didn't know the new president, and why would someone in that high position want to speak with me? I answered the phone, and in a humorous manner asked who was playing a joke on me. The president, William Richardson, laughed and assured me he was indeed the new president of JHU. He had called to encourage me to accept the dean's offer. He invited Jim and me to his home that evening, to discuss his feelings about the position in the dean's office.

At his home, he told us that he knew there was a serious paucity of women leaders in the School of Medicine, and he thought I could add substantially to the administration. He seemed to know a great deal about me, and (despite that?) spent a long time telling me about his plans for the university, how I might fit in, and how much he admired Dean Johns.

With that kind of encouragement, how could I resist the opportunity? Besides, is it not a woman's prerogative to change her mind? On the following Monday morning, I told Mike (as he insisted I call him either way) I would accept his offer, and I called the California institution to tell them of my decision. The chair of that search committee kindly understood my decision. He knew I had not known about the Hopkins offer until after I had told him that I would probably accept the pediatric position. Fortunately, because I had not formally accepted the position, there had not been a public announcement from the search committee.

I promised him I would not tell anyone else about my decision and that I'd ask Dean Johns and President Richardson not to disclose the name of the institution. They readily agreed, hence making it easier for the search committee of that institution to name another person for the chair without making that person feel like he or she was not the first choice. As I soon learned, selecting the finalist for high-level academic positions is somewhat of a crapshoot, with decisions being made based on some things that are not necessarily logical. Thus began another unplanned adventure. Once again, the adage that humans plan and the Great Comedian laughs proved to be true.

DEAN MICHAEL JOHNS (AKA DA DEAN)

As I anticipated, working with Mike was a joy. I told him that he was an otolaryngologist–head-and-neck (née ENT) surgeon who had the heart of a pediatrician. He retorted that I was a pediatrician who had the heart of a surgeon. Whatever—we worked very well together, along with the rest of his team. There was a great deal to be done, and he attacked every problem with vigor. Soon after I started working with Mike, I began referring to him as Da Dean, a title appreciated by him and his staff . My administrative assistant, Roni, came with me to that office, making the move much easier. Her organizational skills and good humor made my office a place where everyone felt welcomed, no matter what the reason for the visit.

I think Mike and I made all the administrative assistants and secretaries laugh and then duck. Because my office was down the hall from his, whenever he or I came up with some bright idea, one of us would tear down or up the hall to share the idea with the other. Usually that resulted in the resolution of a pending problem or the initiation of another project. I'm sure that's how he responded to his other senior deans, but perhaps in a much less dramatic manner.

The one difficult encounter with Mike occurred very soon after I went to the dean's office and witnessed how many personal interactions he was having with the other (all male) deans, such as playing tennis or having drinks together after work. When I discussed this with him, he said he would be happy to do either of those things with me. I laughed and suggested he ask his wife, Trina, what she would think of our having such interactions, especially because the Hopkins and Baltimore gossip communities paid close attention to such social interactions. Rumor mills abound, in almost all such settings. The next morning, Mike told me that Trina told him I was correct. I told him that although we were honest, faithful, and loving spouses, there were those with not-so-benign thoughts who were looking for trouble.

That is just one more reason that makes it difficult for women to function in what is very much a man's world. One way to counter such biases and rumor mongering is for women to have drinks or play tennis or whatever with their superiors together with a few other men and women. In any case, the world must stop belonging primarily to men. Equity must be prevalent in all such situations. To function otherwise would be to give up half the world's intellect and creativity, which resides in women.

WOMANIZING THE ATMOSPHERE

One of the first physical changes I made to my new office was to "womanize" it. It was situated on the ground floor and had two walls that were floor-to-ceiling windows. They had been covered with closed heavy curtains, making for a dark, gloomy atmosphere. As a lover of the outdoors, I couldn't bear it. I opened all the curtains and put planted flowers all around. I would have liked planted tomatoes, but that requires bees. I also hung cheerful paintings on the walls. I believed that no one was interested in my diplomas, which were and still are stored in a closet somewhere. The sunlight effect was glorious and made for a great place to work long hours. Also, I could wave to people coming into or going out of the building.

At that time, Academic Affairs consisted of seven offices, including Admissions, the Registrar, Medical Students, Graduate Students, Postdoctoral Students, Continuing Medical Education, and the Welch Medical Library. Thankfully there were a number of associate and assistant deans, who were responsible for daily activities of six offices, and the library had a chief librarian. After a few months, Mike asked me if I would also be willing to be the senior associate dean of Faculty Affairs, because the person who had that position wanted to do something else. I saw no problem doing that, because I knew many of the faculty members, and it added to the many experiences of my position(s).

I made sure to visit each of the offices at least once a week to speak with as many staff who were present at those times. After a few weeks, I learned a great deal about them and we had fun exchanging funny stories or jokes once they became accustomed to me.

A HAIR-RAISING EXPERIENCE

At some point, all senior associate deans were elevated (by title) to vice deans (VDs). There were four of us, including the executive VD, VD for Clinical Affairs, VD for Research, and VD for Academic Affairs and Faculty (me). We all worked very well as a team, and once again I experienced the importance of close collaboration.

One incident that occurred a few years after I had become vice dean for Academic Affairs and Faculty was very traumatic to many but proved the resiliency of the Hopkins spirit. I was in my office one afternoon when I received a call from the supervisor of a graduate student. The graduate student's girlfriend, a medical student, was being held hostage in one of the ravaged abandoned houses very near the School of Medicine. The man holding her had allowed her to call her boyfriend after she promised that if he would release her, her boyfriend would draw out $200 (the maximum amount allowed at that time), from his bank account and leave it in a spot designated by the man. The graduate student was on his way to place the money in the designated spot, where he would wait for her to be released. I told the supervisor that I would take over and would fill him in as soon as I could. I then ran to Mike's office and informed him that I was going to wait with the graduate student. I warned Mike that if a security guard was seen with or near us, it would further endanger the medical student.

Fortunately, the medical student was released after we left the money in an envelope in the designated spot as instructed. We soon learned that she had been raped and that the man had told her that he was HIV positive. Her boyfriend and I immediately took her to the University of Maryland Hospital, where fortunately I knew many physicians. I didn't want her treated at Hopkins, where she was, or would soon be, known by many with whom she would later work.

After the woman was treated at the hospital, I took her to our home and cared for her for a few days until she felt comfortable going to her own apartment. I was never more grateful for having a Jacuzzi, where she spent hours, as she said, "trying to get clean." The man who kidnapped her was obviously a drug addict, and we never found out if he was actually HIV positive or was just frightening her. Fortunately, she remained negative. She later married her boyfriend, and the last time I saw them, they were very happy and thriving.

One very difficult follow-up I had to do, the day after the kidnapping, was report to an assembly of the Hopkins medical community. That assembly had been called by Mike to allay the fears of those who had heard about the incident. The auditorium was packed with students, residents, faculty, and security officers. Hopkins Hospital is located in a high-risk neighborhood, but there is a usually highly effective security team present. However, the security officers can't possibly be present in every place, so rarely incidents such as what happened to the woman medical student occur. Everyone was relieved and happy to hear that the medical student was doing well.

PROBLEM SOLVING

It was interesting to observe and experience how the faculty, residents, and students approached expressing concerns to me. As a Eucharistic minister, I attended Catholic mass every morning at 7:00 a.m. at Hopkins Hospital. The hospital chapel, where mass was held, was situated across the hall from the cafeteria. When I left mass, frequently there was a faculty member waiting to speak with me. The faculty member would walk with me down the hospital hall and across the street to my office. In that five-minute walk (sometimes prolonged to many more minutes), I would hear some concern I might be able to allay or problem I might solve. The same thing frequently happened, when I made my daily walks through parts of the hospital.

One of the first challenges involved several faculty members, each waiting for me separately, on a few consecutive days. Each one imparted more pertinent information about the same problem. The word went out that I expressed an interest in doing something about the specific problem. The problem involved a high-ranking male faculty member who was harassing women with inappropriate language and touching. Amazingly, all the original complaining faculty were men, because they told me women were afraid to come forward. I told them that it was impossible for me to do anything substantial unless at least one woman came forward with a formal complaint. I knew it could be perceived as a great risk for a woman, and that the woman or women had to trust that I would protect them. I would then force a legitimate investigation with appropriate results.

The faculty member involved in the allegation was a full professor, who brought in a great deal of money to the institution. I had to first convince the male faculty, who brought the complaint to me, that I was serious and concerned by what I heard. They were doubtful that it would be possible to do anything, because of the position and prestige of the offending faculty member. After discussing what I planned to do, they convinced a senior faculty woman, whom I had known for many years, to come forward, together with a junior faculty woman. These women each rendered official an complaint, trusting that I would do something and would not betray their confidence. Sometimes forcing equity requires trust and the power to remedy an inequitable situation.

With Mike's complete cooperation, and after my full investigation, the offending faculty member was "allowed to" resign. Even skeptical faculty members were impressed by the results of that case, which set the stage for a number of other issues to be investigated and resolved. One of those involved a telephone request from a resident who asked if I would meet with him and several others early in the morning. In addition, would I please close my curtains for the meeting? My ground-floor office allowed for anyone coming into or going out of the building to easily observe anyone in my office.

To allay obvious fears, I agreed to close the drapes, and the next morning at 6:00 a.m. I met four young men. I immediately knew what the issue was, and as I served them coffee and muffins I had brought in for the meeting, I said, "I didn't know you guys were bigots." They looked at me somewhat shocked and asked what I meant. I asked them where the lesbian representatives were.

The resident who had called me then laughed and told the others, "See, I told you we could trust her."

The problem for which they sought a solution was how they feared repercussions if they revealed their homosexuality. I promised to make sure that there would be no such treatment and that they were immediately to inform me if that happened. No such reports were made to me, and that year we initiated Gay and Lesbian Day, in which various presentations including research papers about homosexuality and other related topics such as bigotry were presented at the Medical School.

Looking back, that seems so pedestrian, but this was long before gays and lesbians could be so open. Promoting human understanding and equity takes many forms and occurs in many places.

ADVANCING WOMEN FACULTY MEMBERS

In 1989, before I moved to the dean's office, then dean Richard Ross had asked my opinion about a study he had received from the Hopkins University Provost. The Provost requested a response as soon as possible. The report, prepared by members of the School of Public Health, showed that women in the medical school were paid at a much lower rate than men. Dean Ross was concerned that the department chairs might scoff at the findings, especially because the study had been performed outside the School of Medicine. I told him that I thought the methodology in the study was flawed, because allowances had not been made for salary differences in various specialty departments, in faculty rank, and time in rank, but I said the general outcome was very likely accurate.

We then discussed how the flaws in the study might be remedied, and he asked if I would perform the study, so he would know if the finding was indeed true. I agreed to do so providing three conditions were met: (1) He would allow me full access to all faculty salaries, which I would certainly keep in confidence. (2) He would inform all department chairs of the provost's study and that I was conducting another study for him, to verify the accuracy of that study and needed to meet with each of them within the next few weeks. (3) He would provide funds, so all salaries would be equitable, if that was needed. I had no interest in spending a lot of time and effort doing something that had no "curative" outcome.

I considered most such research in the same way I considered ordering diagnostic tests. Therefore, I held to what residents I had taught referred to as "the DeAngelis rule" of ordering diagnostic tests: Ordering a diagnostic test is like picking your nose in public; you must first decide what you will do if you find something.

Dean Ross agreed to all conditions, and I got to work. First I outlined the study I wanted to perform. Next, I met with each department chair, discussed their concerns about the provost's study, and presented my proposed study methodology to gain their confidence and support. I was prepared to make any reasonable changes suggested by the chairs, but nothing significant was suggested; thankfully, they found the new study methodology sound.

I then reviewed all faculty salaries by department (surgeons made more than pediatricians, etc.), rank (professors made more than assistant professors, etc.), time in rank (salaries were raised by some percentage almost every year), and for appropriate additional responsibilities (directing a program, etc.). Most of this information I learned from the department administrators. I considered statements like "she has a husband, who makes a lot of money" to be nonsense at best and offensive at worst, and certainly not appropriate or acceptable.

The final outcome was that women's salaries were indeed found to be inequitable, and that women were not being promoted in the same manner as men. I presented the final study to Dean Ross and then to the Faculty Advisory Committee. Over the next two years, at a cost of almost two million dollars to the fund that Dean Ross had put aside, salaries became equitable.

Because I had also shown that women were not being promoted in an equitable manner (big surprise!), I wanted to get that problem solved after I moved to the dean's office. At that point (1990) I believed it was important for all to understand that the goal was to achieve equity and not equality, in promotions for women faculty. Because until men could bear children (not likely to occur), equality would not be achievable. The Great Comedian obviously has a good reason for only allowing women to bear children. However, we could achieve equity more easily if men would at least share equally in the caring, if not the bearing, of children. That step of fathers sharing the care of children is achievable, and some progress has been made, for example, with couples sharing residencies and men sharing in carpooling.

Because of my personal experiences as a woman trying to succeed in a profession that was very much a man's world where men made the rules, I wanted to do whatever I could to make the rocky road to success much smoother for women. If I couldn't help to shatter the glass ceiling, I at least could help crack it. My goal was to do so without acquiring a bad concussion.

One of the most important initiatives to be accomplished was to provide a program for women faculty, so they could be promoted at the same rate as men. I knew this was essential after performing the study for Dean Ross several years before. I knew that would be a major goal for me when I accepted Mike's offer to join him in the dean's office.

I took a two-week vacation just before I started in the dean's position in July1990, during which Jim and I went on a photo safari in Kenya, Africa. As the time to return from Africa came closer, I began to think about how I might be able to help women faculty achieve promotion fairly. The day before we left to return home, we took a hot-air balloon trip across the Masai Mara National Reserve, a truly awesome experience.

We left the ground just before sunrise and were able to watch the sun rising as we rose in the balloon. The ground below was covered with a mist that slowly lifted above the high grass below. As we watched this magical scene at dawn, I noticed that the female elephants emerged with their young from their various night quarters, traveling through the grass to join together in a herd. I had been fascinated by how the female elephants stayed together during the day. In the evening, they would separate, and each mother-calf pair would head off to its own "home." I had been told that female elephants would respond to a bull's cry for help when he was approached by poachers seeking ivory and would surround the bull to protect him. I guess some things are the same for females in all species.

At any rate, as the elephants converged, a network pattern formed in the wet, high grass, and I was struck with an "aha" moment. Of course, what I needed to do, back at Hopkins, was to form a network of women, pairing senior with junior faculty for mentoring. One problem was that in 1990 there were only sixteen women full professors at Hopkins, and many more junior than senior women faculty. By comparison, there were 186 male professors.

When I returned, I met with all women full professors, and showed them that the number of women professors easily fit on one page. They liked the effect that presentation made, and one woman jokingly asked what we would do when we had too many women professors to fit on one page. I told her we would use a smaller font, until we had a good pipeline of women to be promoted in the system. We decided to first concentrate on the women associate professors and work from there. We also augmented the one-on-one mentoring and group session discussions.

Another initiative was to place at least three women on every important committee, including promotion, important-position selection, and those that involved budgetary issues. The reason for three is that one woman would be considered "token," and with two, they might disagree and cancel out their votes, so I considered three to be the minimal number. I advised each woman on how she could work to convince at least one man, also on the committee, including especially the promotions committees, thereby doubling the number of women's votes. That seemed to work quite well in giving women a real presence in the school.

I also met with the professors' and associate professors' promotion committees and discussed the paucity of women candidates who were considered to be associate and full professors by their promotion committees. In addition, I searched faculty records for women who had been in associate professor positions for what seemed like many more years than expected. I met with them, and their supervisors when necessary, to speed up the promotion process.

As a result of these initiatives and the cooperation of many women and men, by the time I left the dean's office in December 1999, the number of women professors had increased to fifty-eight. Equally important, the number of associate professors in the pipeline to become professors was substantial. I felt confident that there would soon be many more women professors. This initiative continues to this day, and there are now over two hundred women who have been named professors at Johns Hopkins School of Medicine.

A NEW CURRICULUM

Another initiative that needed to be undertaken was an updating of the medical school's curriculum, which had been in place basically unchanged for seventy-five years. I was eager to do this, especially because of a potential grant being offered by the Robert Wood Johnson

Foundation. Because I had a great deal of experience working with that foundation, I knew what a terrific opportunity this could be.

Despite it being unusual for a dean to seek grant funding, I was encouraged by Mike to write the grant proposal. I did, and I used ideas from a number of faculty and students to complete the grant. Much to everyone's delight, in 1992, we were awarded a five-year grant of $2.5 million dollars to change the curriculum.

With the help of this generous grant, we were able to (1) eliminate the emphasis on passive classroom lectures and replace that activity with students reading and learning more, using computers and discussing their findings in small groups with a faculty member; (2) introduce clinical experience from the first week of class by having each student spending a half day a week in a physician's office or clinic; (3) decrease laboratory time, especially in Anatomy; and (4) introduce a four-year course on the role of physicians *in* society but that I named Physician *and* Society, so students would refer to it as the PAS, not the PIS, course. Sometimes anticipating students' probable behavior prevents problems or embarrassments. The PAS course was essential because that was where the emphasis on treating patients and colleagues with equity was to be taught.

Reducing so much time from working on the cadavers in the Anatomy labs was met with great negativity by most of the Anatomy faculty. They balked and behaved badly toward the students, resulting in more than half the class failing the midterm examination. The class members asked to meet with me, because of their concern that they were not learning and the fear that they would fail the course. The faculty had told the students that I was to blame, because it was impossible to teach Anatomy in the time allotted.

I remembered only too well how tedious it had been when I had spent essentially the same amount of time, as a student, dissecting a cadaver in the Anatomy lab. My classmates and I had learned very little of value from that time-consuming exercise. Consequently, I met with the anatomy faculty. I told them that before I had made the time allotment, I had discussed time needed for Anatomy labs with colleagues from London, who had one of the best Anatomy courses in the world. They had assured me that what I allotted for Anatomy labs, in the new curriculum, was sufficient time. Therefore, I told the Hopkins Anatomy faculty if they could not teach Anatomy in the allotted time, I would outsource that responsibility to the London group, at much less expense.

In the meantime, I would judge the success of their teaching by how our students fared on the final exam, and how they succeeded in the Anatomy portion of part one of the National Board Exam. Needless to say, our students did quite well on both exams.

To allay fears of the Anatomy faculty that we might see no need for so many members to teach fewer hours, I told them I would work with them to augment their teaching time. For example, they could teach anatomy to nurses and some advanced undergraduates. This helped the group to understand that I meant no threat to their positions but only wanted a better experience for our students, who were very bright and highly motivated.

We also initiated the four-year Physician and Society course. I knew it was going to be difficult to emphasize the importance of this course to a group of students, who had medical science on their minds and little appreciation for medical equity and the true meaning of the art of medicine. The course involved professionalism and medical ethics; the history of medicine; legal, political, and financial issues; and fine arts, including literature and the theater.

Keeping this course for all four years, allowing a half-day each week, was difficult. This was especially so when the students began their clinical rotations, so we changed the time to a half-day each month for third- and fourth-year students and provided light refreshments for each session. The food, plus that time being the one chance for students to get together with their classmates, provided good incentives for attendance.

Especially in the first three years after initiating the new curriculum, we sought advice from the students who had just completed the courses. It proved to be very wise and effective to have that information.

It made for a much stronger educational experience for all of us and especially for the classes that followed. In the spirit of sharing experiences, I edited a book about this new curriculum entitled *The Hopkins Curriculum for the 21ˢᵗ Century.* The faculty members in charge of the courses and I wrote the various chapters.

This was yet another example of how team effort can result in advancing change, as evidenced by the continuing success of our students.

THE BUSINESS OF MEDICINE CERTIFICATE

Another issue that sorely needed attention was the general paucity of financial and business knowledge of most of the department chairs and division chiefs. At that time, Hopkins University had no school of business but did offer some basic courses in accounting and business management. Based on what I had learned from the economic courses I had audited while working on my MPH at Harvard and the experience I had over the years as a division chief and deputy chair, I outlined a set of four basic courses I thought every medical leader should have. They consisted of Accounting, Finance, Management/Leadership, and Managed Care. I discussed each course with the person I thought best to be responsible for teaching it and then presented the idea to Mike.

I suggested that the Medical School could offer these courses as a certificate program through our Continuing Medical Education (CME) office and charge tuition for each course. A percentage of all Hopkins University faculty salaries were set aside for our education benefit. The salaries were different between the various schools in the university and physicians in the clinical departments had higher salaries than the faculty in other Hopkins departments, such as the basic sciences whose faculty members did research and didn't earn clinical fees. Therefore, physicians contributed more to that financial pool. However, Medical School faculty used the education benefit far less than the nonmedical faculty. Happily, the proposed certificate course would not only increase our faculty's knowledge but would also allow tuition remission, and would be no cost to them. In addition, the dean's office could benefit financially through the Continuing Medical Education office, which would offer the program and collect the tuition. How could Mike not agree to such a deal?

I explained that the "Business of Medicine" certificate program, as we agreed it would be called, could be offered over the course of one year. Classes would be held in the Medical School, in the early evenings, twice a week for twelve weeks each. That would require no extra travel for the faculty, and we could serve light snacks and beverages so they would not be hungry before a delayed dinner at home.

However, much to our surprise, at the next Dean's Advisory Council meeting, one of the department chairs advised that he had a different proposal. He proposed to allow some of our department chairs to have special tutorials with a business expert, at the cost of several thousand dollars each. Obviously, many of us were well aware of the need to upgrade the financial and business knowledge of our leaders.

At Mike's request, I explained to the group what I had proposed to him. The chairman who had discussed the possible tutorial stated that my idea would never work and that one-on-one teaching would be much better. After a discussion with the whole group, Mike decided to try my idea first, because it would cost nothing at the least but might even generate funds for the School of Medicine.

After initiating the program, I took each course the first year and made only minor adjustments. The courses were well received by the first fifteen faculty members who signed up for the certificate program. Much to my dismay, only one department chair opted to take the course. He was one of the very few department chairs who hardly needed it. However, almost every department had a representative leader who did take the course.

Within two years, many of the faculty graduates of the certificate program requested more courses. We eventually developed a master's degree program with the four courses from the certificate program counting toward the master's degree. Over the next years, the certificate and the master's courses became so popular we accepted many physician leaders from within and outside our faculty. The program was also moved to another site in the community.

Oh´yes, the dean's office did make a nice sum from the tuition charges. Some ideas have a number of benefits.

ANOTHER NEW DEAN

In 1997, Mike decided to move on to be the vice chancellor of Health Affairs at Emory University. He had had many successes in an environment fraught with the politics of academic medical centers. He had been a very strong Medical School dean, who had to deal with an equally strong hospital president, and there was no overseeing vice chancellor to solve difference in an equitable way. Mike and I remain good friends and close colleagues to this day, and I'll write more about that later.

The next dean was Dr. Ed Miller, who had been the chair of Anesthesia, and whose personality and leadership style were quite different from Mike's. His new title was chief executive officer of Johns Hopkins Medicine *as well as* dean of the School of Medicine. Apparently the board of trustees had learned much about the need for one person to oversee both the School of Medicine and the hospital. In addition, a wonderful new president of the hospital, Ron Peterson, was named to report to Ed (as he asked me to call him). I had known Ron since I had come to Hopkins on the faculty. At that time, he was the administrator of the Pediatrics Department. In fact, we had coauthored a paper, published in 1986.

At last there was to be one person with the ultimate responsibility of the medical school and the hospital or, more accurately, all educational, research, and clinical services. More importantly, the two main characters were very fine gentlemen whose singular goal was to make Johns Hopkins Medicine and the School of Medicine as great as possible.

It took a while for Ed and me to work smoothly together, because he seemed to be interested primarily in the CEO part of his title. I thought he didn't really appreciate the importance of the dean part, and my role was clearly centered on that aspect. In fact, he once told me that he really appreciated that I kept all the messy stuff (that's not a quote of the actual word he used) out of his office. Also, early on, I had almost resigned my dean's position because of an equity issue. Ed hired someone with generally unproven credentials as vice dean of research, at a higher salary than mine. After all the effort to get women's salaries equitable with those of men, I was not about to allow this to happen with me. It took the intervention of the provost to settle the situation amicably.

I truly believe Ed didn't realize what a bad decision he might have made regarding my salary and that of the incoming man vice dean, and once he understood, he became a true advocate for women. Our relationship from then on was smooth and successful, as I observed and greatly appreciated his leadership skills in building and renovating the physical infrastructure of Johns Hopkins Medicine by raising the money to build several new buildings. No one could have succeeded more in adding needed buildings. He changed the entire structural face of Hopkins Medicine and was a respected and well-liked administrator.

Time to Move On Yet Again

Throughout my time at Hopkins, I had always decided that my position there was best for me. I didn't much care about titles; I'd never been a department chair or a dean prior, although I'd been offered several such positions. What mattered most to me was what I might be able to accomplish in a position. Over the years, and especially the last few years in the dean's office, I had been offered several deanships, a vice chancellorship, and a presidency of a medical university but turned them all down. However, by 1999, I felt it was time to move on, and it would be only a matter of to which position and at what institution. I had pretty much settled on a deanship at an institution where a former Hopkins colleague was the vice chancellor. However, the Great Comedian had other plans.

When I finally made a decision to leave Hopkins, there was a special dinner, sponsored by Ed and attended by a number of my special friends, mostly from the dean's office. In addition, there was a general reception sponsored by the dean's office, to which many of the faculty and friends were invited. I was shocked when several hundred people showed up to say good-bye and good luck. At one point in the evening, one of the kitchen staff members asked if I might come into the kitchen. I immediately went with her and was greeted by dozens of the kitchen and maintenance staff members who also wanted to say good-bye. A number of them had worked the day shift and had waited several hours so they could be there.

These individuals represent the backbone of any institution, and I was so moved I could barely speak. I hugged each of them and told them how very much I appreciated their friendship and support over the years. That tearful good-bye remains in my memory as one of the most wonderful days I spent at Hopkins.

My Hopkins Portrait

During my years at Hopkins and *JAMA*, and much to my surprise each time, I received a number of national awards. Like so many women, I suffered the same feelings of not being worthy of those awards, or not really belonging with the other awardees. Especially early in my professional career, I felt like an intruder, even though I had dreamed of being a doctor from early childhood. I knew I wasn't the smartest or most creative among my peers. Therefore, each time I was told that I had received a coveted award, I was taken by surprise and had a hard time understanding what I had done to be so acknowledged. I learned a great deal about how men took such accolades for granted, and I spent much time trying to teach women to accept deserved awards and salaries. Along the way, I was teaching myself to do the same. However, that lesson did not come easily.

The award that, in many ways, meant the most to me, came from my colleagues and friends at Hopkins. Soon after I left Hopkins, Dr. John Niparko stimulated a fund to have my portrait painted. Amazingly, he is not a pediatrician, but an otolaryngologist–head-and-neck surgeon. The fund was supported by the dean's office and many of my friends. I was amazed that hundreds of individuals contributed to that fund, and I was asked to choose an artist, which I did based on how that artist painted women.

I couldn't imagine sitting still for the time I imagined would be necessary for a portrait. I anticipated that this was to be even more difficult because I was no longer living in Baltimore and spent only some weekends there. However, when I met the artist and his wife, who is also an artist, my anxiety was allayed. She took many candid pictures of me while he discussed a number of things with me regarding what I wanted to wear and where I wanted to be painted.

He asked if I wanted to dress in full academic regalia and I laughed, stating, "Do I look like a formal regalia person to you?" He and his wife laughed and admitted I probably should wear something else. Now the problem would be having my sisters choose something fitting, because I did not have the time or interest for choosing such clothes. In the end, I wore a business pants suit with a silk green blouse, much as I did for all academic presentations. By that point in my life, I only wore dresses and gowns to formal affairs.

Next was my desire to be painted outside, possibly in our garden. It is much more difficult to paint a portrait outside than in a studio, but the artist agreed to paint in our garden. I was greatly relieved when he told me that I would only have to sit three or four times, because he could do the rest from the pictures his wife had taken.

The final resulting portrait was officially dedicated in 2009 at an annual alumni meeting at Hopkins, much to my delight and that of Jim and my family, colleagues, and friends. That dedication was followed by a dinner for my family and all donors, at my then-favorite Baltimore restaurant.

That night I thought of the first visit Poppie and Nannie had made to Hopkins, just before I started my residency there in 1970. After I gave them a tour of the institution, Poppie (obviously impressed with the portraits on the various walls of Hopkins buildings) asked me when my picture would be "up there with the big shots." I told him that would never happen, because all those men (all of the portraits were of men) were giants, and I was only five feet four inches tall. He shook his head and winked at me with that knowing smile he reserved for special occasions. I only wish he and Nannie had been alive to celebrate with us and to see my portrait hanging in the hallowed halls of Hopkins.

In any case, it was now time for me to transition to the next phase of my academic life, which proved to be something I'd never dreamed of doing. Chicago, here I come.

CHAPTER 13

JAMA Mama: A Reluctant Editor

How I became the editor in chief of *JAMA*, the *Journal of the American Medical Association* is a very complicated story. The groundwork for this new role began in 1994, when I became the editor of *Archives of Pediatrics and Adolescent Medicine* (née *American Journal of Diseases of Children*, a name that was to be changed with the new editor, namely me). I had worked in that editorship, with Modena and Alain serving as the deputy editors, while all of us continued our full-time positions as Hopkins pediatric faculty members.

That was possible because *Archives* was a monthly journal owned by the American Medical Association (AMA), and we could pretty much work on it during evenings and weekend hours. We met only once a week in person, to discuss journal-related issues. We had a very efficient and effective journal administrator (actually two, because the first returned to her former job and was replaced by another "whiz kid"), and that made the work so much easier.

All editors of the several Archives specialty journals served on the editorial board of *JAMA*. In March of 1999, the AMA, owners of *JAMA* and the Archives journals, publically fired the editor of *JAMA*. The editor had published a survey of college students, investigating whether they considered oral sex to be sexual intercourse. Ordinarily, the AMA would have ignored the publication of this survey. However, some members of the AMA senior staff and the board members believed it could be interpreted as reflecting on the impending impeachment of President Bill Clinton.

By what many believed was probably the editor's design, the article appeared in press the week of the impeachment. Whatever the motive, the article had been peer reviewed, and the firing of the editor was a clear interference by the AMA on editorial freedom. An essential prerequisite for any editor publishing refereed articles is to be unhindered by political or other interests of the journal's owners or anyone else. That kind of policy information is supposed to be published in the organization's bylaws or another house organ, such as a newsletter.

A search committee was chosen to name the new *JAMA* editor, and the clear requisite of the AMA, cited by the search committee and editorial board members, was that the new editor was to have complete editorial freedom assured. We all believed that, otherwise, no one with sound credentials would even consider the position.

Actually, considering the record of the AMA's historical treatment of the *JAMA* editors to that point, the preference of the search committee members was to make *JAMA* a limited liability corporation (LLC), or similar independent entity. But that would have taken at least two years to enact, because it would have required changing the AMA bylaws. As a result, that idea was abandoned. Instead, the search committee chose to strongly advise the AMA board of trustees (BOT) to sanction a journal oversight committee (JOC) to be composed of academic peers of the editor, to whom the editor would report for all editorial issues. This JOC would then interact with the BOT of the AMA.

At the May 1999 annual *JAMA* editorial meeting, a closed session was held for all Archives editors and the *JAMA* interim editors and deputy editor. At that meeting, the chair of the search committee announced that the AMA BOT had refused to agree to the JOC proposal. We all were appalled. I then moved that if the BOT refused to sign on to the proposal for a JOC, all eleven specialty (Archives) journal editors would resign. This would force the BOT to find twelve editors, instead of only one. This would be a great embarrassment and financial setback, because the journals were an important source of income for the AMA. All Archives editors enthusiastically voted yes, and we all walked out of the meeting.

Paul Blackney, the recently appointed AMA senior vice president (SVP) for business, who had just retired from a very prestigious position with a big company, followed me out of the room. He was shocked at what had just happened and asked me why the editors had made such a decision.

I explained that we worked as editors because we believed in the worthiness of publishing good medical science and other health-related manuscripts, unencumbered by the policies of the AMA. We certainly did not receive much financial reimbursement for our work, and we were editors because of our desire to contribute to making patient care better. We could hardly do that if encumbered by the policies of the AMA.

I am not sure what transpired within the AMA, but the next day all attendees at the meeting received an e-mail message from the search committee chair. The message stated that the AMA BOT had agreed to having a JOC. I was delighted, as I was sure were the other editors. The new administrative flowchart, with all changes, was to be published in the first available issue of *JAMA* a few weeks later.

The day (a Friday) after the e-mail message was sent, I received a phone call from the search committee chair. He told me that the committee wanted me to be the next *JAMA* editor, whose responsibilities also included all of the Archives specialty journals. I almost fell off my chair and laughed at the suggestion, asking why they wanted me. He responded that it was for many reasons, including they knew of no one who would better "take on the AMA and make the JOC work."

I told him that I was honored by their confidence, but that I was about to accept a position as a dean. I had no desire to be the full-time editor of *JAMA* or any other medical journal. He asked me to please consider the position over the weekend and to call him on Monday. Out of respect for him and the other members of the search committee,

I agreed to do so, but at that point I had no intention of accepting the position.

THE WALK

The next day, Jim and I went for a walk around a reservoir just north of Baltimore. About halfway around, Jim asked, "How many medical school deans are there in the United States?" to which I responded, "One hundred twenty-six."

Jim then asked, "And how many editors of *JAMA* are there?" to which I laughed and said, "One."

He then said, "And where do you think you could have the greatest chance of making a real contribution to medicine?" I stopped walking, thought for a while, and then called him a bad name. He looked at me with that innocent look of his and claimed that he was only trying to get me to think carefully about how I wanted to spend the next fruitful years of my professional life.

Jim's question did stimulate my thoughts. On the one hand, I had spent all my professional life as an academic physician and loved it. Whereas I found caring for one patient at a time enjoyable and rewarding, I really loved teaching, research, and being able to lead teams in projects that provided good care for many.

What would it mean if I could successfully lead a team using clinical knowledge, teaching, and research as the basis for editing a journal that published sound information? If a multitude of physicians and other clinicians would read articles that helped them to provide good care for patients, wouldn't that also be something I could accomplish and love? Also, it would definitely provide a wider platform in which I could champion for equity and for the health of women and children.

However, another consideration was that I had no experience as a full-time editor. My experience as editor of *Archives of Pediatrics and Adolescent Medicine* was part-time, for a monthly journal. It did not have anywhere near the range of responsibilities that editing the weekly

JAMA and overseeing all of the Archives specialty journals would involve.

Also, my background in proper use of words and grammar was primarily based on what I had learned from Mrs. Wozniak, my high-school English teacher. She was a terrific educator, who knew how to use the teachable moment to accomplish a great deal. For example, every week she would write a famous saying on the blackboard (it was 1954, after all) that made two points. One example I'll never forget was, "Don't waste time; that's the stuff of which life is made." The grammatical lesson was not to end a sentence with a preposition, but the philosophical point, made by the sentence, is a very good way to think about time. The more I thought about Mrs. Wozniak's teachings, the more confident I felt about being a full-time editor. I will be forever grateful to that beautiful woman.

My Response to the Search Committee

On Monday morning I called the search committee chair and told him I would consider the position. However, I would first meet with the then executive vice president and chief executive officer (EVP/CEO) of the AMA to discuss terms of agreement. He told me he was thrilled and immediately arranged for my visit with the EVP/CEO, Dr. E Radcliff Anderson Jr., at AMA headquarters. (I apologize to the reader for all the alphabet soup, but that's the shortest way to get the meanings across, and it saves a lot of space and trees.)

I was reluctant to give up an academic position to work for the AMA, an organization I had never joined, much like the majority of American physicians, and especially academicians. Like many of my colleagues, I was not in agreement with various AMA (national, state, and county) stances on social medicine, especially in the 1950s.

In fairness, historically the AMA had played a very substantial role in establishing professional and educational standards for American medicine. However, the AMA's leadership had promulgated almost all these standards during the first half of the twentieth century. That leadership served on a part-time basis and had been composed of primarily academicians, unpaid by the AMA.

Those academic leaders had left their leadership roles in academia, and the AMA, to serve in the military during World War II. Thereafter, the academicians lost their leadership roles in the AMA, having been replaced by a group of physicians who had been in private practice and also had not been eligible for the draft. These new AMA leaders allegedly alienated the academicians by making it very difficult for them to assume any leadership roles upon their return from military service.

Because academicians educated and trained future physicians, these academicians and certain decisions subsequently made by the AMA leadership, influenced many young physicians not to join the AMA. I also was not happy with many of the AMA decisions, such as voicing disapproval of free school lunches in the 1920s. This resulted in pediatricians forming their own specialty organization, the American Academy of Pediatrics. I wondered if I could work within the AMA to make the changes in *JAMA* and the Archives journals I felt were necessary.

Soon after I agreed to consider the editorship, I was visited at Hopkins by Paul Blackney, the AMA's SVP for business, whom I mentioned earlier. I was very impressed that he visited me and had not waited for my visit to the AMA headquarters in Chicago. In addition, I liked him very much, even from our first meeting in May. We spent almost four hours in my office, discussing many issues. Most were related to my ideas to take *JAMA* from a good journal to an even higher-impact, international journal.

I was also impressed by Paul's (as he asked me to call him) concerns for the journals and the AMA. He wanted to use his corporate expertise and experience to help make the journals successful and the AMA a great association for all physicians. I felt he would be a wonderful partner, because we shared so many goals. Unfortunately, he retired from the AMA about six months after my arrival there. I can only imagine what we might have accomplished had we worked together longer.

I felt more confident about my upcoming meeting with the EVP/ CEO, because of my positive interactions with and feelings for Paul. My original caution was based on what I had read about the illustrious academic and military careers of the EVP/CEO. I had been expecting a difficult meeting with a man I assumed would be accustomed to working with men and having no great respect for women's leadership abilities in a working environment. However, my meeting with this true gentleman was a revelation to me, because it began with his asking me to call him Andy. That meeting proved to me, once again, how wrong it is to prejudge someone.

MEETING THE EVP/CEO

Before this meeting, I had discussed my potential AMA contract with my completely unselfish and close friend, attorney Estelle Fishbein, who was then the vice president of Legal Affairs at Johns Hopkins University. She had taught me a great deal about law and how to handle difficult people and difficult situations. Her advice about my potential contract was, as usual, perfect.

It took Andy and me only an hour or so to agree (1) on a salary (that I determined must be 10 percent higher than my current income); (2) that, as a SVP, I would report directly to him (or specifically to the AMA EVP/CEO in case he should leave before me), for all administrative issues (the previous editors had reported to the publisher, who was a vice president, who reported to the SVP for business, who reported to the EVP/CEO—way too many bureaucratic levels for my taste); (3) that I would report to the JOC for all editorial issues; (4) that I could spend a day a month back at Hopkins, where I would retain my faculty position; and (5) that I would have a five-year contract stating that if I were to be fired for any reason other than legal cause (that is I would commit a crime or injure another person...both hardly likely), I would be paid the entire remaining salary and benefits of my five-year contract.

The last item was very important, considering that I had been warned to be careful because of the alleged track record of the AMA with previous *JAMA* editors. I had been told that every previous editor of *JAMA* essentially had been fired or forced out. While I was not sure this was true, I wasn't taking any chances.

It was not easy for Andy to arrange the salary, which would have been the highest in the AMA. As the SVP for Human Resources told me, there was a rule that the EVP/CEO had to be the highest-paid employee. It was also difficult for Andy to arrange for me to have a contract, because no one employed by the AMA at that time had a contract, much less a five-year contract, with the specifications I required. However, with the assistance of the then SVP for Human Resources, who unfortunately also left a few years after I arrived, Andy made it happen.

My salary was to be a base at an acceptable level for the AMA, plus an annual bonus for the rest, which would be paid annually, if I was successful in my role with *JAMA*. How that was to be judged was left open, but I felt that if I was not successful, or if there was a backtracking on our understanding, I wouldn't want to stay anyway.

The bonus would not include benefits (thus saving the AMA some money), but I didn't care about that. My main point with the salary was that I would not move without a 10 percent raise. That was still lower than what I would have received as a dean, but I had never made decisions based on principal (money, per se) but always on principle (fundamental belief). The actual salary was important to me as a woman, because I had learned that salary was one determination of how important a position, or person, was considered to be by the employing institution. Salary is one area where equality in funds is part of equity (fairness).

The issues of my SVP title and reporting directly to the EVP/CEO were questioned by several of my AMA (but not *JAMA*) colleagues. They saw no reason for change in titles, because there had been no big problems with the situation as it had been. They would soon learn how vital that arrangement would be for the success of *JAMA* and the Archives. A leader must always look to the future, hoping for the best but planning for the worst.

Another important person with whom I met before starting at *JAMA* was the chairman of the AMA Board of Trustees. He and I had a very cordial and friendly meeting, and it was clear to me that he wanted to have a highly regarded journal that helped physicians take good care of patients. One of the things he asked was my opinion on the potential members the BOT had chosen for the JOC. I told him I thought they were all excellent, but I wondered why there was no woman on the committee list. He smiled and said, "Good point. Who would you suggest?" I gave him the name of a highly qualified woman, who was immediately invited to the committee, and much to my delight, accepted the offer. Perhaps my worries about working with the AMA group were unfounded?

My written contract was deemed acceptable by my friend, Attorney Fishbein, so I agreed to start my editorship on January 1, 2000. The new millennium was to have great meaning for me. In December of 1999, I was invited to attend the annual interim meeting of the AMA House of Delegates, where Andy wanted to introduce me as the new *JAMA* editor.

When I arrived at the meeting, he asked me for my e-mail address, and I jokingly responded, "*jama*mama@ama-assn.org." He thought that was hilarious and announced to the delegates that that was to be my e-mail name, much to their delight. It was nice to know the House of Delegates members had a sense of humor, because I often like to joke to make a point. At the time I had no special point with that moniker, but it stuck. Be careful what you say in jest.

POPPIE'S AND UNCLE FRANK'S REACTION
The announcement of my becoming the new editor in chief of *JAMA* was made at a press conference. Amazingly, it was reported in the

October 9, 1999, issue of the *New York Times*, along with my picture on page two. When Poppie saw it, he said, "That's not bad for a little shitpot from Old Forge." He was a man of few but colorful words.

On the other hand, his brother Frank, who had driven me to Wilkes College so I could work in the laboratory in the summers, heard the news on the Paul Harvey radio show. He called and told everyone he could think of about the great news. Great joy prevailed in my extended family, all of whom took pride in my accomplishment. One public journalist was not so pleased, for reasons beyond me, and wrote a mean-spirited article about my working for the AMA. That article only added to my will to succeed in improving a great academic journal, which would help physicians provide good care to patients.

A Happy Editor

When Jim left me at the airport on January 3, 2000, the day after my sixtieth birthday, I felt trepidation similar to what I had felt as an incoming medical student many years before. I really had no idea what to expect or even if my ideas for *JAMA* were possible or would prove to be successful.

As the plane flew over the Chicago skyscrapers in preparation for landing, I felt a great loneliness for Jim and for my colleagues at Hopkins. Jim and I had decided that one of us would visit the other at least every other weekend. I hoped that would be enough time together, but as we learned it wouldn't be. After six months, Jim took a leave of absence and came to live with me in Chicago returning to Baltimore once a month to attend in his clinic.

One of my fears was that I had just spent more than thirty years working with some of the world's brightest and most accomplished physicians and staff, and I had no idea about the abilities of the awaiting editors and staff. Of course they also had no idea about me and what I might change. There was also the issue of my being the first woman *JAMA* editor; what might it be like for them to work with a woman?

One thing that had provided me with some comfort was that Phil Fontanarosa, one of the former interim editors and now one of the deputy editors, had invited me to his home on one of my negotiating visits. He hosted a reception at which I met the other editors and staff. He and they all seemed to be a cohesive and accomplished group, but I knew I'd only really find out when we worked together. Little did I know just how terrific this group was and how well we would work as a team.

As I walked onto the tenth floor of what was then known as the AMA building (although the AMA no longer owned it, but leased about a third of the floors in the building), I was greeted with nervous smiles from most of the staff. Phil and Annette Flanagin, the managing editor, led me to my cozy corner office, which had a great view of Chicago.

Annette stayed with me while Phil continued back to work. After all, *JAMA* was a weekly journal, and the fast-paced schedule had to be maintained. I later found out that Phil had been offered the full interim editorship. Phil requested that the editorship be shared with another senior deputy editor, Richard Glass, who had been at *JAMA* longer than Phil. The worthiness of such unselfishness was not lost on me, especially because it has continued throughout all my interactions with Phil.

Annette, who also proved to be a tireless, unselfish individual, proceeded to orient me in a way that immediately allowed me to relax. I knew that I was in for a great experience in which I could lead *JAMA* and the Archives journals to greater heights. Who better to have as the managing editor than a nurse? Like so many nurses, Annette was incredibly well organized and kept the wheels turning while developing new ways to make things better and more efficient. In addition, she appreciated my weird sense of humor, and we soon were laughing at a number of things that might otherwise have been problems.

Rounding out the senior team was Richard Glass, another deputy editor, who I believe used his skills as a psychiatrist to help us through some difficulties. It also probably helped him to understand my sometimes what-might-be-considered bizarre behavior. Maggie Winker, also a deputy editor was our computer guru and geriatrician in residence.

Drummond Rennie, the fourth deputy editor, was the sage not in residence (he lived on the West Coast). Roxanne Young, an associate editor, was the overseer of the art (as opposed to the science) aspects of medicine. Teresa Southgate, another associate editor, was the "mother" of the *JAMA* art covers. Rona Henry Siegel, also an associate editor, was the expert on tables and figures.

Stacey Christianson was the director of the *JAMA* manuscript editors, and Cheryl Iverson, the director of the Archives manuscript editors. Marsha Goldsmith was the director of the news section. I also needed a knowledgeable, trustworthy, and efficient administrative assistant to deal with the daily functions of my office. I found her in Helga Fritz, who proved to be a gem. My gal Friday editorial assistant was MaryAnn Lilly, a quiet antidote to my noisiness. There were more than seventy others to complete the team, the vast majority of whom were well suited to their jobs.

My next decision was to select a *JAMA* leadership team of editors and staff to assure the highest performance possible. I wanted to assign individuals with the best credentials and track records to serve in the positions most appropriate for their skills. I knew that unless it was absolutely necessary, it was not wise to make any major changes in the first six months of a leadership position, so I used that time to watch and consider how the team members functioned in their current roles. It didn't take me more than a few weeks to know that Phil was going to be my executive deputy editor. I had made this decision even though Richard and Maggie had seniority, and Richard had also been the interim coeditor with Phil.

How would I make an equitable decision? Richard was quiet and steady, very much like the body's spine, without which the body (*JAMA*) could not function. Maggie was tireless and quickly mastered new challenges. However, I needed someone who essentially agreed with my objectives but would provide a counterargument if he or she disagreed with me. In addition, I needed someone who understood my mode of operation and would buffer it when necessary. When Phil told me he was vanilla, I responded, "That's great, because I am tutti-frutti." That pretty much summed it up.

After six months, I announced that Phil was to be the executive deputy editor. Fortunately, I had anticipated that Richard and Maggie would be upset. I met with each of them before the announcement to explain my position congenially, but firmly. Those are the moments that make leadership so difficult, but they are to be expected. I was able to allay their concerns by explaining my decision. I also assured Richard that he could keep his corner office with windows, which seemed to be very important to him. Maggie also had a very nice office with windows. I tried very hard thereafter to make sure they both knew how much I valued their work and friendship.

EARLY-DAYS PLANNING

Having control of my budget was essential and one of the major reasons I had insisted that, unlike the former editors of *JAMA*, I would report directly to the EVP/CEO for administrative and business affairs. I would not report to the publisher, who reported to the SVP for business, who reported to the EVP/CEO. I didn't want to be twice removed from the person who was ultimately responsible for financial and administrative matters. I am a firm believer in the golden rule: he or she who controls the gold...rules.

Another reason for my negotiated administrative arrangement of direct reporting to the EVP/CEO was that I needed control of other administrative tasks. For example, when I ordered new stationery with appropriate changes, the administrative assistant to the publisher approached me and informed me that I could not do that without the approval of the publisher. I politely told her that I did not need permission for anything from anyone, except the EVP/CEO, and he certainly was not concerned about such small items as stationery for his SVPs. She looked shocked; obviously no one had bothered to tell her about the new administrative arrangement. I should have realized that the new reporting arrangement would have to be published in *JAMA* soon, but that was not to come until later.

I also made a few other changes with the staff, switching jobs within *JAMA* for a few who were not performing as I required. The majority did much better after changing positions in *JAMA*, but I encouraged the two persons who still were not working out to look for other employment. I assured them that I would help them find new jobs for which they were better suited. In the end, all of the staff had jobs at the AMA and apparently were doing well.

I was delighted that the few who moved to other departments of the AMA were not angry. Perhaps it was because I had helped them obtain their new jobs by accentuating their strong points to potential future supervisors. To be equitable (fair), I had also disclosed their weak points—the ones that made it difficult for the individuals to succeed in their *JAMA* positions—but I knew these points would not be a problem in the new positions. Not to have disclosed the weaker points would have been dishonest and unkind to the other supervisors and to the two individuals. It also would have led to others mistrusting my word, which I never wanted to happen. Equity does not include dishonesty.

Working with the now fully assembled team was a joy. We all worked hard but had fun and reveled in the ensuing success of *JAMA* and the Archives journals. I considered us to be a family, with all the characteristics of most families: good people who cared for one another, settling disagreements fairly easily and working together to solve problems. There was also the issue of how careful I had to be not to show favoritism, especially among the editors, while assuring I had the best person doing the job for which he or she was best suited.

It was necessary to have editors with expertise to handle the major medical specialties that were the topics in the submitted manuscripts. It was impossible to have that many full-time editors, so we employed a group of contributing editors who worked part-time for *JAMA*. This allowed for the coverage of all the major specialties. Each of these editors had full-time academic positions in various medical schools, almost all of which were in the United States, but a few were in Canada.

None of these terrific editors were paid their worth, but they obviously enjoyed the positions they held. I tried to make sure they had fun and learned from the interactions with the other editors, reviewers, and authors. I certainly learned a great deal from them and from the reviewers and authors with whom I interacted.

ORGANIZING THE WORKING SPACE

The *JAMA* and Archives staff offices were located on most of the tenth floor of the AMA building, sharing the floor space with Human Resources. We also occupied a relatively small but important part of the eleventh floor of the building. This was adequate space for our needs, but it was very important to organize the space well to ensure good working relationships and productivity. Therefore, at one point I moved the group responsible for the art, tables, and figures to the eleventh floor. While geographically removed from the main *JAMA* space, the quietness allowed that group to function well. One thing I know is that people work better in space and facilities conducive to their responsibilities.

There are always restraints of resources, one of which is the square footage of allotted space. At the AMA, having a real office, especially one with a window, was considered to be an indication of so-called "higher rank." This is probably true everywhere; the only time I had an office with a window at Johns Hopkins as vice dean. All deputy editors and most senior editors had such offices, but most of the staff had cubicle offices.

A week or so after I had arrived at *JAMA*, several of the editorial assistants who worked in cubicles near my office, asked if they might have a high outer wall to their offices, instead of the lower outer walls they currently had. The traffic flow to my office was substantial, and it was difficult for them to concentrate.

I thought it would be simple to meet this request until I discussed it with Phil and Annette. They said they had been trying to arrange for these high walls for some time, without success. I called the person in charge of such infrastructure and was told that there were no high outer walls in stock and that he did not know when they might be available. I explained that it was essential for some editorial assistants to have these walls, for work efficiency. He told me he would let me know when the high walls were received and that I could then have the three I had requested. My staff told me not to hold my breath.

I knew that the husband of one of the editorial assistants (not one in need of a high wall) worked in the shipping-and-receiving department. I asked if she would alert her husband of our need, and she happily agreed to let me know when such a shipment arrived. I asked why she was smiling at my request, and she replied that I would find out. I thought that was a peculiar answer but shrugged it off, guessing it was something I would learn, as I soon did.

A few weeks later I was told by the editorial assistant that a shipment of walls had arrived the day before, but to please not let anyone know how I'd found out about it. Again I was perplexed but assumed it was a political thing involving hierarchy. I knew only too well about hierarchy issues from my experiences as a woman in a field that had been very much considered belonging to men.

I thought the director of the shipping department would soon contact me, as he told me he would, but I had a plan B in case that didn't happen. So two days later, when I still hadn't heard from him, I went to his office. I knew it would be much more difficult for him to play games with me in a face-to-face interaction.

When I arrived at his office, I saw that he was down the hall, speaking with two men. I went up to him, apologizing for interrupting, and asked when I could expect the high walls he'd promised. The director smiled and reminded me that he would send them as soon as he received some. I told him that I knew he was a very busy man and probably didn't know that a shipment of high walls had been delivered three days ago.

I noted that his secretary and the two men looked down and were smiling, whereas the director looked as if he was about to have seizure.

He stammered that he was unaware of the shipment but would certainly check on it. The next morning, the high walls were delivered to our area and put up. I had a very happy staff, and I overheard one of them telling another that she thought things were going to be interesting with the new editor in chief. If she only knew!

The Ladies' Room

One thing that really surprised me was the reaction of the female staff regarding using the ladies' room. I noticed that when I entered the room, anyone, except deputy and senior editors, who was not in a stall would immediately leave. This was perplexing to me, and at first I thought it might have been the result of the staff not wanting me to think they were slacking off.

After about a week of this, I stopped two staff members who were about to exit the room right after I had entered even though they had entered the room just before me. I asked them why they were leaving. They both turned red and told me they had never been in a bathroom with the chief editor and were embarrassed to stay there while I was in the room. I thought that was one of the funniest things I had ever heard and told them so. I also asked them to please pass that word along to others, so I wouldn't feel lonely in the ladies' room. We all had a good laugh, and that crazy behavior stopped immediately. Life is sure full of interesting incidents. I wonder if men feel that way with male leaders; after all, there is much greater exposure in that situation. Oh well.

Manuscripts

Manuscripts selected for publication are the very foundation of a journal. So it is essential to attract the best and select from that pool. It was also essential that we treat all submitted manuscripts equitably—for example, allowing extra consideration to a young author.

ATTRACTING THE BEST STUDIES

In order to make *JAMA* a better journal, one thing we had to do was attract the best possible research studies. That would require knowing where very good studies were being conducted. After we found out where key studies were being conducted, it was important to personally contact the principal investigators. The goal of those contacts was to entice them to submit the studies to *JAMA*.

That was not an easy task, because at that time, most academicians and others—including myself—considered the *New England Journal of Medicine* to be the top general medical journal. That journal clearly had the highest impact factor. That notwithstanding, I knew that if we worked hard, we would be another leading high-impact general medical journal, where many academicians would be proud to have their best work published. *JAMA* was a very good medical journal, but we wanted to make it better and more competitive.

We planned for the full-time editors and the contributing editors to alert me about impending important studies of which they were aware. They then would contact the principal investigators directly, especially if they knew them. In addition, I would contact the investigators, many of whom I knew from attending various national and international meetings and serving with many of them on national and international panels. These interactions evolved as *JAMA*'s impact factor increased, and the authors required much less convincing to submit to *JAMA*.

For many reasons, I hate the journal impact factor and will address that issue later. The problem is that every editor strives to have the highest possible impact factor for his or her journal, because many professionals judge the relative importance of journals by that factor, even though it is only one of many indicators of quality.

SATISFYING THE AMA-MEMBER READERS

One problem I had to anticipate, which would occur as a result of increasing the number of research studies published, was that *JAMA*'s print circulation included all members of the AMA. The vast majority of those members were private practitioners, who were very good clinicians but who had limited backgrounds—and interest—in evaluating research. I joked that some of them could barely differentiate a P wave from a p value. (A P-wave is part of an electrocardiogram [EKG or ECG], and a p value is the term used in statistics for a determination that helps to show the significance of a study's result.) Of course, I was only kidding about the knowledge of some members.

So in order to make sure that the AMA members not skilled in research methodology would enjoy reading *JAMA*, we initiated the "Clinicians' Corner." That new section consisted of at least one article in each issue that was clinically relevant to most practicing physicians. In addition, that article was almost always the topic chosen for the "Patients' Page," which was published on the last page of *JAMA*.

The "Patients' Page" contained information about a specific illness or medical problem. Physicians and other readers were encouraged to copy it and make the "Patient's Page" available to patients. I assumed that the practicing physicians would read the clinically relevant study featured on the "Patients' Page" and be able to answer questions on the topic more easily. I hoped this was true, especially for those questions raised by the patients to whom the physicians had given the "Patients Page." I hoped that physicians would appreciate the opportunity to educate their patients and themselves with a single read.

Another change to *JAMA* was the expansion of Commentaries, which are short opinion pieces about important current medical issues and other interesting topics. We employed a number of well-known physicians and other health-care experts to write several of these pieces annually. These solicited Commentaries were published in addition to those submitted spontaneously to *JAMA*. In that way we published at least two or three Commentaries in each issue. I thought these Commentaries would also be of interest to the practicing physicians.

A few other high-impact journals also published such commentaries or perspectives, written by authors who were paid. However, the editors of those journals did not disclose such payments, because they decided the amounts (usually $500 to $1,000 for each manuscript) were minimum amounts not worthy of disclosure. I decided that any amount of payment should be disclosed. So we published an editorial in which we revealed that we were going to employ contributing writers, whose names were to be listed in our masthead. However, we did not pay the authors of spontaneously submitted and published "Commentaries."

Selecting Articles for Publication

One of the most enjoyable aspects of the *JAMA* editorship was having the privilege of choosing which studies and articles would be published in our journal. Of course this was a double-edged sword, because it was also necessary to decide against publishing many very good articles that simply were not at the level that *JAMA* required. We just did not have the room to publish more articles. We had to make choices based on current interests, avoiding articles similar to those already published or those accepted to be published in upcoming issues.

One advantage we had over other high-impact journals was that we were a family of journals. We could offer the author of a very good article the opportunity immediately to relay his or her manuscript directly to one of the Archives specialty journals, including any external reviews available. That would save the author a great deal of time and effort, and the article already would have been "triaged" by one of the *JAMA* editors. There was no guarantee the article would be published by the Archives journal, but we knew the chances were quite good, especially for those articles that had received favorable external reviews. A substantial number of authors accepted our offers, so this was also beneficial for the Archives journals.

When I arrived at *JAMA*, about 3,500 manuscripts were submitted annually, and about 350 were published. Of those published, about 280 were research studies counted by Thompson ISI (now Thompson Reuters

ISI) to calculate our impact factor. After a few years, we were receiving approximately 6,000 manuscripts and publishing about 400, of which Thompson counted about 240 studies in the denominator for calculating our impact factor. The reason for the decrease in articles counted by Thompson, despite an increase in the number of articles published, will be discussed under the heading "Impact Factor" in chapter 14.

The reasons for the increased number of submissions were at least twofold. First, the number of submissions increased immediately after we set up an online submissions site, which made the process much easier. Of course the number submitted leveled off rapidly when it became obvious that the percent of published articles did not increase accordingly. That is, we did not publish more articles. Second, and more important, *JAMA* became a very high-impact journal, with very good readership, and this encouraged more authors to submit their best work to us.

The Process of Selecting Manuscripts for Publication

Most individuals have no idea about how manuscripts are selected for publication. They know that manuscripts are submitted, and then somehow a committee or the editor or *someone* selects those articles to be published, based on whatever. Usually, the authors of a manuscript that gets published believe that, whatever the process, it is fair and even-handed. However, those authors whose manuscripts are not published often believe the opposite. Some of the latter even make that point directly to the editor, making it essential for editors to have patience and thick skin.

What actually happened at *JAMA* is as follows: Each manuscript was assigned to a specific editor who had expertise in the subject covered in the manuscript. No manuscript was rejected without an editor seeing it. The assigned editor then read the manuscript and determined whether or not to pursue it further. This decision was based on the quality of the study or writing, the topic, the fit for the journal, the existence of other similar articles already published in any journal or scheduled soon to be published in *JAMA*.

Those that passed that first step, about 40 percent, were then sent out to a number of peer reviewers (and a statistical reviewer for research studies). *JAMA* was one of the few journals in which all data-based articles were reviewed by a biostatistician from the start. We did that because I believed, especially because all the deputy editors and I had faculty positions at academic centers, that one of our duties was to educate the authors as best we could. This was true whether or not the author's paper would be published in *JAMA*.

Then the wait began for return of the reviews. *JAMA* had a sequence of reminders for those reviewers who were tardy. When all reviews were received, the editor managing that manuscript determined whether to go forward. If so, that editor presented the manuscript at one of the twice-a-week manuscript meetings. Those meetings were attended by the editor in chief and a number of other editors, almost always including a statistical editor. The Part-time editors were also present on the telephone when they presented one of their papers or upon special request because of their expertise for another paper being presented.

Each editor had access to each complete manuscript online, or at a minimum, paper copies of the abstract and all tables and figures. During these meetings the editor who was responsible for the paper reviewed it and the peer reviews of the paper to the other editors. Attendees discussed questions and comments about the submitted manuscript and then made a decision either to not accept the manuscript or to request that the principal investigator / corresponding author revise the manuscript. That author was to respond to the external reviewers' and the editors' questions and suggestions.

Virtually no article was accepted without some changes to make it better. For some smaller journals, the editorial board members serve as the journal editors, as described above. The editorial board for *JAMA* and most of the other high-impact journals serve in a different capacity, which I will describe later.

The next step for an accepted manuscript was to be represented at a future manuscript meeting, after the author had made changes and answered all questions. Most authors are anxious to have their papers published, so the response time is relatively short. For those who were tardy, reminders were forthcoming. When the managing editor presented a rewritten manuscript at the next meeting, the same process ensued as for the first presentation. If appropriate changes had been made and all questions answered, the manuscript was then accepted for publication by the editor in chief, who is responsible for all final decisions.

Except for those manuscripts rejected without review (about 60 percent), manuscripts not accepted for publication in *JAMA* at any subsequent step in the review process required a letter sent to the principal author, explaining why the manuscript was not accepted. It is not easy to tell an author that his or her manuscript will not be published in your journal. Most manuscripts represent a great deal of time and work, so it is essential that the letter of nonacceptance be as kind and encouraging as possible, without being false.

This effort is made especially difficult when a reviewer states in the comments to the editor (not seen by the author) that the manuscript is "terrible" or some similar term and then in the comments to the author states that the manuscript is well written and a sound study. Whereas I always stressed to reviewers to be kind and gentle with criticism, that sort of behavior was not easy to deal with.

The next step in the manuscript process was for the manuscript editors (formerly known as copy editors) to edit a manuscript and for the editor in charge of tables and figures to work on that aspect. I derived great pleasure on occasions when I showed authors what they first submitted as tables or figures and then what we ultimately published. I consider the entire process of medical journalism, at its best, as akin to making a short movie: you start with the story and then add the various aspects to produce a publication (or a movie).

The Human Side of the Manuscript Process

The requirement for attention to quality and integrity of what we published, while also considering the feelings of the authors, could have made the process arduous. So one important consideration for me during the manuscript meetings was that the editors and staff have good senses of humor. That is, they were encouraged to laugh at my sometimes stupid jokes or quips. I especially liked their reactions to how I handled the manuscript meetings.

I really hate the word "reject," so I called such decisions "sorry, hon," a term used in Baltimore (or Balimer, as it's pronounced there). If it was clear that the manuscript was not going to be published in *JAMA*, I cut the discussion short by tossing candy at the editor presenting (if she or he was physically present) or squeezing a stuffed toy kookaburra bird I'd picked up in Australia, which sounds very much like hysterical laughter. You've probably heard that bird song in Tarzan or other African movies, even though the kookaburra bird is found only in Australia. Ah, Hollywood.

These manuscript meetings often lasted three to four hours, and when I first arrived I was appalled to discover that there was no coffee pot or other goodies in the manuscript room. The staff told me that coffee pots were forbidden because they were considered to be a fire hazard.

Knowing that they certainly did not present a fire hazard and that the probable reason for the rule was to increase revenue in the cafeteria, I immediately placed a coffee pot, coffee, and condiments in the manuscript room. When I saw the reaction of some staff, I told everyone that if someone objected to the so-called "fire hazard," here or she was to be referred to me. I never received any such referral. Perhaps rumors about my "Uncle Guido" had already circulated. Of course, Uncle Guido was a make-believe character, who I warned people was always handy to protect me.

We asked anyone who wanted a mug of coffee to put a quarter in the coffers, from which I replaced the supplies. I also personally purchased chocolate candy (stating that "vitamin chocolate" is essential to good health), peanuts, and gummy bears. I learned from my Italian heritage that important discussions should occur over food sharing. In addition, all editors at various times purchased muffins and other breakfast foods for occasions such as birthdays and always for the theme (special topic) issue meetings.

We reviewed each *JAMA* issue before sending it to press, at a separate, short weekly meeting.

THREE IMPORTANT PUBLISHED ARTICLES

The most important thing in medical journalism is to publish the best studies and articles, which are honest and whose integrity could not be questioned. All editors want to publish practice-changing studies, but no editor wants to discover that what he or she published is false or that the data were manipulated.

Practice-changing publications are rare, because clinical science is a slow, repetitive process, with the objective of proving that something is good for patients; that some clinical practice is wrong; or that the medical community should adopt something new and better. Even then it usually takes years for physicians to accept anything new and change their practices.

A published article, which later is found to contain false or missing important data requires clarifying corrections as soon as possible in a future issue. In the worst case, a retraction of the article might be necessary. Unfortunately, articles with false or important missing information occur too often and seem to be increasing in frequency. Fortunately, however, most of these errors can be rectified by publishing corrections in future issues and do not require retraction. Retraction of an article means that what was written in that publication is not true or correct, and the publication is treated as if it were never published. An example of each of these types of publications, which occurred while I was the editor in chief of *JAMA*, follows.

The practice-changing article published during my editorship, and probably the one for which I am proudest, is the Women's Health Initiative study entitled "Risks and Benefits of Estrogen Plus Progestin in Healthy Postmenopausal Women." The study, published on July 17, 2002, included data on 16,608 women whose average age was 63.3 years and ranged from 50 to 79. It was a diverse group of women, and the study involved forty medical centers in the United States.

In this randomized clinical trial (the best type of clinical study, and the only type that proves causation and not only association), women were given either a medication, which was a combination of estrogen-progestin, or a placebo. The women and the investigators were unaware of which pill (the medicine or the placebo) each woman received. There also was a safety group of individuals, who kept track of which women had the medication, which had the placebo, and who had side or bad effects.

The pharmaceutical companies that sold these medications had promulgated the use of these and similar medications, known as hormone replacement therapy (HRT), for postmenopausal women to prevent heart disease. The most popular brands were Premarin and Prempro.

The study had been planned to last 8 years but was stopped after 5.2 years, because it was found that the overall health risks of the HRT exceeded benefits. The study revealed an increased risk of heart disease, stroke, blood clots, and breast cancer in the women who took the medication. The final conclusion was that the regimen of estrogen-progestin, the most popular form of hormone replacement at the time, should not be initiated or continued for the prevention of coronary heart disease.

We had been in contact with the authors for a long time, trying to convince them to publish the study, which we knew was ongoing, in *JAMA*. When we received the manuscript, we were overjoyed but cautious. We knew the probable ramifications the study would have on women who were taking or who planned to take HRT medicine. We also anticipated the negative reaction we would receive from the drug companies who sold these medications. We worked very hard to have the manuscript reviewed thoroughly but with as much speed as possible. We personally contacted the reviewers, who assured a thorough but rapid response.

The published study was highly publicized in the media, and women almost immediately stopped taking the medications. In 2001, before the study was published, there had been over 91 million prescriptions for all forms of HRT, resulting in $2.04 billion in sales. In 2002, after the publication of the study, prescriptions for Premarin decreased by 38 percent, and by 78 percent for Prempro. Both medications were used in the study. In 2002, a reported 18.5 million women used some form of HRT, and this decreased to 7.6 million by 2004.

I expected the overwhelmingly negative reaction forthcoming from the pharmaceutical companies, but I was surprised by the negative reac-
tio̶   many gynecologists. These physicians claimed that providing
         ̶omen in their practices was not a problem. I politely asked
         refully read the study and to check its validity with colleagues
         ̶miliar with clinical research. When some of them balked at
         ̶tion, I carefully explained the clinical scientific validity and
         of the study, which I considered time well spent.

         some form of HRT was medically indicated for some
v   ̶t not for those represented in the study. Like many other
p̶   ̶, I spoke with a number of women's groups, explaining that
HRT was medically indicated to allay symptoms such as hot flashes during menopause, but not thereafter to prevent heart disease. It was also important that the replacement of hormones be taken in the lowest possible doses for effect and to avoid those that caused unnecessary problems. We continued to publish many follow-up studies on HRT, which investigated various aspects of the study.

One publication during my editorship that contained false information, requiring a published correction, caused me a great deal of concern. That was the Class Study, published in *JAMA* in 2000, soon after I became the editor in chief. That study reported that the incidence of gastric ulcers and ulcer complications was significantly lower with celecoxib than with nonsteroidal medications (such as ibuprofen) used in the study. These medications were commonly used for pain, especially arthritic pain.

Importantly, the study was supposed to be conducted over twelve months, during which the side effects were to be monitored. When we received the manuscript, the report included only six months of data. We were so concerned about the timing that I requested the editor handling the manuscript to ask the authors three times if they had the six-month results. Each time, including the last one in writing, the answer was no. However, the reported results and peer reviews based on these results were such that we published the paper as a "Preliminary Report" (not a final report) with an accompanying editorial from a respected expert in the field.

About a week after the paper was published, I received a phone call from another investigator who reported that the authors did have the twelve-month results and that the results were also in the hands of the FDA. I worked to find these results, which showed that indeed at six months the report was accurate, but by twelve months, there was no difference between the different medications. I was irate about the authors' deliberate lying and went for a long walk before I called the principal author to demand an explanation. The end result was that we published a letter from the authors clarifying the issue and apologizing to the readers.

Incidences like these cause nightmares to editors, and it further tainted my trust in studies supported by pharmaceutical companies, as the Class Study had been. I certainly have published many studies supported by pharmaceutical companies, but I am especially careful with those studies, as I will discuss later.

The publication of which I am least proud to have published was the only article I retracted during my eleven and a half years of editorship. That publication was "Chemoembolization Combined with Radiofrequency Ablation for Patients with Hepatocellular Carcinoma Larger than 3 cm: A Randomized Control Trial" by Cheng B-Q and colleagues from China. It was published in *JAMA* in April of 2008. The study proposed a treatment for liver cancer.

Soon after publication, we received information that raised concerns about the integrity of the study. Following our procedure when such concerns about the veracity or integrity of a study arose, we contacted the lead author and his institution. The response we received from the lead author was not satisfactory so, also per usual procedure, I contacted Yun Zhang, MD, PhD, vice president of Shandong University and dean of the School of Medicine, where the study had been performed. I politely requested an investigation of the issue. Dean Yun agreed to do so and conducted an intensive investigation that took almost a year, which is not unusual for such thorough reviews.

The results of the investigation by the dean were that there had been unscientific behaviors by the authors, and the conclusions from the study were not valid. The dean stated that the article should be withdrawn from *JAMA*. We retracted the article in May of 2009. The one good thing about this unfortunate incident is that we found that when the dean had been allowed to proceed according to a reasonable timeline for him, the results were fair.

Equity was given to the dean, the author, and our readers. If we had rushed the dean, he might have raised the Great Wall of China ten feet higher and become agitated with us. Dean Yun became one of my heroes, because it is very difficult for anyone to conduct such an investigation and to admit that someone in his or her institution did a bad thing.

The importance of contacting and allowing the dean as much time as he needed proved to me that our approach to investigate allegations was proper. This had great significance in an unfortunate earlier case following another allegation involving a researcher, a dean, and the media, about which I'll write later.

Theme Issues

JAMA was published forty-eight times a year, so there were a sufficient number of issues to allow for special themes to be showcased. We published the annual medical education issue in September, and the biennial HIV/AIDS issue corresponded with the international HIV/AIDS conference. Each theme issue, except medical education, was accompanied by a press conference, where several authors published in that issue presented their work.

Five months after I arrived at *JAMA*, we published a call for papers that, if accepted, would be published in the upcoming special issue on Woman's Health. This was my first theme issue, and even though *JAMA* had published Women's Health theme issues in the past, I knew I wanted to put a special emphasis on the health of women and children as part of my editorship. This was one way of doing so, and we soon did a special theme issue on children as well.

A humorous thing happened when I told people on my podcast about the press conference of the Women's Health issue, to be held at a very nice New York City hotel. Not to offend the male audience, I told them about an upcoming special issue on Men's Health. I jokingly said that press conference would be held at Hooters restaurant. You can imagine the responses I received to that joke.

The General Atmosphere

The pace at *JAMA*, as I'm sure is true for any weekly high-impact journal, was brutal, so maintaining good humor was essential. The first week there, I placed a sign outside my door, which was kept open except for the rare confidential meeting. That sign was a going-away present from one of my Hopkins colleagues, whose humor matched mine. It was a sign she purchased from the San Diego Zoo that read, "Please do not annoy, torment, pester, plague, molest, worry, badger, harry, harass, heckle, persecute, irk, bullyrag, vex, disquiet, grate, beset, bother, tease, nettle, tantalize, or ruffle the EDITOR" (the last word had replaced the original word, "animals). That sign stopped a number of individuals in their tracks at first, but that didn't last very long, because everyone soon realized it was a joke.

I also kept a big jar of chocolate candy on my desk, which I encouraged the editorial assistants to share. That brought them into my office where I could also share a smile or a quip with them. Because only a few took advantage of that invitation, I frequently walked around the office space occupied by the *JAMA* staff. While it took me a half hour or so to stop and speak with most of the staff, over time I learned the names of their spouses and children.

I wanted to know about them, and that seemed to make the staff happy. It also made me happy, and I learned a lot about what was really on the minds of individuals. Sometimes that knowledge allowed me to alleviate potential or real problems while they were small. In addition, those tours contributed nicely to the ten thousand steps that I walked every day to keep my weight down, what with all that "vitamin chocolate" being present all over the place.

One thing that surprised the staff was that I'd never eaten a Twinkie. One day they presented one to me at a manuscript meeting. Because I wanted to make a point with them about why I'd never eaten one, I tacked it on the bulletin board outside the manuscript room. A decade or so later, when I was about to leave, the cake was still on the bulletin board, looking no different than the day I'd tacked it up. Everyone laughed, but they still ate and enjoyed Twinkies, and I still haven't tasted one. I just might be missing a delicious treat. So be it!

Late Friday afternoons were sometimes very quiet, in fact too quiet, because we all were suffering from the rapid pace of the past week. I had a stereo radio and CD player in my office, where I played classical music almost all day. One especially quiet Friday afternoon, I put on one of my favorite pieces, the *William Tell* Overture, and turned the volume up to full sound (read "blasting"). I went outside my office and saw everyone standing outside his or her office or cubicle, looking at me as if I had just lost my mind. That was probably an accurate assessment.

So I shouted, "On your horses, and let's go," as I began galloping up the aisle to the music. I was soon joined by a number of people. We had a good laugh, and everyone was certainly awake by the end of the musical piece. I repeated the music, at full volume, periodically on Friday afternoons, just to remind us all that there was still work to be done. It was effective in stimulating a final burst of energy to get us all through the last working hours of the week. I've always been very fond of music therapy.

THE ARCHIVES JOURNALS

Every previous editor (all of them men) of *JAMA* had chosen the editors of each Archives journal, and they all reported to him. However, there seemed to be no close involvement of the *JAMA* editor with the Archives journals. I knew that from my experience as editor of the *Archives of Pediatrics and Adolescent Medicine*.

I vividly remember the first *JAMA* Editorial Board meeting I attended; all of the Archives editors were members of the *JAMA* board. By custom, the *JAMA* editor gave each member of the board a small gift. That year the gift was a tie tack, which was not much use to a woman. So I raised my hand and told the editor that I had received only one earring. He looked shocked, but the other board members recognized my humorous point, and most of them offered to give their tie tacks to me. I jokingly took one and put that one plus mine in my pierced ears, much to the delight of the board. Even the *JAMA* editor laughed. I knew he had realized that the gift was not appropriate, because future gifts were gender-neutral.

The covers of the Archives journals contained the AMA logo, and there was no indication of affiliation with *JAMA*. That always bothered me when I was the editor of the Archives journal. Once I was at *JAMA*, I wanted to remedy that situation and promote the Archives journals as much as possible. Actually, what I really would have liked to have done was to rename the Archives journals. The name *Archives of Neurology* would be changed to *JAMA Neurology,* and the same would be done with the appropriate name of each specialty. Naming the Archives journals as such would have emulated the Nature journal series and later the Lancet series.

The deputy editors and I discussed this possible change. However, I did not want the Archives to restart with an impact factor of zero. That's what would happen when the name changed, because the journal would be considered a different, new journal. That's what had happened when I became the editor of the renamed *Archives of Pediatrics and Adolescent Medicine* in 1994, despite my having been assured that would not occur. It had taken me years to get that journal's impact factor to a decent level, from the zero at which I started.

So, instead, we changed the logo on the Archives covers to read as follows:

JAMA
&
Archives Journals
American Medical Association

The letters decreased in size as they went down the four lines it took to display the full logo. Now we had a real family of journals, which we displayed proudly. This change also pleased the Archives editors.

I had discussed this planned change with the EVP/ CEO, Andy, to prevent problems with some of the AMA staff, who might not like the change. You really can't please all of the people all of the time, especially if change is involved. I now officially became the editor in chief of *JAMA* and the Archives journals, to differentiate me from the editors of the Archives journals.

Another thing we did was to promote the Archives journals in *JAMA*. We published a section called "From the Archives," in which one of the Archives editors would highlight an article to be published in an upcoming issue of his or her journal. We published the abstract from that article and accompanied it with a commentary on the article, written by whomever the Archives editor chose. The commentary put the specialty article into perspective for the *JAMA* readers, most of whom were not specialists in other fields. We also encouraged the other Archives journal editors to do the same thing by publishing appropriate abstracts from another Archives journal in their own journals. Also, the Archives journals could publish pertinent *JAMA* abstracts. This kind of cross promotion proved to be very successful.

Another change with the Archives journals was a sad one, and it involved the *Archives of Family Medicine*. We had a well-known, highly respected editor, who worked very hard to make that journal a high-impact and well-read publication. However, no matter how hard she tried, and I tried to help, the journal simply did not receive a sufficient number of publishable research studies to maintain a monthly schedule. Moreover, we did publish some very good studies by family physicians in *JAMA*. I thought some of the authors of those *JAMA* articles might be interested in having their studies published in our *Archives of Family Medicine* journal, but virtually all whom I asked declined.

Because that Archives journal was losing money, I needed to decide if we should continue to publish it. That would only make sense if it was considered necessary by family physicians. We conducted a survey among the readers of the *Archives of Family Medicine* and found that, for the most part, they were not very interested in research studies. They preferred review and guideline articles. They read and preferred the journal published by their own academy, which provided many such articles.

I met with the editor and the publisher of *American Family Physician*, the journal of the American Academy of Family Physicians (AAFP), to see if they might be interested in our joining the journals together. That way each issue would contain reviews and scientific articles. They had no interest in that potential plan, so the AMA publisher and I decided to stop publishing our *Archives of Family Medicine*, probably much to the pleasure of the AAFP. I could hardly blame them for wanting to promote their own journal, but I felt very bad to lose the close working relationship with our Archives editor, who had worked so hard.

Over the years, I had to replace several Archives editors, primarily because they retired. Only one asked to be replaced, because he lost his deputy editor and was too busy with other interests to continue as editor. Much to my pleasure, I never had any trouble finding excellent editors, all of whom worked to advance the Archives journals.

CHAPTER 14

The Fully Engaged Editor

I CONSIDER TWO INCIDENTS, EACH of which occurred within the first six months after my becoming editor in chief of *JAMA*, to have been tests of just how far certain people would go in attempting to manipulate me. The first dealt with a rule we had that no advertisement for a drug or device could be placed adjacent to an article dealing in any way with the same topic. For example, no advertisement for a cardiac drug could be placed adjacent to an article on cardiology. It did not matter whether or not the drug in the advertisement was mentioned in the article or could be used for the cardiac problem described in the article.

The issue of advertisement placement was mostly handled by having an editorial "well" in *JAMA*. That is, all research studies were placed in a series of continuing pages, with no intervening advertisements. If the first or last pages of the published studies required an advertisement to be placed on an adjacent page, the advertisement would be for *JAMA*, an Archives journal, or a free advertisement. (We provided free advertisements to nonprofit organization, such as organizations for the blind or deaf.)

We also would not allow any advertising agency to specify the particular issue in which their advertisement would appear. Most companies purchased a number of ads, for the same drug or device, to be published in upcoming issues, and they had no idea of which articles would appear in those issues.

I received a phone call one morning from a person in the publishers' ad sales office. She reported that she had just received a request to buy a four-page (read "expensive") advertisement from a pharmaceutical company, requesting that their advertisement appear in a specific upcoming issue. I looked at what was scheduled to be published in that issue—we planned issues several weeks ahead—and I saw that there was a study, sponsored by the drug company requesting the advertisement, to be published in that issue. Clearly and understandably, the author of the study had informed the pharmaceutical company that had sponsored the study about the planned publication date.

I told the ad sales person that the advertisement could not be published in the requested issue. The pharmaceutical company could have any issue except that one. She called back a little while later and said the company wanted only that issue (big surprise!), noting also that it was a very big advertisement (again, read "expensive"). I thought about it for a short while, and said, "OK, they can have that issue." She was obviously pleased but surprised by my decision.

What she and the company did not know was that I moved the study to be published to a different issue. The advertiser was not happy, despite getting its requested issue. Later, when questioned about this decision, I "innocently" explained that the drug company, the publisher's advertisement office, and I all got what we wanted. So what could possibly be a problem? This was the first of what was to be many situations where pharmaceutical companies and I had "issues."

The advertisement incident also showed the importance of the wall between the editor, who is responsible for assuring the integrity of what is published and therefore the physical and mental health of the public, and the publisher, who is responsible for assuring the financial health of the journal.

I will later write more about the attempts of for-profit companies to use *JAMA* and other journals to market their products. The companies' goal was to have the public believe that, because their products were advertised in issues with peer-reviewed articles about problems for which one of their products could be used, it showed the benefits of their products. Thereby, the journal supposedly supported the use of their products. That form of influence peddling has no place in medical journals—or anywhere in medicine.

The second test came soon after the one just related. I received a phone call from a distraught principal investigator, about a study dealing with an HIV-vaccine study. This was a multicenter study, and he had received only 85 percent of the data. The sponsoring pharmaceutical company refused to provide him with the remaining data when he told them that the vaccine did not work. He was very concerned, because without the missing data, his study did not have the necessary statistical power to prove that the vaccine was not effective. However, the investigator was certain that the data he had showed the clinical failure of the vaccine. This meant that many HIV-positive patients in the study were now not taking medications that were effective in controlling the disease, because they believed that the vaccine they'd been given was possibly working.

The author asked if I would review the manuscript of the study and possibly consider it for publication, despite the lack of statistical power. I told him to submit the manuscript, and I had it reviewed by a number of HIV experts and several biostatisticians. It was clear that the study, although statistically incomplete, should be published, along with a discussion about why some data were missing. The study contained important information for physicians and for patients with HIV, especially those involved in the study.

This experience taught me the vital importance of the principal author (investigator) having access to all data from the study in which he or she was involved. Allowing the for-profit sponsor to control the data can be dangerous, as it was in this case. There must be a clear, and unmovable, wall between the scientific and the marketing aspects of producing, testing, and selling products that are to be used for human purposes.

Several days after I told the investigator that we would publish the revised manuscript, with an accompanying commentary, I received a phone call. The caller was a man (gentleman he was not), identifying himself as someone from a law firm. He wanted to discuss my decision to publish the manuscript. I informed him that I didn't speak about upcoming articles with anyone except the authors and especially not with lawyers, because I didn't understand "legalese." I did offer him the telephone number of our *JAMA* attorney. He refused that offer and said, "Lady, you don't understand. We will sue you and *JAMA* if you publish that paper." I thought about that threat for a few seconds and responded with my newly made up, and now-favorite, "Japanese" word, "So-sue-me."

We published the study, and that failed vaccine never came to market. This was another example of how medical journal editors can help to preserve the health of the public.

The drug company didn't sue me, or *JAMA*, but did sue the author's medical school. The attorneys at the institution in question had had a similar experience with another pharmaceutical company, years before this episode. They had learned important lessons. Specifically, their previous experience also involved a study that was to be published in *JAMA*.

That clinical trial had the opposite outcome to what the pharmaceutical company expected for the drug being tested. In that case, the institution where the study was being performed, had signed a contract allowing the company to have the final decision on when and where the study could be published. Because of this, the pharmaceutical company had been able to delay publication for three years, while the issue of publication was being fought legally. The result was that the public was not made aware of the failed clinical trial until three years after it was known.

For the HIV-vaccine study, the lawyers for the same institution, having learned a vital lesson, had signed the contract in which they made sure the institution, and not the pharmaceutical company, had the final say on when and where the study could be published. Therefore, the pharmaceutical company lost the case.

This experience taught me how important it is for the institution where a study is being performed or where the principal author is a faculty member to have the final say on when and where a study would be submitted for publication.

After Istanbul

After my hair-raising experience in Istanbul in March 2001, which I related in the introduction, I had to stay in Baltimore for at least a week in order to recuperate. My physicians wanted to make sure I was healing well after I was discharged from Johns Hopkins Hospital. I was very weak physically but enjoyed short walks and sitting outside in our beautiful garden.

One trip I had to make during the time was the scheduled annual meeting of my editor colleagues from the International Committee of Medical Journal Editors (ICMJE). I'll write much more about that committee later. This meeting was special because we were going to discuss the problem of industry or agency sponsors of clinical research controlling all data, and deciding if, when, and where research studies would be published. As discussed previously, I found this to be an unacceptable situation, as did my editor colleagues.

Because I was still very weak, and Jim was not about to let me travel alone, even on the relatively short train ride from Baltimore to Philadelphia, he went with me. At that meeting, the editors decided to publish a joint editorial in strong opposition to contractual agreements that did not allow investigators to independently examine all data or to require permission from the sponsor before submitting a study for possible publication. To emphasize this issue, we also revised and strengthened the section on Conflict of Interest in the ICMJE Uniform Requirements. These requirements are used by many editors, investigators, and reviewers.

The trip was well worth my time and energy, not only because we accomplished something very important to help assure the integrity of clinical studies, but also because I had the opportunity to be with some of the finest editors in the world.

After spending a week at home in Baltimore recuperating from the results of the Istanbul adventure and gaining back my strength—but happily not the fifteen pounds I'd lost (there is a silver lining behind every cloud, after all)—I was anxious to return to *JAMA* and get back to work.

This time, when the plane flew over the Chicago skyline, I smiled and felt like screaming, "Yippee!" The next morning, when I arrived in the office (as usual being the first to arrive), I found a path of "Welcome home" and "Happy you're back" signs that began at the tenth floor elevators and ended in my office. If I ever doubted that my staff loved me as I loved them, any such foolish thoughts disappeared forever.

The morning meeting was a joy, with virtually everyone from the *JAMA* staff and many AMA staff coming by to say hello and welcome me back. My desk was covered with cards and flowers, providing even more evidence of the caring nature of my friends and colleagues. However, it was time to get back to work. Phil had led the team in my absence, and not a single beat had been missed in publishing the journal. This was no surprise to me, but it meant that getting back into my *JAMA* rhythm was a lot easier than it might have been.

I'll Never Be a Diva

Over the next week or so, I noticed my inability to sing while attending daily mass; my range was greatly diminished, especially for the higher notes. I once had a decent voice and even had sung in the church choir during high school. I called my anesthesiologist friend, who had delivered anesthesia to me, during my recent care at Hopkins. I asked him if there had been any problem passing the tracheal tube for anesthesia, and he assured me there had been none. However, he was concerned and suggested I see an otolaryngologist. He asked me to keep him informed about the problem. I then spoke with my dear friend and former dean, Mike Johns, who you might remember was an otolaryngologist–head-and-neck surgeon. He referred me to a colleague of his who cared for the members of the Chicago Opera.

Many years previously, when I spoke at the New York Medical College graduation, I jokingly sang a very short greeting to the graduating class, in Carnegie Hall, where the graduation had taken place. I told the audience that I'd always wanted to sing in Carnegie Hall. The audience laughed, of course. Despite that earlier comical foray, I felt completely out of place when Jim and I went to the Chicago Opera House, where Mike's colleague had an office.

The otolaryngologist visualized my vocal cords, while Jim watched on a nearby monitor. Actually, I was gagged while the physician and Jim discussed how my vocal cords were functioning…or not. It turned out that, because I had lost so much weight so rapidly while in Turkey, the muscles to my vocal chords had shrunk.

He prescribed vocal exercises, which I was to sing in the shower every day until I no longer felt improvement. I did as instructed, and although there was great improvement, I still can't reach the higher notes I once could. But what the heck? I can still make a joyful noise.

PHONE CALLS

It was now mid-2001, eighteen months into my editorship, and things were in full swing. Our plans to have all submissions and manuscript review performed online were moving ahead. Also, the result of the many phone calls, e-mail messages, and visits made by all *JAMA* editors, including myself, with investigators performing good studies were bearing fruit. We were definitely receiving more very good manuscripts. I spent an hour or so almost every day, often including weekends, calling potential authors. Many of the calls were to solicit studies, and others were to solicit commentaries. As I quipped to the *JAMA* staff, "I'm a woman who shamelessly 'solicits'…manuscripts, that is." The Sisters of

No-Mercy, who trained me, would not approve of such an admission, no matter how innocent.

Quite a few of my calls were to authors, especially to young investigators whose manuscripts were not accepted for publication in *JAMA*. I personally read, reviewed, and completely managed about three hundred of the six thousand manuscripts we received annually, and many of my calls were to those individuals. I never ceased to be amazed by the responses I received when I made those calls.

A number of potential authors were surprised that I had called them. Their surprise concerned me, because a personal call from an editor should not be unusual. I understood the time constraints, but most editors are professors and therefore should profess—that is, teach. How better to teach than by personal interactions with someone who could learn from what he or she might be told about a manuscript?

Some of the calls, especially with the older and more experienced authors, were humorous. For example, once I called a senior author to discuss something in the manuscript he had submitted. As is customary, I always introduced myself by name and title. This time, after I had started to explain the purpose of the call, the person said with an eastern-European accent, "Is this really the big cheese?" I responded that perhaps I was a bit like Swiss cheese, having some holes in my head, but otherwise I was not a "big cheese." I told that story to the *JAMA* senior staff, and thereafter, on appropriate occasions, in jest they would call me "da big cheese," and we'd all laugh.

The Impact Factor

The next few years continued to be a joyous ride. The impact of *JAMA* increased with each issue. Note I did not say "impact factor," because even though that also continued to improve, I became aware of how that number could be manipulated and its significance misunderstood. The impact factor number was supposed to be a measure of the quality of journals, but that was not necessarily the case. I did not, and still do not, think it was right to make editorial decisions in order to achieve higher numbers on something that is only one measure of the quality and effectiveness of a journal.

For those who don't know what an impact factor is, it is a number for a particular year, determined by dividing the number of times a journal was cited over the previous two-year period, divided by the number of items the journal published in those two years. I mentioned earlier that Thompson ISI (now Thompson Reuters ISI), a for-profit company, decided which articles were counted in the denominator, and they still do. Clearly not all articles are counted.

To be fair, the company uses the same formula for all journals. However, most people don't understand how the impact factor is calculated and believe the denominator is determined by simply counting the total number of articles published in a journal over the two-year period. Despite Thompson ISI determining which articles are counted in the denominator, how that decision is made is not evident or readily available.

Several journal editors, including yours truly, have visited the Thompson ISI offices to discuss this issue. There are some interesting differences of opinion about what should be counted in the denominator. However, because it is Thompson ISI's impact factor, the decision is theirs, so the journal editors must live with it, at least for the foreseeable future.

Our visit to Thompson ISI included attorney Joe Thornton, who happened to be the newest member of our senior team. We found out generally what criteria were used to determine the articles counted in *JAMA*'s denominator. Thereafter, we made sure that the short articles ("Commentaries," "Perspectives," etc.) followed their rules about length and number of authors. This resulted in our denominator number decreasing despite the total number of published articles of all varieties, including data based studies, increasing.

I was and remain most disturbed by how the impact factor could be manipulated by editors to increase the impact factors of their journals while not actually increasing the quality of the journals. Certain articles, such as reviews, clinical guidelines, and randomized clinical trials, generate the highest number of citations. Almost all editors seek to publish as many of those types of articles as possible, after peer review, to assure quality.

However, there are manipulations that raise the impact factor without necessarily raising the quality of the journal. For example, citations for any article could be counted for as few as thirteen months, for those articles published in December of the first of the two years used in the calculation, or for twenty-four months, for those published in January of the first year. An editor could hold publication for what would likely be a highly cited article until January, rather than publish it in the last few months of the year. That would increase the journal's impact factor. Most authors favor rapid publication, so there is a downside to such decisions. This has become a lesser issue with rapid online publishing before print, but it remains a possible manipulation to increase a journal's impact factor.

Other manipulations involve choosing only those articles likely to be cited often, or to publish fewer data-based articles, which are counted in the denominator, and filling the pages of the journal with nonstudy-based commentaries, viewpoints, and other short, mostly opinion-based articles that are not counted in the denominator. Of course, this is a double-edged sword, because good editors of journals that receive many submissions want to publish as many data-based articles as possible while maintaining the highest possible quality.

In any case, I still believe the impact factor is not the best criterion to determine the real value or quality of a journal, and I am joined by many other editors and authors.

LETTERS

JAMA's influence on medicine in general and the impact factor continued to increase, and my interactions with *JAMA* staff, investigators, authors, the media, and the public were a constant source of good feelings and were often fun. Examples of fun interactions with the public include some of the letters I received. There were so many enjoyable examples I shared with the *JAMA* staff at our weekly meetings that a few of the other editors began to contribute examples of their own, much to our good cheer.

I'll share two of my favorites with you. The first was sent by a gentleman in his senior years. (I should point out that I only allowed the word *elderly* to be used at *JAMA* when referring to someone over ninety years of age. You can guess the reason for that decision; remember, that I was sixty years young when I started at *JAMA*.) In any case, the gentleman began his letter by explaining that he had lived with his elderly mother, and when she died he had paid for all the expenses, despite having several siblings. He then explained that he didn't want his children to have the same experience when he died, so he wanted to place an ad in *JAMA*, stating that his body was for sale for medical research or "convention," whatever that meant. "Why get bodies illegally and pay top dollars, when I'm offering mine for a small price?" his letter stated. Needless to say, we did not place such an ad in *JAMA*.

The second letter was also from a senior gentleman, and it was handwritten on a sheet of lined paper taken from a notebook, like those used by children in school. He explained that he had shrunk his prostate by eating peanut butter every day. He had also decreased his nightly visits to the bathroom, from four or five times a night to once or twice. He explained that he had begun eating peanut butter after he had a tooth repaired. He decided to stop eating peanuts and to eat peanut butter instead, and this resulted in a shrunken prostate.

He then asked that I publish this in *JAMA* and to please send him a complimentary copy of the issue in which his letter would be published. The letter was signed, "end of story," followed by the person's name. The envelope also contained the label from a peanut butter jar. Needless to say, we did not publish the letter or the peanut butter label. I wonder how many male readers are considering this dietary plan after reading this; strange things do happen.

In addition to these humorous letters from the public, some letters to the editor submitted for possible publication in *JAMA* and other letters accompanying manuscript submissions were frequently sources of mirth. For example, I had long made it clear to anyone who would listen that all letters to the editor should be addressed using proper gender and the correct journal title. When I would receive a letter or e-mail message addressed "Dear Sir" (almost always sent by a man), I'd respond by addressing the return letter or message "Dear Madam" and would await the response to that hint. Occasionally I would receive a phone call or message appreciating the humor and usually an apology for the oversight.

Sometimes I would receive a letter addressed to the incorrect journal. I'd respond by stating that while I was not the editor of said journal, I'd be happy to forward the manuscript to the other journal for the author. No one ever requested that I do so, but almost all authors requested that I accept their apologies and proceed to review their manuscripts for possible publication in *JAMA*.

Of course, another journal's title in the letter to *JAMA* provided me with a clue that the manuscript probably had already been submitted to the other journal and had not been accepted for publication. That fact was not necessarily a bad mark, but the carelessness in not having made the correction in the letter was a definite no-no. Consequently, the manuscript was usually scrutinized even more closely than it might have been without that mistake in submission.

I share these episodes as examples of important things I learned from receiving such submissions: the general public was reading *JAMA*; many individuals had interesting, if somewhat peculiar ideas about the role of *JAMA*; and most importantly, I learned more about the beauty of human nature. Oh, and that the Great Comedian is ever present.

REVIEWERS

An issue that faces essentially all journal editors is procuring enough good reviewers to assist as advisors in the decision process for manuscripts.

Although all final decisions regarding whether or not to publish a manuscript rest with the editor in chief, reviewers play an essential role in peer review. They contribute greatly in determining the quality of articles and assist by generally knowing what has been published and what is currently being discussed and researched in their fields of specialty. They also frequently alert the editor if they have already reviewed manuscripts in question for other journals and whether or not their suggested changes have been made.

The problem for editors is that the very good reviewers are requested to review manuscripts by many journals, and they are usually very busy individuals. There is little, if any, reimbursement for most reviewers, so editors must depend on their good nature to offer their honest opinions regarding the quality of the material being reviewed. JAMA only paid some statistical reviewers to review studies, because there are relatively few statistical reviewers available, especially in subspecialty fields such as genetics. The reimbursement is not very much, but since many, if not most, statisticians are not physicians, even the relatively small amount helped them financially.

Because most reviewers are not statisticians, I sought other ways to provide them with at least a token of our gratitude for their assistance, in addition to the usual publication of their names in *JAMA*. One issue that concerned me at that time was how the Accreditation Council on Continuing Medical Education (ACCME) was providing continuing medical education (CME) credits to physicians. The ACCME was allowing for-profit companies to sponsor conferences for which CME credits were given. All physicians in the United States are required to have a certain number of specific types of CME credits in order to renew their licenses, so it is necessary for all physicians to earn these credits.

Many times, physicians would attend conferences though actually not be present at the specific CME sessions but were given CME credits anyway. I thought that physicians who served as reviewers must read and learn from the manuscripts they reviewed, so why not allow them to receive CME credits for reviewing manuscripts? I worked to get this accomplished not only for *JAMA* but also for any journals that followed the rules for being accrediting entities. There now was something of value that editors could offer reviewers in return for their reviews.

The journal editors would have to grade each review and the grade recorded online. The criteria used by *JAMA* for credit were: (1) the reviewer had to receive a score of at least "good" for the quality of the review as determined by the editor managing the manuscript, and (2) the review had to be submitted on time. The editor handling the manuscript recorded his or her "grade" online, and the reviewer could download and print a copy of the CME credit certificate for his or her records. The reviewer would receive one CME credit for every article he or she reviewed.

These online records also assisted the editors in selecting reviewers, because no one wanted to invite a review from a reviewer who had a fair or poor score or who had taken too long to return the review, often despite several requests from the *JAMA* office. Once again, doing the right thing for individuals (reviewers) also benefitted the person or entity benefitting from the right thing (authors and editors). It's funny how that works.

Reviewers sometimes disagreed with one another about the quality of an article. That was why we used at least three reviewers for every article. For difficult or controversial articles, we would request the advice of four or five reviewers. We also had an automatic "nudge" e-mail for reviewers who were late with their reviews.

PODCASTS

A problem requiring solution was how could we compete with one of our rival journals, which had hired a professional company to help advertise the articles published in their journal. This was accomplished by our rival journal by providing a free podcast for each issue. These digital media consisted of an audio file, downloaded on the web each week. A professional speaker would briefly describe key articles in each week's issue, thereby generating interest in the articles.

I knew we needed to do something, but I did not have the funds to support a professional speaker or company. So the deputy editors suggested that our media staff could record and make the audios available on our website, and that I should do the speaking. I was dubious about the idea, but I decided to try it because it would cost us nothing, except time. Hence was born the "From the Editor" podcast.

By some miracle, the podcasts were a success. I would begin each session with, "Hello out there." I was amazed when I began to pass obvious listeners on the street, or especially at meetings or in the airport, who would wave and say, "Hello out there," to me. We'd both laugh and, usually, stop to chat. Hidden joys of meeting people were everywhere.

THE MEDICAL LIBRARY

A year or so after I arrived at *JAMA*, a relatively new SVP for business, Robert Musacchio (or Bob, as I called him, and he called me Cathy), replaced Paul Blackney, the wonderful man who had helped to recruit me. Bob had been at AMA for many years, holding several senior positions. As a cost-cutting exercise for his budget, Bob suggested that the medical library be closed. We frequently used the medical library's books and journals to find information needed for an article. That information was not available on line.

I couldn't believe he was serious about that suggestion. I thought only someone who had no knowledge of how a journal, much less eleven journals, functioned on a daily basis would make such a suggestion. I was sure Bob was very smart, so probably his suggestion was based on economics. Indeed, he had a doctorate in economics. So I requested a meeting with Andy and Bob to discuss this issue. Closing the medical library could have caused a great deal of trouble and extra work for the editors and staff. At this point, *JAMA* and the Archives journals were not yet functioning fully online, as most of our competitive biomedical journals were.

Bob told us that, because there were several medical school librar-ies, one of which (Northwestern Medical Center) was only ten or so blocks away, he thought we could simply use one of those libraries. I then asked, "So why are you keeping the law library open, when the American Bar Association is only a few blocks away?" Bob stated that, unlike the medical library, the law library was quite small and cost very little to maintain.

Not stated, but evident, was that the medical library was adminis-tratively part of the business office and therefore part of Bob's budget. Like a good economist, he was simply trying to cut his expenditures. I could understand and respect his request. However, I pointed out that, assuming we could negotiate a formal relationship with Northwestern, if someone from the *JAMA* staff had to go to that library to retrieve books, journals, or other material, we would need more staff. All *JAMA* staff currently were fully occupied to make sure the journals were pub-lished on time. I said extra staff would not eliminate the disorganizing effect such a plan would have on *JAMA*'s functioning.

To his credit, after considering all the issues involved, Andy decided that the medical library would remain open. I understood Bob's desire to cut expenditures in his budget, and I was concerned about the future of the library functioning under the business office. Therefore, I volun-teered to have the library supervision and budget transferred to me in the upcoming fiscal year. Bob readily agreed, and Andy immediately approved the move, resolving the problem.

The next fiscal year, the library became part of the *JAMA* family. Of course the transferred budget had been cut somewhat. The library staff members were so happy to still have jobs that they agreed to our plan for eliminating some journal subscriptions, book purchases, and services. To make up the difference, we would expand some services, which involved more time and effort of the staff but no or not much money. For example, *JAMA* received several hundred books annually sent to us for possible selection for our "Book Review" section. The vast majority of these books were not reviewed, so we sent these to Loyola

Medical library, and in return, the librarian at Loyola would send us copies of articles from journals not kept in our library.

I wanted to work out a mutually beneficial plan for Bob and me, especially because I had to work closely with the publisher, who reported to Bob. The resolution of the issue was an example of mutual aid at its finest, I thought. Darwin would have been proud of us for finding ways to help each other rather than allowing something valuable to die. It was an equitable solution.

The Fishbein Fellowship

JAMA offers a one-year paid fellowship for physicians. It is designed for those who are interested in possible careers involving the various aspects of medical editing, including understanding how clinical research is evaluated by journals. When I arrived, I was not exactly sure what the fellowship involved. But I knew that the fellowship had trained some wonderful editors, including Phil, Maggie, and several part-time *JAMA* editors.

Over the following years, we continued to train one fellow each year, except for one year when we decided none of the candidates met the requirements we sought. It took a fair amount of time and energy to train fellows, so we wanted to make sure our efforts would be fruitful. We wanted to be proud to have the *JAMA* name behind a physician who might become an editor after completing the fellowship. Of course the fellows also contributed to *JAMA* work when they were well prepared. We therefore reaped some real benefits for our efforts.

As is true for all training programs, the major benefit of training fellows is the pleasure they generate with their enthusiasm and ideas, which stimulate our desire to teach. A few of the fellows trained during my editorship became part-time editors at *JAMA*. Two became "Art Story" editors, another the "Book Review" editor, and another a "Clinical Correlation" editor. A few became editors for other journals.

When I first started at *JAMA*, Richard Glass was the editor who coordinated the fellowship program. After a few years, Richard assumed

Pursuing Equity in Medicine

other duties, and a new editor, Rob Golub, assumed the responsibility for the fellowship. That assignment was a natural for Rob, because he spent a small percentage of his time continuing the medical-education program he already directed at Northwestern, which included research methodologies.

The fellowship primarily involved learning about all aspects of medical-journal editing. That included evaluating, presenting, and working with the authors of submitted manuscripts, all the way through the process, from initial submission through final decision, including publication. The Fishbein fellows took courses at Northwestern in biostatistics, epidemiology, and other elected courses, as they chose, to help them in evaluating the studies submitted to *JAMA*. After a few weeks, they each were assigned a submitted study that they managed completely, with Rob's oversight. After a few more weeks, they assumed responsibility for more studies and became more independent.

Other experiences included learning about the art and poetry sections of *JAMA*, and the section called "A Piece of My Mind." Several fellows wrote stories for the cover-art pieces, with the assistance of at first Terri Southgate, the editor responsible for *JAMA* cover art. After Terri retired, the next art editors (it was now a shared editorship) were former Fishbein fellows. The Fishbein fellows also spent time with the editors in charge of "Medical News", with the tem responsible for perspectives of editorial graphics (tables and figures used in the articles), and with the manuscript editors.

Having a trainee in the midst of the *JAMA* group added so much to the general awareness of how younger physicians were thinking and what they believed to be currently important. Young, fresh "blood" keeps the circulation, no matter how defined, brisk.

AMA Obituaries

When I began as editor in chief of *JAMA*, I was advised that there were two things I should not consider eliminating: the art on the cover and the obituaries of AMA members. The obituaries consumed one page of *JAMA*, published in almost every issue. I completely agreed with keeping the art on the covers, which for so long had been such an important part of the *JAMA* image. The suggestion regarding the obituaries of AMA members was another matter.

To use one editorial page per issue of our allotted pages for obituaries seemed wasted space, especially because we wanted to publish as many good articles as possible. Many of the obituary announcements were old; the individual involved having died as much as a year prior to *JAMA*'s publication of the obituary. Also it seemed much more appropriate for the AMA house organ, the AMA newsletter, to publish them.

JAMA is a journal dedicated to publishing biomedical science, discussions regarding medicine, and health care. I could understand why the editor of the AMA newsletter was reluctant to use one of his allotted four-or-so pages for obituaries. In the end, the AMA decided to publish the obituaries online, in order to assure more timely notification. This decision saved *JAMA* about fifty pages a year and no pages lost to the AMA newsletter.

When I stopped publishing the obituaries, the reaction regarding their omission in *JAMA* was far less than I'd expected. Most of the objections came via phone calls and handwritten letters from older AMA members. I personally responded to each one essentially the same way, by telling the member that it was better for the AMA to publish the obituaries of the AMA members in a timely manner, online.

Many older physicians told me they didn't use computers, and I told them I could empathize with their reluctance to use computers, because I was part of or close to their generation in age. Being a digital immigrant—unlike the younger generations, who were digital natives—made me partners with the older members.

To provide them with some idea of my background with "newfangled things," I explained that, when I was a child, my family had a four-foot-high console radio; we purchased our first black-and-white TV when I was a preteen; I had used a slide rule in college; my first purchase of a calculator was for my college-bound nephew, when I was a medical resident, and it had cost three days' worth of my pretax salary; and I had used my first computer was when I was an associate professor faculty member.

That explanation helped with most of the complaining readers. I advised those who still balked, because they claimed they did not even know how to turn on a computer, much less to own one, to purchase one. I advised that they should then ask one of their grandchildren to teach them how to use it, thereby democratizing information technology. Many seemed to like my way of explaining the situation and even laughed.

I told them I was sure they would find that the computer had many uses to make their lives easier and even more enjoyable. A number of them actually bought computers and told me that it was a lot of fun to be with their grandchildren and to be able to brag about how bright they were.

This was another example of never knowing what would come of doing what I considered to be the right thing and responding to negative reactions by sharing personal experiences, which made my humanism, like theirs, very apparent. By becoming an ally, I could allay their concerns. Isn't it interesting how the words *ally* and *allay* seem to go together?

NUMBER OF PAGES

When I began my editorship, *JAMA* was allotted one hundred editorial pages per print issue, of which there were forty-eight per year—that is, four issues per month. Up to that point, the number of pages had been determined by the publisher. Since the previous editors reported to the publisher, there had been little, if any, discussion on this topic. Each page cost a fair amount, depending on the number of journal copies printed per issue, postage, price of paper, printing, etc. Therefore, the number of pages per issue determined a substantial proportion of the publishing cost. Since the publisher was responsible for the financial security of the journals, it was understandable that he or she would want to keep the costs as low as possible while maintaining quality.

As the number of good manuscript submissions continued to increase, it was essential for me to obtain every editorial page possible while considering the cost. That was why I eliminated every page of content that did not meet the mission of *JAMA*, which is, "To promote the science and art of medicine and the betterment of the public health."

Besides eliminating the AMA obituaries, we also eliminated the so-called "blue pages," which were dedicated to AMA news. Whereas the mission statements of *JAMA* and the AMA were essentially the same, how that mission is accomplished is far different. It was also clear that the inclusion of AMA news and policy statements was clouding the sense of *JAMA*'s editorial independence. Perception is reality to many, and I certainly did not want there to be any question about our editorial independence, especially after what had happened with the previous editor.

Eliminating those pages and the obituaries saved two or three pages for each issue. That helped, but because the average study or full article covered seven to nine pages and some even more, it was necessary to obtain more editorial pages or better utilize the pages we had. It was essential to meet the increased demand for publishing more good studies and articles.

This same page problem was obvious for the Archives journals. The Archives editors were clamoring for more pages because their submissions of good articles also increased. I was allotted a total number of pages for all journals, so I could manipulate some page allocation to the various Archives journals, depending on the relative number of submissions, circulation, and impact.

I did not want to reallocate too many pages, because I didn't want to unnecessarily frustrate some Archives editors, all of whom worked very hard to maintain excellence. I also did not want to solve *JAMA*'s page problem by allocating pages from the Archives journals to *JAMA*.

That would not be fair, and I did not do it. Instead, we planned another approach: to decrease the number of words, figures, and tables per manuscript.

Each journal page contains approximately 850 words or one to three tables and figures, depending on their sizes. We found it was quite easy to describe studies and articles, allowing seven and not eight or nine pages, for most full articles. Of course, some studies required more, and some articles required fewer pages.

The director of the manuscript (copy) editors required my permission to allow more than seven pages for an article, if needed. We also allowed extra tables and figures to be published only online, as supplements to the article. In addition, we shortened the "Commentaries" and "Editorials" to two pages. I also tried to negotiate more pages from the publisher, especially because the journals provided substantial profits to the AMA, with some success, at least early in my editorship.

CIRCULATION

The circulation of *JAMA* was well over 300,000, and the Archives circulations varied by the specialties involved. *JAMA*'s circulation was the highest among general medical journals. This was mainly because the journal was a benefit of AMA membership, which was about 230,000, including residents and medical students. The other 100,000 or so were mostly complementary, so-called "controlled circulation," the number determined by the publisher to increase potential ad sales. The advertising companies wanted the largest reach to high prescription-writing physicians and paid for ads based on circulation. Very few physicians wanted to pay for journal subscriptions, because they received so many journals free of charge or could access journals via their medical libraries.

Pharmaceutical companies determined in which journals they would place ads, based on a journal's reach or, in other words, how many physicians (prescribers) received a journal. Therefore, the complementary subscriptions went to physicians who were considered high prescribers, almost all of whom were in private practice. It seemed illogical to me not to also consider academic physicians, who frequently wrote for many prescriptions and were training future high prescribers. That should have been considered a "twofer."

With academic physicians, the advertising companies could reach current and future high prescribers, because academicians and their trainees prescribe many drugs. Moreover, many academic physicians were involved in research, which we wanted to be submitted to our journals, so therefore we wanted to assure that *JAMA* and the archives journals were in the hands of the researchers.

No matter how much time and effort I expended explaining this to the external groups, which sold ads, even deemphasizing the research part, they continued only to consider private practitioners. The high prescriber category was determined by how a physician classified himself or herself, as primarily being a clinician, which most academicians were not. Pharmaceutical companies partially paid their sales representatives by the number of prescriptions the physicians to whom they were assigned wrote for the representative' products. The pharmaceutical companies paid for such information, which was compiled by data-collecting companies.

I had a very close relationship with the AMA director of ad sales, Jeff Bonastelli, who worked for the publisher. I would meet with the external ad sales groups he would bring into AMA headquarters to discuss *JAMA*. Most importantly, he understood my reluctance to accept ads that were clearly advertorials (those ads formatted by the advertising companies to look like editorials); or that were company commentaries—that is, not naming a product but advertising the importance of needing a drug for a specific medical problem, (and of course the company would soon release such a drug for sale); or that the company didn't make it clear that the ad was indeed an ad by showing the pharmaceutical company name or logo only in a very small size.

In any case, among all general medical journals, *JAMA* had the highest income from ad sales, if total income was considered, and not by number of ad pages sold. *JAMA* did not sell ads by bulk pricing—that is, "buy three and get the fourth free" or similar, as did some other journals.

It should be noted that circulation and readership are two distinct entities. Circulation is the number of subscribers, but many individuals might read one issue of a journal, such as those placed in physicians' offices to be read by patients. Also, the number of readers who accessed the journal, via their libraries or online, could be substantial.

SPECIAL FEATURES OF *JAMA*
THE ART OF JAMA

One distinguishing feature of *JAMA* was the art on every cover, which was accompanied by an essay about the art and the artist, published inside the journal. That cover art was considered to be such a special feature that, when I was advised it was one of the things I should not eliminate, I couldn't imagine why anyone would even contemplate such a change. Fortunately, because I reported to the JOC for editorial matters, and to the EVP/CEO for administrative matters, and not to the business office, I was able to maintain the art on the cover throughout the time I was editor in chief. This was accomplished despite the wishes of the business office to place the table of contents on the cover. So much for the art of medicine!

When I started at *JAMA*, the editor in charge of art and other literary features was Roxanne Young, who had started her career at *JAMA* in 1977. *JAMA* began placing art on the cover with the April 20, 1964, issue. In 1974, Terri Southgate began selecting the art to be published and occasionally wrote an essay to accompany it. The accompanying essays about the cover became more frequent, and by 1988 essentially all cover art was accompanied by essays.

Although Terri had not practiced clinical medicine after her medical training, her ability to touch the hearts of physicians, other health professionals, and anyone who read *JAMA* was truly amazing. The one feature of *JAMA* I had read long before becoming editor in chief, was the essay accompanying art on the cover, which many considered to be one of the highlights of *JAMA*.

I was so taken with Terri's work that I called her soon after accepting the *JAMA* editorship. She immediately struck me as a grand lady, and over the years of working with her, that first impression struck true at all times. Like so many physicians, my original understanding of art emanated from reading Terri's stories. Later I learned much more about art and artists from Jim, who began writing the essays accompanying the cover art on the *Archives of General Psychiatry*, at the request of its editor. It was great fun to visit many museums throughout the world with him and return with postcards of potential art for the *JAMA* covers, which I turned over to Terri.

It only took about a year's experience at *JAMA* for me to consider the cover art and accompanying essays to be the heart of *JAMA*. Having a painting or picture on the cover was emulated by a number of very good journals; emulation is a high form of flattery that we appreciated. I negotiated with each of the Archives editors about putting paintings or pictures on the covers of their journals. The one rule was that if a painting (rather than a photograph, figure, etc.) was to be used, the painting and an accompanying essay must be related to the specialty represented by the Archives journal.

The *Archives of General Psychiatry* began publishing art and an accompanying essay for each issue, and *Archives of Pediatrics and Adolescent Medicine* published a painting and an accompanying short paragraph or two for a few issues each year. It was expensive to obtain permission to use paintings, so most journals did not use them.

The "Art of *JAMA*" was so popular that the AMA Press published a book in 1997 containing a selection of the art covers and essays. Terri planned to publish eventually all the *JAMA* art and essays, which was a very ambitious plan considering the time and effort needed to publish just one book. It was not easy to find a publisher because of the cost to obtain museum and copyright permissions for the various pieces of art and to reproduce color prints of each art piece. Nevertheless, two more Art of *JAMA* books were published in 2001 and in 2011 by Oxford University Press, after a contract had been negotiated for them to publish and sell all three books.

Terri seldom traveled, which at first surprised me because her love of art and museums was so great. I soon learned that she was a soft-spoken and private individual, who enjoyed a very private life. Terri worked from home, where she had two adjoining condominiums; one was her office with an art library and the other, her living quarters. She literally would leave her home by going out one door, and arriving at her office by walking a few steps down the hall and opening the door to her office. Who could question how any individual prefers to function, especially when she is so successful?

POETRY

In addition to the art on the cover, Roxanne Young also was responsible for supervising the poetry published in *JAMA*. The person who, like Terri for the art, handled that section on a day-to-day basis was Charlene Breedlove. Very few medical journals published poems, so physicians submitted many poems to Charlene, and some were quite good. Charlene was a master at choosing those worthy of publication in *JAMA*.

I had no idea about what made for a good poem, other than how it made me feel reading it. So I pretty much left the choices to Charlene and Roxanne and only responded to requests to provide opinions. I knew when to step aside and take the word of the "experts" while still accepting full responsibility for the publication. After all, I had chosen the "experts".

A PIECE OF MY MIND

The other *JAMA* feature I thought was special, and distinguishing, was "A Piece of My Mind." Roxanne personally handled the editorial role, and after a few months of reading all the essays to be published in this category and a number that we decided not to publish, I realized just how special this feature is. I say "we" decided on what was to be published because, while nothing could be published in *JAMA* without my permission (the buck did stop with me, after all, and I accepted full responsibility for everything published in *JAMA*), I tried to use the knowledge and experience of a number of individuals who knew more about a subject than I in almost all decisions.

I considered myself to be much like an orchestra conductor who knew the music produced was dependent on the expertise of each musician. Like any good leader, the good conductor surrounds herself with individuals who are better than he for each specific instrument or task to be accomplished. My role as the editor in chief conductor was to assure that all were playing the same tune and in synchrony. It takes many minds to create greatness.

No one knew more about the manuscripts submitted to "A Piece of My Mind" than Roxanne, who had been at *JAMA* a very long time. In fact, she had become the general "archivist" for *JAMA* and remained so at least up to the time I retired from *JAMA*. It was great fun to discuss the various submissions with her. After a while, I told her that my decisions for publication of those essays were gauged by how much I became emotionally choked up or how much they made me laugh.

It took only a short time before I labeled "A Piece of My Mind" as the soul of *JAMA*. Now *JAMA* had a soul, a heart (the art on the cover), and a brain (the scientific articles). We were a full-body journal. Who could ask for more—besides the SVP for business, I guess, who probably also wanted a full cash register? Why not?

GRAPHICS
One feature of *JAMA* I thought could be upgraded was the graphics. Ronna Siegel was the editor who managed the graphics (mostly tables and figures) by herself. Although her work was very good, I knew the

figures could be made much better if we hired a professional medical artist, and she readily agreed.

My interactions with the faculty and students in the Johns Hopkins School of Medicine's acclaimed Art as Applied to Medicine Department, had been an eye-opening experience for me. I believed that program to be so important that, while I was the vice dean for Academic Affairs and Faculty at Hopkins, I allocated money for the department to train one additional student annually. That, of course, endeared me to Gary Lees, the director, and pleased me very much, because he is such a great person who directs a world-class program.

Therefore, I rearranged *JAMA* funding so I could hire one of the Hopkins graduates, and I called Gary for some suggestions. He was delighted that one of the graduates of that program would work at *JAMA* and suggested Cassio Lynm. Cassio began working with us in the fall of 2000. He worked out so well that, a few years later, we hired Allison Burke, another graduate of the Hopkins program. The figures in *JAMA*'s science articles were greatly upgraded, and the art on the "Patient Page" was wonderfully enhanced.

It was fun to experience the reactions of the authors, who submitted their own figures for publication with their articles, some of which had been crafted by professionals at the authors' institutions. At first, almost all authors balked at our desire to have our own artist recreate the figures for their articles. However, when they were shown the final products, they were very impressed. After a while, authors requested the *JAMA* art team to create their figures. Familiarity breeds content.

CHAPTER 15

Groups and Organizations

DURING ALL MY TIME AS editor in chief, in addition to my relationship
with certain people such as the EVP/CEO and the publisher, other close
relationships with a number of groups and organizations were essential
to assuring my success as the editor in chief and, therefore, the success
of *JAMA*.

THE JOURNAL OVERSIGHT COMMITTEE

Having a journal oversight committee (JOC) was one essential criterion
without which I never would have accepted the editorship of *JAMA*,
and that proved to be very wise. I reported to this committee for all
editorial matters, so it was important that the members be very familiar
and experienced with issues related to medical journals and editorship.
Because the chairman of the AMA Board of Trustees had discussed
with me which individuals to name as the founding members of the
JOC, and I had known and respected all of them, I knew I could count
on them to be fair and understanding of any editorial issues that might
arise.

The AMA representative member on the JOC was Bob Musacchio,
the SVP for business, whom I did not know prior to my editorship but
whom I assumed also would be fair. The first chairman of the JOC
was Dr. Joshua Lederberg, a molecular biologist/geneticist with expertise in artificial intelligence. He was the former president of Rockefeller

University, who at age thirty-three had won the Nobel Prize in physiology/medicine. The dear man set a standard for the JOC members based on integrity, intelligence, excellence, compassion, and a healthy sense of humor. I will be ever indebted to him for his guidance.

The JOC met annually at the *JAMA* headquarters in Chicago, for which I would provide a general report about all of the journals. I would call Josh, as he requested I call him, and other JOC members periodically during the year for advice and sometimes just to keep in touch.

After several years with no problematic issues, Josh suggested that the JOC be disbanded, because it did not seem to be necessary. I explained to him and the other JOC members that they served as a kind of vaccine, which provided the immunity essential to prevent problems from arising. If a problem did arise, they would be readily available to help me sort it out. Little did I know just how important the JOC would become, as I will discuss later.

Josh and the next chair, Dr. Frank Davidoff, the former editor of *Annals of Internal Medicine,* chaired the JOC through mostly serene times. Unfortunately, that was not true for the third chair, Dr. Jordan Cohen, a former dean and president of the American Association of Medical Colleges. Like the previous two chairs, Jordie, as he requested I call him, also provided sound leadership for the JOC. I can never adequately express my gratitude to him for the guidance and unyielding support he provided through some very difficult episodes. But I'm getting ahead of myself.

The Media

Interacting with the media was another great learning experience. Soon after I arrived at *JAMA*, I needed to hire a new director of *JAMA* Communications. After interviewing Jan Ingmire, the choice was easy, and Jan proved to be an invaluable source of warding off possible media harassment and trouble. I quickly learned not to respond to almost any call from media persons and to have all of those calls referred to Jan in the Communications Office. She and her staff were masters of diplomacy and protected me just as well as, or even better than, my imaginary "Uncle Guido," who I kidded was my ever-present protector.

Toward the end of my editorship, there were only three reporters whom I trusted enough to call me directly and not have to go through the Communications office. Subsequent experience with one of them was so traumatic that it caused me great sadness. However, at this point in time, the Great Comedian was obviously only in the planning stage for mischief.

Interacting with the media was time consuming, but they were very important in making the general public aware of the articles we published and in advancing the reputations of *JAMA* and the Archives journals. Having a media story about a study or article we had published not only provided the public with important medical information, but it was also great publicity and heightened the importance of the study in the public's eye. In addition, the media provided authors with exposure, which was appreciated by them, their institutions, and of course their mothers. Such public exposure of our articles also provided impetus for other investigators to consider submitting their important studies to *JAMA* and the Archives journals.

In order to promote such coverage with the media, every week Phil and I, along with the Archives editors, would choose a few studies that were scheduled to be published the following week and alert Jan of our choices. She and her team would then write short summaries of the study, in language easily understood by the public. Phil or I—after a while Phil did the vast majority of them—would review what Jan's team had written to assure scientific accuracy.

Finally, those summaries were put on a special website available only to media persons approved by the communication team. The special site was to assure only trusted media persons had early access to our upcoming articles. The summary information was put online for them a few days before the embargo time expired, to enable reporters to have time to prepare their stories for print or broadcast. Of course, we made the entire articles available to them also, but it was surprising to me how many times the media reports were very close to the summaries we had provided.

The embargo was a ban against publishing *JAMA* material before we published it. Embargo was used by *JAMA*, and almost all biomedical journals, to assure that something we would be publishing in our next issue would not be published or "scooped" in the public media before we our issue came out. It was a means to assure fair access to journal material by all media outlets.

Some reporters were upset by that rule and believed they had the right to publish or publically discuss a journal article as soon as they were made aware of it. That hardly seemed fair, considering the time, energy, and funding expended by journals to have the articles peer reviewed, revised, and published. Therefore, if a reporter broke the embargo without a legitimate reason, he or she would be removed from our special online service for prepublication alerts. That almost never happened, because on the rare occasion of an embargo break, there usually was a logical explanation. One example involved a young reporter from a European newspaper who published an article based on the local time in his country, and not on US time.

Another interesting aspect of the required embargo time was my erroneous assumption that only the smaller news outlets benefitted from and wanted it. When I discussed possibly eliminating the embargo with various reporters, they all were in favor of keeping the embargo. When I questioned this response from reporters who worked for the big newspapers, they said that it protected them because if they were "scooped" by another newspapers, their editors would be very upset. Also, they appreciated having the summaries provided. I told them that if we eliminated the embargo, we would still provide the summaries, only they would not be released until just before we made the articles available directly from *JAMA* and the Archives. That did not please the reporters, because it would mean extra work for them, even though sometimes they wrote more extensive reports based on articles. It also would mean that they had much less time to prepare their reports.

The importance of our summaries became even more evident as news media eliminated some of their staff. Often reporters had to cover several areas and were not as knowledgeable as those assigned only to medical or scientific areas. In any case, our relationship with the general media via our Communication Office was vital.

Presentations at Meetings

Another way of getting national and international exposure for *JAMA* was oral presentations—that Phil or I primarily delivered—at meetings. I had a flash drive with PowerPoint presentations (godsends, after experiencing the former slide-show paraphernalia that had once been needed for such presentations) and actually enjoyed speaking at these meetings. I had plenty of experience speaking publically as an academic.

One problem for me was that, from my Italian genes I suppose, I spoke while using both of my hands for emphasis. So when I was handed a microphone, along with a remote control to advance the slides, I would look at the audience and ask how they expected me to speak with both hands tied up. That usually stimulated a laugh, and the rest was simple. I knew that laughter from the audience was one way to assure their attention, so I peppered my presentations with jokes or puns. I continue to do that and still receive many requests to speak at national and international meetings. I am convinced it is at least partially because audiences like my jokes and puns, which usually make specific points.

A New AMA EVP/CEO

In mid 2001, Andy left the AMA after a disagreement with the AMA Board of Trustees, the nature of which I still don't understand. Notwithstanding my lack of understanding, I knew I would miss him a great deal. Our relationship had been conducive to working hard and promoting *JAMA* and the Archives journals while being assured that the AMA appreciated our efforts.

The AMA Board of Trustees selected a search committee to find a new EVP/CEO. All SVPs were asked to interview the candidates, and I looked forward to meeting the candidates for this very important position. I was curious to find out what sorts of backgrounds the candidates would have. I was certain the position would be filled by a physician, but beyond that, I could imagine a variety of experiences the new EVP/CEO might bring.

At that point AMA membership was decreasing annually. Of the approximately 900,000 physicians in the United States, only 230,000 or so, including medical students and residents, belonged to the AMA. It was clear that whatever else, the new EVP/CEO would have the task of increasing membership numbers at the top or close to the top of his or her list of things that must be done. I was happy that *JAMA* and the Archives were thriving and were a good source of sound reputation and revenue for the AMA.

The day after I met with the first candidate, Dr. Michael Maves, I received a call from the then-SVP for Human Resources (I worked with three of them at the AMA). She asked for my opinion of the candidate for the EVP/CEO position. I told her that I could not provide an opinion, per se, and all I could do was give my reaction to a half hour interview with Dr. Maves. Based on my experiences of having interviewed hundreds of candidates for all sorts of positions, the cursory interview, in the time allowed, was very limited in providing information necessary to help make a hiring decision.

In retrospect, my opinion, and that of others who were provided the same time frame in which to make determinations, were not really going to make much difference, but were mostly a courtesy. That way of hiring for key positions is not all that unusual for many organizations. In addition to its being a courtesy, the interviews with non–board members was to make sure there was no fatal flaw unrecognized by the board members. This way of hiring someone, of course, was the prerogative of the AMA BOT members, who were responsible for supervising the EVP/CEO.

Not realizing at first what was expected of me, and in order to provide better information for the search committee to consider along with the other information they would have, I wanted another day to make some calls to my colleagues who had knowledge of Dr. Maves. I also wanted to find out what other candidates there were. That was how I had contributed my comments after interviews in the past.

The Human Resources SVP told me that there were no other candidates and that my opinion, based on the half hour, was all that was requested of me. My reaction was that I couldn't believe the search committee could only find one candidate for such an excellent and high-visibility position, but if there was only one candidate, he already was chosen for the job, and my opinion wouldn't really matter.

Given that was all I was expected to provide, I told the SVP for Human Resources that Dr. Maves seemed to be an affable gentleman, who was very polite, dressed appropriately for the interview, and had some basic knowledge of *JAMA* and the Archives. I did not tell her that I had already called a few colleagues, prior to meeting Dr. Maves, who provided mixed reviews about how successful he had been in his previous two positions. Because I had only had time for one conversation about each of his previous positions, I didn't think it would be fair to state what I'd been told. Besides, I assumed the search committee had already performed due diligence and knew what characteristics they wanted in the new EVP/CEO. I decided time would tell how successful Dr. Maves would be in his new position, and I looked forward to working with him and helping him to succeed.

After he was hired, he asked me to call him Mike. One of the first things I did with Mike (not to be confused with Mike Johns, whom I will refer to by his full name going forward) was to coauthor an editorial, making my reporting relationship clear. As previously mentioned, I reported directly to the EVP/CEO for all business issues and to a JOC for all editorial issues. It was very important to officially publish that in a *JAMA* issue, so there would be no misunderstanding by anyone. To report the reporting relationship turned out to be a wise decision, especially for some future AMA Board of Trustees members and some AMA delegates.

AMA HOUSE OF DELEGATES

I attended most of the biannual AMA House of Delegates (HOD) meetings, and especially the main annual meetings, which were held in Chicago. At the Chicago meetings, we discussed and voted on major issues, and the new officers were officially announced. All previous AMA presidents who could attend were present on stage in formal dress at the closing session. A formal ball, which was quite a gala affair to honor the new president, was the closing event of those meetings. I attended the interim meetings, not held in Chicago, for only a day or two, in order to give my *JAMA* and Archives journal report to the AMA BOT members.

My second Chicago meeting (the first had been when I was introduced to the HOD, which I discussed previously) was a fascinating experience for me. I thought it resembled a political convention, at least as I had seen them on television. I assumed that was because there were about a thousand delegates, representing all fifty state medical societies, and each of those various medical specialty societies that had representative delegates.

At my first dinner with the group, Jim and I were assigned to sit with the incoming AMA president and his wife. The president's wife told me that her husband had told her, the day he graduated from medical school, that his wish was to one day become president of the AMA, and his dream had now come true. I am grateful to her for sharing that story, which helped me gain much better understanding of the workings of the AMA, and especially its leadership.

An incident involving the HOD taught me a great deal about the importance of having published the joint editorial including the administrative flow chart in *JAMA*, which specified to whom I reported for business and to whom for editorial matters. In 2003 I published a peer-reviewed article dealing with physicians accepting gifts, and that article differed from the AMA policy. The members of one state society, including the main delegate from that state, objected to that article. They wanted *JAMA* to publish only articles that agreed with AMA policy.

The publisher, the SVP for business to whom the publisher reported, and I had a cordial meeting with the state representative and several other delegates from his state. We attempted to explain why *JAMA* couldn't publish only articles that agreed with AMA policy. We showed them the published administrative plan, and I showed them the following statement printed on the masthead of every *JAMA* issue: "All articles published, including editorials, letters, and book reviews, represent the opinions of the authors and do not reflect the policy of the American Medical Association, the editorial board, or the institution with which the author is affiliated, unless that is clearly specified."

That did not satisfy the delegates, and they submitted a resolution to the HOD's next meeting. That resolution would require that when *JAMA* published an article not in keeping with AMA policy, an article stating the AMA policy must be published in the same issue. This was simply not acceptable for an editorially independent journal. Therefore, two members of the JOC came to the annual AMA meeting in Chicago, where that resolution was to be discussed and voted on, to speak against the resolution.

I also attended the meeting, expecting a major verbal battle, as did most members of the BOT and the JOC. When the resolution was introduced to the HOD, a number of people got in line to speak. The first to speak was the main delegate from the state that had introduced the resolution. He argued that because the AMA owned *JAMA*, it had the right to dictate how editorial freedom was to be interpreted and rendered. He stated that it seemed that editorial freedom should be only for scientific articles. However, I had explained to him that defining "scientific" would be arguable, and that editorial freedom was for all articles.

He therefore thought it was fair to at least provide equal coverage by the AMA for articles that didn't follow AMA policy.

The second speaker was also from the same state and essentially presented the same arguments. At that point I walked to the end of the line of speakers. I noticed that the BOT members seemed nervous when I joined the line. I thought surely they knew I would never embarrass or denigrate anyone, especially being a guest, so to speak, in their house. However, I did want to explain why I disagreed with the resolution.

Neither the BOT nor I should have worried, because the next half dozen or so speakers spoke avidly against the resolution. Notable to me one was a delegate from the Massachusetts Medical Society, who stated that despite their ownership of the *journal*, no such requirement was made by their state society for the *New England Journal of Medicine*. The final speakers before me were the two members of the JOC who discussed why complete editorial freedom was essential for *JAMA*.

I then spoke and thanked the HOD for allowing me to speak. I told them I was very proud to be the editor in chief of the editorially independent *JAMA* and Archives journals and would continue to work hard to make the AMA proud of the journals. I meant every word, and the reaction of the HOD was to clap loudly. At that moment, I could not have been happier. Later, one of the BOT members told me that they had been concerned when they saw me get in line to speak, because they thought that I was going to resign. I told him that I was a fighter, not a quitter, he told me that he certainly knew that, and we both laughed.

Because I respected the main delegate from the state that had made the resolution, at a break, I gave a *JAMA* sweatshirt to him saying that I hoped he would wear it someday. He immediately hugged me and said he would be proud to wear it. Several members of that state delegation later told me that he did wear it. Such is the nature of individuals who believe in something sufficiently to work hard for it, but who respect others who feel as strongly for an opposing view and work equally hard for it. That is equity at its finest.

The ICMJE

One of the most enjoyable experiences I had associated with being the editor in chief of *JAMA* was that I became a member of the International Committee of Medical Journal Editors (ICMJE). When I first joined *JAMA*, this organization—or group would be a more accurate term—was composed of the editors of the *Annals of Internal Medicine*, the *Australian Medical Journal*, the *British Medical Journal*, the *Canadian Medical Journal*, the *Danish Medical Journal*, *JAMA*, the *Lancet*, the *Netherlands Medical Journal*, the *New England Journal of Medicine*, the *New Zealand Medical Journal*, and the *Norwegian Medical Journal*. The committee also had a member from the National Library of Medicine, and the *Croatian Medical Journal* was added a few years later. The *Medical Journal of Chile* and the *Chinese Medical Journal* were added much later, in an effort to be more globally representative.

The ICMJE is a well-respected committee and has published guidelines for medical publications that are of great value to editors, authors, reviewers, and many others. The committee meets annually, hosted by one of the editors at his or her journal's home city. Occasionally, a guest who presents an issue of current importance to the group attends the annual meeting. In the summer of 2004, we met in Dubrovnik, Croatia, and I asked the group to discuss a problem I found to be especially troublesome.

Many randomized clinical trials, considered to be the highest level of medical research studies, are submitted to journals. They are the only studies that show cause, not just a statistical association, and are welcomed by editors. I was disturbed because, although many of the clinical trials I received seemed to be well designed and scientifically conducted, I was certain there had been other clinical trials testing the same drug. However, I could find no reference of those trials in the submitted manuscripts or any record of the trials in the National Library of Medicine clinical trials site, <u>clinicaltrials.gov</u>.

The law in the United States stated that all clinical trials were to be registered at clinicaltrials.gov, at the time the first subject was enrolled in the trial. Although there were many clinical trials under way or completed, only a very small number were registered. Clearly no one was enforcing the law.

I was delighted when every one of the international editors agreed that this was a significant problem. After discussion, we all agreed that, whereas we had no legal jurisdiction, we could facilitate clinical trial registration by not publishing or even reviewing any submitted clinical trial that had not been properly registered. It was a minor miracle that twelve editors could agree on anything, much less something that would affect publication of highly sought clinical research studies.

We agreed that we would announce our plan in a joint editorial, to be published the same week in all our journals. We would allow the clinical-trial investigators one year from the date our joint editorial was published to register all ongoing clinical trials. Thereafter, all new clinical trials would have to be registered when the first human subject was enrolled. That joint editorial was published in October 2004, and the reactions it caused was amazing. The reactions ranged from near apoplexy by the pharmaceutical company executives to applause from the National Library of Medicine leaders, who had been trying to enforce the registration of clinical trials for years.

As soon as word got out that we planned to publish that editorial, there was such an outcry from "Big Pharma," (a term I will use to mean pharmaceutical and medical-device companies, unless otherwise specified) that I asked the officials of the Institute of Medicine (IOM) of the National Academy of Sciences to host, not sponsor (that's a very important distinction), a meeting. Invitees were the Big Pharma company representatives, the ICMJE editors, and any government officials interested in the issue.

Hosting our meeting meant only that the IOM allowed us to use their facility. Sponsoring the meeting would have implied that the meeting was funded or supported by the IOM. The IOM president very kindly agreed to host the meeting, which they held in the Washington,

DC, headquarters of the IOM, several months after the joint editorial had been published.

A number of members from the major pharmaceutical companies and representatives of the Federal Drug Administration (FDA) attended the meeting. I represented the ICMJE, at the members' suggestion and with their permission, of course. The pharmaceutical representatives claimed that the ICMJE editors were attempting to restrain their companies from conducting research in a secretive environment, which is necessary to prevent competitors from knowing about their plans for new drugs. I said that was ridiculous, because as soon as the first human subject was enrolled, any interested party had easy access to information that such a study was underway. Also, as per the law, we were not requiring the registration of anything that would interfere with the protection of their products.

When they hinted that the editors' behavior might be bordering on restraint of trade, I pointed out that there were thousands of biomedical journals where they could publish their studies, whereas we represented only twelve of them. A representative from the FDA asked me why I cared about this issue. My response to him was first to clarify that he was from the FDA. When he assured me that he was, I said, "Sir, I care because I don't think the FDA does." A gasp went up from those present. I ameliorated my bold statement by pointing out that US law required registration of clinical trials when the first patient was registered, but no one, including the FDA, was doing anything to assure enforcement.

I further explained that the pharmaceutical companies were using the peer-review process and reputations of our journals to market their products. They distributed printed copies of research studies about their drugs, published in our journals, to promote their drugs to physicians. If the companies wanted to use the integrity of our journals and the editors' personal integrity to promote their products, we had the right to make rules for what we would publish.

The meeting ended cordially after more discussion, but with no change in what the joint editorial had clearly stated. During the next few months, there was not very much action with registration of clinical trials. We assumed the investigators were waiting until the last minute to register their ongoing clinical trials. Procrastination seems to be human nature, especially when we are required to do something that is either unpleasant or not deemed important. I was becoming a bit worried when the week before the deadline, there still was not much action in clinical trial registration, which I checked periodically on the clinicaltrials.gov site.

Early in the last week before the deadline, a manuscript dealing with a clinical trial was submitted to *JAMA*. That study looked strong and we normally would have sent out for peer review, but it had not been registered. I called the corresponding author / principal investigator and told him I would like to have his manuscript peer reviewed, but that was not possible because it lacked documentation of having been registered. To my surprise, he claimed ignorance of the requirement, so I referred him to the published joint editorial.

After he had read the joint editorial, he called me back and told me he would get right back to me after he'd registered the trial. I didn't hear from him until the next day, when he told me that he couldn't register the trial because the study's sponsor, a pharmaceutical company, wouldn't allow it. That was no surprise to me.

I told him I was sorry but could not accept the manuscript without registration, though I mentioned that he had two more days until the deadline. Because I didn't want to harm him for a decision that unfortunately was not under his control, I advised him to withdraw the manuscript. He was very upset, especially when it became clear that he would receive the same response from eleven other high-impact journals. All authors want to publish in high-impact journals because of their reach, and academic promotion and reputation are often based on where their work is published.

The morning of the deadline I received a call from the happy author with the registration number. He told me that, after a somewhat-heated discussion with the pharmaceutical sponsor representative, they both agreed that the ICMJE editors were serious about what we had published in the editorial, and they decided to register the trial. What I didn't know at the time is that the same scenario was being played out with another ICMJE editor, involving a different study and another Big Pharma sponsor, with the same result. I assume the pharmaceutical company sponsors were testing us, and much to their chagrin, we passed that test with flying colors.

The following week, I received a call from the director of the National Library of Medicine, a member of the *JAMA* Editorial Board, who was thrilled with the response regarding the registration. He jokingly told me that he couldn't decide whether to hug or to choke me, because thousands of studies had been submitted for registration just before the deadline. In fact, in the two weeks between September 4, 2005, and September 23, 2005, about six thousand clinical trials were registered. Because of this onslaught of submissions, he had to employ additional, part-time staff to manage the increased work.

As a result of this action on clinical-trial registration by a few serious editors, published randomized clinical trial articles could now include information about previous other trials, involving the same drug or device. This could be accomplished in two ways. One way was to have the published clinical trials include the results of those previous clinical trials, if they had been published. Another way was simply to state that the other trials had been conducted but were never published. This nonpublication could have been the result of the clinical trial having been stopped earl, because the results were not what the sponsors (Big Pharma) had wanted, inability to register a sufficient number of subjects to attain power of proof, the study having been rejected for publication by journals, or for some other reason. Importantly, this information now would be available to the readers, who could determine the results of the newly published trial in full light of all trials on the product.

Forcing the registration of clinical trials along with the other ICMJE editors, is one of my proudest accomplishments as editor in chief of *JAMA*. It resulted in equitable reporting of drug and medical-device trials, thereby protecting the public's health.

A New Place to Live

In November of 2003, the end of my fourth year of editorship, it was time to consider signing a new contract. By mutual agreement with the AMA, my new contract had to be signed twelve months before the expiration of the current contract. Because I reported to Mike for all business issues, I met with him to discuss my new contract. Our meeting was short and cordial, and we reached an agreement immediately.

At that point in time, I planned on being the editor in chief of *JAMA* until about December of 2009. That would mean serving ten years, plus perhaps a year or two more if appropriate. I believed that would be about the right amount of time for anyone to stay in such a position. Overstaying in a position of power is probably one of the biggest reasons there is so much trouble with politicians who stay in power so long. As I have quoted Mark Twain previously and what bears repeating, "Politicians and diapers should be changed often and for the same reason."

The new contract meant that Jim and I had to plan for a more permanent place to live. We had been living in an apartment in downtown Chicago, on a floor high enough to see the beauty of Lake Michigan and the Chicago skyline. When I first started at *JAMA* in 2000, we had planned for Jim to stay in Baltimore, and that we'd commute on weekends to see each other. However, it soon became clear that was a bad plan for us.

Back then, on one of my weekend trips back to Baltimore, after a few weeks of being away from each other most of the time, I took one of his T-shirts out of the laundry and took it back to Chicago with me. I put it on the pillow next to me and would curl up to the pillow when I went to sleep. While this helped a little, it wasn't nearly enough, and Jim wasn't faring much better. Perhaps other couples can tolerate being away from each other, but that was not possible for us. As I mentioned earlier, Jim and I are like two old shoes; we do not look so good anymore, but we surely feel very comfortable together. I suppose that feeling is what love is all about.

Jim took a leave of absence from Hopkins and moved to Chicago about six months after I did. He returned to Baltimore once a month to conduct his special clinic at Hopkins and to spend a day or so working on the part of his research project that could not be managed from Chicago. That plan and living in an apartment worked well, until we knew that we would be in Chicago for at least another six years. In addition, we were about to lose the beautiful view of Lake Michigan because another high-rise building was being constructed across the street from our apartment.

It was also very difficult to maintain our beautiful, but old, house in Baltimore. We decided to sell it and buy a condominium in Baltimore for when we returned to Hopkins. We also wanted to purchase a condo in Chicago, where we would live until I finished my editorship. We knew the wonderful memories associated with our Baltimore house would remain with us forever, but change was necessary.

We soon purchased a condo in Chicago in Lake Point Tower, a beautiful building on Lake Michigan, which had been designed by the famous architect Ludwig Mies van der Rohe. We had a friend in Baltimore who was a real estate agent and who helped us find a very nice condo on the first floor of a building only few blocks from our former Baltimore house. We purchased it without my seeing it. Jim had sent me pictures, and I fell in love with the walled-in garden; that was good enough for me.

We sold our Baltimore house to the Calvert School, the private school that was located right next door whose headmaster had built or house originally. Our real estate agent told us our selling price was much lower than the market, but we wanted the children of Calvert School to have the property where we had so enjoyed their presence next door to us. In the end, we all were happy with the sales and purchases, Jim and I were together in in our Chicago condo, and we had our condo home in Baltimore for the future.

CHAPTER 16

Dr. De Hits a Bus

AFTER OUR ADVENTURES IN ISTANBUL and with the required registration of clinical trials, everything continued to function well at *JAMA* and the Archives journals. I continued to travel as the job dictated, although I was only able to accept about a third of the invitations I received to speak at various meetings.

I tried to choose those most important to advancing *JAMA* and the Archives. So it was that on a Friday afternoon, in mid-December of 2004, I was preparing to attend a meeting in Puerto Rico, where Jim and I both had been invited to speak. After the frightening incident in Istanbul, except for Canada and London, he and I never travel alone outside the United States.

I left my office about five thirty that afternoon, so I could pack for the next morning's trip. While I was walking home from the office in the rain, I had another life-changing event. No matter the weather, I always enjoyed the one-mile walk from my office to our condo. I was standing on the sidewalk on the corner across from our condo building, waiting for the light to change so I could cross the street. It was a dreary, cold December day, and the drizzling rain and wind were coming from my left side, where I had tilted my umbrella for protection.

The last thing I remember is looking at the red hand alert on the traffic light across the street, thinking that I was going to get wet when the light changed. I planned to lift the umbrella and look to my left, to make sure it was safe to cross the one-way street. Childhood lessons about crossing the street don't disappear easily, especially when repeated almost daily by your mother.

The next thing I remembered I was in the emergency room of Northwestern University Hospital, lying on a gurney. I was very dizzy and nauseated, and a nurse was holding an emesis basin, telling me not to close my eyes. I again blanked out and awoke to see Jim standing at my side. The ER staff had notified him that I had been hit by a Chicago Transit Authority (CTA) bus. He had run to the emergency room, located about a half mile from our condominium. He walked into the radiology suite, where I was about to have a CT brain scan, and called my name.

I looked at him and was very confused. He said, "Are you in pain? You've been hit by a CTA bus." I told him I was very dizzy, nauseated, had a bad headache, and my left side hurt a lot. After the various tests were completed that evening, we were told that I had a bad concussion, with small subarachnoid and subdural bleeding in the right parietal area of my brain. Also, my pelvis was broken in two places on my left side. Fortunately, these fractures would allow weight bearing, and I didn't need surgery. Over the next eight hours or so, serial CT brain scans showed that the bleeding remained minimal and did not progress.

I was admitted to the hospital, and by the next day, when I knew that I could walk with the assistance of a walker, and that the bleeding was not progressing, I wanted to go home. After one night in the hospital, I thought I could heal as well or better at home. The pain, dizziness, and nausea continued, but I knew I could control them at home.

The nurses and doctors were wonderful, but anyone who has ever been admitted to a hospital will understand my desire to go home. I was released from the hospital that afternoon and given an appointment for a few days later, to meet with the neurologist and with the physiotherapists.

The morning before discharge, Mike visited me in the hospital and was relieved that I was doing well. That was a very kind gesture on his part, especially because I had requested that the *JAMA* staff not visit, even though they were very worried about me. I planned to go to the office the day after I was released from the hospital, in order to show the staff that I was OK. The next morning, my administrative assistant picked me up in her car. Jim and I had never taken our cars to Chicago, because I walked the mile to and from my office, and public transportation was excellent (except, of course, for when the CTA buses were hitting pedestrians).

Annette met me outside the building with a wheelchair. I have no idea where she found it, but leave it to a nurse to have done so. She wheeled me into the manuscript room, where all the *JAMA* staff waited apprehensively. It was clear that they were not certain how badly I had been injured and did not know what to expect.

I assured them that I was just fine, except for continued dizziness from what turned out to be postconcussion BPPV (benign positional paroxysmal vertigo). I told them I was just a bit dizzier than usual, and they were not to worry about me. I even got out of the wheelchair and held on to the table to show them that I could walk with support.

I assured them that with time I wouldn't need any support, except the usual support I received from them. We all hugged and ate the chocolate cake someone had brought for the meeting. How better to assure everyone that life would go on than to eat chocolate? They had great fun thereafter telling people, "Dr. De hit a bus." What a bunch of wonderful smart alecks they were.

Jim and I had planned to spend the Christmas holidays with family in Pennsylvania, flying from Chicago a few days after we returned from the Puerto Rico meeting, which we'd missed. We always took a vacation the last two weeks of December, so we could spend the holidays with family. Most of my family still lived in Pennsylvania, where Jim's brother and sister would visit for the holidays.

Usually we'd fly from Chicago, but because of my concussion with brain bleeding, (that thank God had stopped), I was advised not to fly. So Jim rented a car, and we left very early the next morning. He drove for thirteen hours, stopping about every two hours so I could stretch my legs. It was not very comfortable sitting in a car with a fractured pelvis.

We had planned to stop halfway and spend the night in a motel, but we were so anxious to get home, Jim drove all the way. Although I had always enjoyed arriving home for the holidays since I was in college, this time was a special gift for my family and me. We all knew that I would never have been home again, at least not alive, if the bus had hit me in a different way, and I had landed in front of instead of the side of the bus. While I was still on the sidewalk, The driver had made an illegal left turn, but thankfully had hit me on my left side and knocked me to the right and backwards. I had probably hit my heat on the sidewalk causing the concussion.

It was easy to heal at home, surrounded by my loving family and friends. Good food, good wine, and good humor are great healers. I couldn't sleep lying down, because of the vertigo, but as long as I kept my head upright there was no dizziness except, as Jim would say, for my usual state. I was able to keep up with the goings on at the *JAMA* office by calling in for the manuscript meetings and by speaking with Phil every day. The manuscripts could be handled online, so there was no interruption in my work or play. I was confident that I would return to *JAMA* after New Year's Day, refreshed and well on the way to complete healing.

That was exactly what happened. I used two canes to walk for the first two months back at work, one cane for another month, and thereafter I needed no support to walk. I never missed a planned day of work and was able to travel to meetings with no interruption.

The several months' experience of walking with canes and dealing with dizziness allowed me to empathize, on some level, with individuals who lived with those ailments for life. We don't appreciate how lucky we are to have health until some malady or accident takes it away. I know this and other such experiences helped to make me a better doctor.

Probably because it would be temporary, traveling through airports with the aid of a wheelchair was an exciting experience. Getting through the TSA lines with a wheelchair pushed by an attendant was a breeze. Since then, the closest I've come to that expediency is by having TSA Precheck and Global Access. Again, every cloud has some silver lining, but I really wouldn't recommend my particular experience to find one.

Another interesting aspect of being hit by the CTA bus was legal in nature. Soon after I had returned to work, several of the staff suggested that I consider suing the CTA, because the bus driver had hit me while I was on the sidewalk. They also told me about others, including another person in our building, who also had been hit by a CTA bus while standing on the sidewalk. I contacted a very fine attorney, who tried very hard to fight the Chicago political system, which controlled the CTA. He had little success...no surprise there.

Over the next five years, he and another attorney he had suggested, who had more experience with the Chicago legal system, also tried to arrange for a trial, which I wanted. We even went through a process with an arbitrator, a former, very experienced Chicago judge, who believed we had a valid case. He also suggested a fair settlement fee that I might consider negotiating, knowing how difficult it would be to get a jury trial. I wasn't so interested in the monetary settlement, because I thought it was more important that a jury and the public be aware of the CTA workings. For example, the bus was required to have a camera on board, which was very important in my case, because the bus was empty and on the way to the garage at the day's end for that driver. Interestingly, and conveniently, that camera reportedly did not record that trip.

In any case, the litigation dragged on for five years. A few months before I was to leave Chicago, my attorney suggested that I settle the case for an amount nowhere near what the arbitrator, who had died, had suggested. The amount I was to receive was less than what the attorney would receive, which I knew was not unusual, but I refused to allow that to happen. So we had a discussion, and the attorney agreed that I would receive a small amount more than his fee. Because I had intended to donate a significant amount of the settlement to Maryknoll Sisters, the

Medical Missionary Sisters, and to Saint Joseph's Center in Scranton, Pennsylvania, my only regret was that the amount would be less than it might have been. The Great Comedian works in strange ways.

My Second Five-Year Contract Years

I returned to Chicago in January of 2004 with my two canes, enthusiastic to finish the last year of my first contract, and to plan for my second five-year commitment, which would end on December 31, 2009, unless it was extended or terminated by me or for legal cause. I wanted 2004 and thereafter to continue to be banner years, with new initiatives to expand and enrich *JAMA* and the Archives journals. Now that all manuscript management was completely online, we could work more efficiently and effectively and expand plans to make the journals better.

Because I was an AMA SVP directly reporting to the EVP/CEO (Mike), I attended the weekly meetings of those SVPs, who also reported directly to the EVP/CEO. (I hate alphabet soup, but it makes writing and reading easier). During those meetings, each of us reported on the major happenings in our departments, and Mike provided us with his report about general AMA matters, as he saw fit. In addition, we discussed various items Mike and others brought forth.

In 2004, Mike hired a man to assist him in making the AMA more visible and in promoting membership to the AMA. To that end, substantial funding was expended to develop a new logo, which resulted in the new AMA logo being "Together we are stronger." When I jokingly changed the second *o* to an *a*, thereby editing the word *stronger* to read *stranger*, most people laughed, but a few individuals did not appreciate my humor. I have found that because we all have foibles, if you can't laugh at yourself, you'll never enjoy life. But there are some individuals with big egos who cannot endure truth, even when stated in jest. I can only feel very sorry for them because, after all, we all are a bit strange.

Another initiative meant to stimulate membership in the AMA, was to sponsor one Friday evening reception with refreshments for medical students from the five Chicago medical schools. You can almost guarantee attendance by medical students if you provide refreshments. This reception was to feature various booths to promote the AMA. I agreed this was a very good plan, which could demonstrate the interests and workings of the AMA, especially as related to medical students.

There was to be a Blackberry mobile device as a prize, with the winner to be drawn from cards completed by those students who spent time at the AMA Membership booth. I pointed out that the proposed prize cost more than the hundred-dollar limit set by AMA policy regarding gifts to physicians. A few individuals did not appreciate that reminder, but they did change the prize. The person who had these expensive bright ideas left the AMA in 2007, after a number of his other plans proved to be dubiously cost-effective.

I was not trying to be obstructive but did express some surprised at how much money was being spent on these and other such projects, when there were so many other initiatives that needed to be addressed that also could advance the reputation of the AMA. I suppose that, like most others, I could have simply sat back and agreed with everything proposed and complained about it in private. But that simply is not my nature. Fortunately for the AMA, the chief financial officer was a very smart woman who effectively managed to keep the AMA financially healthy.

In late 2005 Mike hired a chief operating officer, who would also report directly to him. This gentleman had just retired from a leadership position in a Chicago-based commercial-property and casualty insurance provider. He was to take direct charge of all business and information technology aspects of the AMA, including those issues pertaining to the journals. Over the years he certainly changed the functioning of those operations. Fortunately, my official responsibilities as an AMA SVP were miniscule compared with the responsibilities associated with the editorship, and we were making great progress on that front. Therefore, my relationship with the COO was mostly indirect, at least at first.

One thing I had learned early in my career was that leaders should always plan for their replacement. After all, you must consider that you might get hit by a bus someday. Oh, that's right, I'd already been there, done that, and survived, but I still planned for the worst. Jim believes that I should not always worry and plan for the worst, but I tell him that for a woman, that is a very good way to prevent disaster. Hope for the best, but plan for the worst, and rejoice when it doesn't happen. In fact, such planning is one reason for much of the success I've had in leadership positions.

I knew that Phil was clearly very well suited for the editorship of *JAMA* or any other similar journal. The only important experience he did not possess at the time was in business. Therefore, we arranged for him to attend a business school, on a part-time basis, to obtain his MBA degree. He decided on the program at Notre Dame University and completed his degree in 2005, having attended classes at the Chicago campus on weekends and nights and twice spending a few weeks on the Notre Dame main campus during his vacation. Knowing Phil's ethics, his choosing Notre Dame was no surprise to me. It also solidified our mutual enthusiasm for Notre Dame football, which continues to border on fanaticism.

HAPPY MEMORIES OF SHARED PARTIES
Some of my fondest memories of the AMA are those times the AMA senior staff (the EVP/CEO, SVPs, chief general council, and the chief financial officer,) got together just for fun, and also when the senior staff met with the BOT members for informal parties, usually on an evening following the formal annual meeting.

One of the best senior staff get-togethers was an event in which we all were invited to cook our best Italian pasta dishes. Essentially that meant cooking (or brewing) our favorite sauces (or gravies, depending on where you grew up in the United States), which would be poured over already cooked pasta. Mike's administrative assistant, who is aptly named Maria, organized this particular evening. Almost everyone submitted his or her home-cooked sauce, and everyone participated in the tasting and voting. Despite there being several submitted sauces cooked by those of us of Italian descent, the winner was someone who had no Italian heritage and was not known to be a great cook. Go figure.

Importantly, we all had a great deal of fun cooking and eating together, with no discussions related to work. The wine and food only added to the comradeship we felt at that and other similar get-togethers. Unfortunately, all those great occasions only happened in the early to mid-2000s, but ceased thereafter for some unknown reason.

Fortunately, the senior staff get-togethers with the BOT continued, and are still going on as far as I know.

The best of those were the ones held at the country home of one of the BOT officers, or at other sites in rural parts of the country. Food cooked outdoors and eaten with friendship, song, and wine does a great deal to engender great human relationships. Especially during those times, I was able to establish solid relationships with a number of very fine physicians who led the AMA. I will always be grateful for those shared, joyful times.

THE OFFICE OF THE GENERAL COUNSEL

One support office I especially appreciated was the Office of General Counsel (OGC), especially because an attorney was assigned specifically to *JAMA* and the Archives journals. When I arrived at *JAMA*, the attorney assigned to us was Wayne Hoppe, who was well versed in legal issues related to journals and very adept when legal questions arose. He also had been very helpful to Jim and me during our escapade in Istanbul. Working with Wayne was a real joy, especially because legal issues could be a real problem. He approached sticky legal matters with an assurance that generated confidence.

In the spring of 2004, Wayne had a major disagreement with his supervisor, the general counsel (head of the OGC). As a result,

Mike came to my office for a discussion, which unfortunately only seemed to happen when he was in need of my help. While I understood the reluctance of some EVP/CEOs to meet in any SVP's office, this particular visit alerted me to be careful. During that meeting in my office, Mike suggested that because Wayne and I got along so well, would I like to have him report directly to me, instead of to the general counsel? I suppose I was to be flattered that he was offering me another opportunity for leadership. However, Wayne had kept me abreast of the unfortunate situation that had occurred between him and the general counsel.

Wayne and the general counsel's major run-in resulted in Wayne's lodging a formal complaint of a hostile work environment with the AMA Office of Human Resources. An outside attorney investigated and apparently found that Wayne's complaints had merit. Having Wayne report to me was obviously Mike's resolution of the unfortunate, irrevocable breakdown in an employee-supervisor relationship, which had resulted in an impaired working environment. Wayne had been a longtime employee, and Mike needed to prevent a major problem that might occur with some AMA members, other physicians, and the media. This situation would very likely happen if Wayne were to go outside AMA channels or make his specific complaints public via a lawsuit.

Wayne and I were quite willing to accept Mike's resolution by having Wayne report to me. However, I would have been happier had Mike been honest with the reason for his request, instead of presenting the proposal as being a special offer from him to me. This sort of manipulation had always annoyed me, because I thought that kind of behavior was well beyond Mike's prominent position.

I told him how his "offer," that was really a request for a favor, in a way offended me, because I knew the real reason for the request. I would happily have helped him with the situation if he'd simply asked me. I believe that direct response was surprising to Mike, and that he'd have preferred that I hadn't disclosed my feelings. So be it, but I generally liked Mike and hoped such honesty would change his approach in the future, not only with me but also with others. I'm not sure how effective it was, but I tried.

In any case, I told him that I would be happy for Wayne to join my staff as a direct report providing that only I completed his annual evaluation and recommendation for salary increase, that I was provided adequate space and a paralegal assistant for him, and that I be given all other items necessary for me to have to have another staff member for whom I would be responsible. Further, if and when Wayne was to retire, all future *JAMA* counsels would continue to report directly to me, under the same conditions. Unfortunately, but understandably, this arrangement did not make the general counsel happy, but he agreed, and Mike arranged for the transfer.

I also discussed with Mike an issue sure to arise with my fellow SVPs, who also depended on the Office of General Counsel for legal support. They would wonder why I was allowed to have my own direct-report attorney, whereas they were not. There was no way the real reason for the transfer could be revealed, but Mike told me that he was sure I could handle that situation and that he'd help if he could. This issue did arise with some SVPs, who kindly took my word that the move was not the result of something I requested. I have no idea if they also checked with others to verify my word, but the issue never seemed to alter my good relationships with them. I guess track records help in those kinds of situations.

I knew the general counsel was not happy with the resolution or with me. I felt very bad about this, because I liked and respected him. Despite the problems I knew this equitable decision would produce, I thought this was one situation that was worth my discomfort. Thick skin is an absolute necessity for any leader, but it is not an easy attribute to acquire.

In November of 2006, Wayne decided to retire. He had accumulated sufficient service time under the AMA pension plan that continuing would not be financially beneficial to him. Because of our close working relationship and mutual respect, after he retired, we became friends socially, and that continues to this day.

I asked Mike what he planned for the next counselor for *JAMA* and the Archives journals, and he told me that would be decided by the general counsel. Because, as always, I had planned for the worst while hoping for the best, I reminded Mike of our agreement and offered to show him the paper trail I'd kept. It's always a good idea to keep a paper trail for future reference.

Upon reflection, he remembered what we had agreed. However, because I did not want to make a big deal about the issue, and because the general counsel had agreed to our previous arrangement, I agreed to the resolution. We would both select the new editorial counselor, and the new attorney would return to reporting to the general counsel. Further, his or her office would move back to the same floor as the general counsel. However, we would both complete the annual evaluation.

This turned out to be a nonissue, because the next *JAMA* editorial counsel was someone we both liked very much. The excellent choice, Joseph Thornton, a.k.a. Joe, would prove to be a real godsend during some troubling times and always a joy with whom to work. He made the transition from Wayne smooth and peaceful. An added attraction was that he is another avid Notre Dame sports fan, along with Phil and me. We have had great times, especially during football season, playing Monday morning quarterbacks.

Joe had experience working for a newspaper, and that helped a great deal with his understanding relationships between the editor in chief and others. While his office was not in the *JAMA* area, as had been the arrangement with Wayne, I never minded going to the floor that housed the general counsel's and Joe's offices. In fact, I enjoyed visiting with his secretary and other staff when I went to see my "consigliere." Like Joe, they had great senses of humor, and even liked (or at least pretended to like) my jokes and humor.

My working so well with Joe on many issues even contributed to my having a much better relationship with the general counsel, much to my pleasure. He now viewed me through Joe's eyes, and we never had a disagreement on how well Joe functioned. Joe is very mild mannered, much like Phil, and their working relationship was also very close. It was great for me to have two close associates who allowed me to be a warrior and not a worrier for things that needed my attention.

Joe found great humor in an episode I related involving something that occurred prior to his arrival. I had been asked to meet with an attorney from an outside firm. He represented someone with an issue concerning something that happened with *JAMA* years before I had become the editor in chief. The AMA attorney who handled that case was not Wayne, because it involved some issue for which the other AMA lawyer had special expertise and experience.

The outside attorney demanded that I produce records that simply were not available, and about which I had absolutely no knowledge. The outside attorney met with the AMA attorney and me and asked me nonstop questions for over three hours one morning, breaking only once. When we returned after lunch, he continued with his questioning, which bordered on badgering me, despite the AMA lawyer's expressed displeasure with the format. I'm not easily frightened or made anxious, and in fact I was amused by the rather clumsy way the outside attorney tried to get my cooperation. He demanded information that I would gladly have provided, had it been available. The AMA attorney knew that I actually was having fun, so he allowed the questioning to continue.

Now, unknown to either attorney, I had a very small, scabbed lesion just beneath the corner of my left eye, resulting from a scratch. About an hour or so into the afternoon session of questioning, I unconsciously rubbed the scab, causing some bleeding. A trickle of blood slowly ran down my cheek, apparently giving the appearance that I was crying blood. The look on the face of the outside attorney was priceless as he sat facing me. The AMA attorney was sitting to my right side and couldn't see what was happening with the scratch, and I was also unaware of the situation.

The outside attorney stopped midsentence and stood up as I reached up to wipe my cheek, not knowing that the tickle I felt was blood running down my cheek. As he said, "I think we've had enough for today, and I'll come back if I need more information," I looked at my hand and saw the blood. The AMA attorney also saw what was happening and was confused and a bit frightened.

The outside attorney quickly gathered his papers and rushed out the door, and we never saw or heard from him again. After I explained to the AMA attorney what had happened, we both had a great laugh. So did Joe and everyone to whom I told about the incident. Some funny incidents come in strange ways.

Joe, Phil, and I were to have many adventures together, which I will relate later.

Big Pharma

I have always believed that pharmaceutical and medical-device companies have substantially contributed to the better health of the general public and to the alleviation of pain, the curing of many illnesses, and the prolongation of life for many. Of course these companies make great profits, as they should if these profits are earned honestly and appropriately. It is important to understand that the development of their drugs and medical devices have benefited from research funded by the National Institutes of Health (NIH) and other federally funded studies. I believe it is the American economic way to make good use of federally funded research findings, with some caveats, which I'll explain below.

Scientists employed by Big Pharma develop these drugs and devices. These scientists are among the best and brightest in the world and work for the scientific-development divisions of the Big Pharma companies. There is also another division for each Big Pharma company called marketing. The individuals who work in that division are also among the best in the world at selling their products. They are paid to sell the drug and device products. The Big Pharma sales representatives, assigned to specific physicians, often receive part of their pay based on how many prescriptions their physician clients write for the companies' drugs.

Some organizations that keep track of this information (how many prescriptions for which products are written by each physician) sell this information to the Big Pharma companies. Naturally, the Big Pharma sales representatives work very hard to make sure the doctors to whom they are assigned, are prescribing their drugs.

Big Pharma stockholders expect maximum profits from the sales of drugs and medical devices. That profit margin has been in the enviable range of 20 percent or higher for many years. How that profit margin is achieved upset me, and therefore I began my arguments with Big Pharma and with physicians who contributed to the methods by which drugs were promoted by Big Pharma to assure their very high profits.

In order to understand my disagreements with Big Pharma, it is important to understand how the representatives manipulate physicians, publishers, editors, politicians, and the public. Developing and bringing a new drug to market is a very expensive proposition. According to the companies in 2005, the cost is $2.6 billion. However, that figure includes the cost of the basic research, much of which was funded by NIH federal funds, and the amount lost if the money had been invested in a money generating account. That kind of cost accounting is beyond unbelievable.

Up until the late 1980s and early 1990s, the scientific divisions of Big Pharma had been provided with substantially more funding and resources than the marketing divisions. Around that time the chief executives of some Big Pharma companies decided to meld the funding and resources of both the scientific and marketing divisions. The result was threefold: first, new drug development over the next two decades or so slowed dramatically; second, drug sales were very high, resulting in great profits; and third, the number of published articles on conflicts of interest soared.

The CEOs of some Big Pharma companies had decided that it would be easier and more profitable to sell products to patients that were already approved by the FDA. Such patients actually could use other, less expensive and just as effective drugs. In addition, Big Pharma could make more profits by selling their already FDA-approved products off label—that is, for illnesses or conditions other than for those approved by the FDA for a specific drug. Now, how could these two goals be achieved?

Physicians in the United States can legally prescribe any FDA approved drug for any illness, not only for those illnesses or ages approved by the FDA. In fact, as with essentially all pediatricians, I frequently prescribed drugs, such as some antibiotics for young children, even though the drugs had been approved only for children older than fourteen years of age.

The reason for the older child approval is that the drug company that owned that drug's patent performed the required clinical research studies only on older children. The companies avoided the relatively greater difficulty and higher expense to perform such studies in younger children. Recently, some drug trials have included young children, in return for the drug company receiving six months more for their patents on those drugs. There are often trade-offs to achieve a goal.

Because most Big Pharma profits derive from sales of drugs prescribed by physicians, or other clinicians in some instances, these physicians must be convinced or enticed to use these drugs. Enter the pharmaceutical sales representatives, with their free lunches, dinners, and sports-events tickets, not to mention pens and prescription pads with the companies' names on them. There is also the so-called continuing medical education sessions, usually held at resorts, and paid for by Big Pharma.

The Sunshine Act, which I will explain below, now has rules that all pharmaceutical and medical-device companies must keep track of such interchanges. This information must be available to the public online. However, this kind of marketing continues, although to a lesser degree, because physicians don't want their patients and others to know how much influence Big Pharma has them.

Some influential politicians receive large donations for their reelection coffers from Big Pharma and are responsible for supporting laws that benefit Big Pharma. Some of these laws prevent federal agencies from negotiating with Big Pharma for bulk purchases of drugs used by patients insured by some federal programs. Hence, for example, the price of drugs used by patients on Medicare is more than the same drugs paid for by other insurance companies.

Some medical journals and other publishers are enticed to sell high-priced advertisements for drugs, with little oversight for how the ads are formatted. Often these advertisements appear to be studies or editorials (called "advertorials") and are supported by data held only by the Big Pharma companies that create them. Look at many medical journals or popular magazines to see what I mean. The latter advertisements are part of the "direct to consumer" allowance, which occurs in magazine, TV, radio, and other media ads. In addition, coupons for drugs are used to entice future use of these expensive drugs. Almost all of these coupons provided are only for the first prescriptions for new, expensive drugs that are required for extensive periods of time.

PHYSICIAN CONFLICT OF INTEREST

Some of the worst offenders assisting Big Pharma in offensive drug marketing are physicians. These physicians have very good credentials and reputations in specific medical specialties and allow their names to be put on studies the companies have conducted and professional writing services have written. Unlike physicians who receive grants from the companies and actually conduct the research, these physicians have no real role in the studies. They can make changes in the manuscripts, with approval of the Pharma sponsors, but the changes are usually not significant. They are reimbursed handsomely for their "names, time, and effort."

The next step is for the report of the study to be sent to a medical journal for publication. Some editors, almost always physicians, allow the papers to be published without appropriate peer review and oversight. These editors might or might not be aware of what has transpired.

Physician experts who serve on Big Pharma's speakers' bureaus, receive pay from Big Pharma. They are invited to meetings or conventions to speak about drugs, using the PowerPoint presentations developed by the Big Pharma sponsors. Those presentations accentuate the positive effects of the drugs, with little information on the negative effects or the relative costs. The companies claim that these PowerPoint presentations must follow specific FDA rules, but I have found no evidence for that claim. *This is not to be confused with other expert physicians, not paid by Big Pharma companies, who present at meetings, using their own slides, which accurately and fairly point out all aspects of the drugs on which they present.*

In some cases, in addition to a potentially biased presentation by a physician paid by Big Pharma, another physician, also well paid by Big Pharma, sits in the audience. During the question-and-answer period, that second physician asks the expert speaker if he or she has ever used the FDA-approved drug being presented for another illness not approved by the FDA for use in that illness. The speaker answers in the positive and thereby encourages the "off label" use of the drug.

All of the above are examples of financial conflicts of interest that occur when there is a conflict between the private interests and the official responsibilities of a person in a position of trust. Surely a physician is in a position of trust. I had assumed that anyone choosing a career in the pharmaceutical and medical-device companies would have chosen this path, because he or she wanted to contribute to people's health and to alleviate pain and suffering. After experiencing the tactics used by many of those who work for Big Pharma, I changed my assumption, at least as it pertains to some of the executives and to others who choose to remain employed by them when they have other choices.

As I review this in 2016, something is being done to inform the public about these practices of Big Pharma with physicians. The Physician Payments Sunshine Act requires manufacturers of drugs and medical

devices that participate in federal health-care programs to report certain payments and valuable items they give to physicians or to teaching
hospitals. As of August 1, 2013, these companies began collecting and
tracking such payments and have submitted these reports to the Centers
for Medicare and Medicaid Services (CMS) annually.

According to the Sunshine Act, companies must record nearly every
transaction with physicians, from sales representatives bearing pizza to
marketers paying physicians to give lectures. An exception is for companies providing funds to institutions for accredited continuing medical
education meetings, as long as the companies don't select the speakers.
Also, manufacturers and group-purchasing organizations must report
certain financial interests held by physicians and their immediate families.

Physicians have the right to monitor and request correction before
reports are made available to the public, if they believe and can prove
information is inaccurate. One can hope this provision exposing to their
patients their relationship with Big Pharma will make physicians reconsider carefully how they want to deal with Big Pharma.

This Sunshine Act has caused some Big Pharma companies to
change their behavior to some degree. For example, a few began post-
ing physician payment data online while I was still the editor in chief
of *JAMA*. In addition, one very large company decreased the amount of
money it paid physicians for fees and gifts from over $195 million in one
year to $173 million the next.

It would be wonderful if all Big Pharma would use the money saved
from such physicians' fees and gifts for increased research for new drugs
or to decrease the price of drugs. If they did, the drug pipeline and,
therefore, patients would benefit greatly.

Lest anyone misinterpret my comments about physicians receiving
fees or funding from Big Pharma, I am enthusiastically supportive of
Big Pharma funding research projects. The companies benefit from this
research and so do patients and investigators, because the NIH has a
limited amount of money for clinical research; most funds are used for
basic research. Also, physicians with special expertise *should* serve as

consultants for drug development and be paid reasonable fees—note I wrote "reasonable." By that, I mean an amount based on their usual incomes and time expended.

Despite the Sunshine Act, I continue to read and hear about Big Pharma tactics that clearly endanger people's health and assure the financial bottom line but that don't involve physicians directly. For example, clandestine methamphetamine production sites use cold and allergy medications sold over the counter. Because of the danger of methamphetamine use especially by youths, many states sought to make pseudoephedrine a prescription drug. However, only a few states have been successful, because of intense lobbying and advertising blitzes paid for by Big Pharma. How can the individuals involved in such behavior sleep at night?

As more examples of shady Big Pharma practices involving the medical profession became obvious to me, I had a member of my staff at *JAMA* count the number of published articles that dealt with conflict of interest in medicine and were listed in PubMed. (PubMed is part of the National Center for Biotechnology Information and contains about 23 million biotechnology journal articles.)

These conflict-of-interest articles were tracked from 1974 on, but we found almost none were published until around 1989. That was around the time that Big Pharma merged their scientific and marketing divisions. The numbers increased steadily until they reached six hundred articles in 2006, and have remained at that level at least until 2013, when I stopped counting. Clearly something bad for patients was happening.

As the editor in chief of *JAMA*, I understood how some studies, openly sponsored by Big Pharma, and other studies, discretely sponsored by Big Pharma, that were submitted for publication had been manipulated or biased. There were so many examples, especially of clinical trials, that I decided to require that all such studies submitted to *JAMA* have their data analysis performed by an "independent" biostatistician, before we would send it out for external review. That meant that either the biostatistician, if an author on the paper, must not be an employee of the Big Pharma sponsor or that an additional statistical review be performed by a faculty member who was acting as a faculty member at the time of the review. In the latter case I required a letter from that faculty statistician stating that he or she had reviewed all of the pertinent data and agreed with the results.

If there was a disagreement among the authors, the published manuscript had to contain the faculty member's analysis. When that happened, the faculty-member biostatistician would have discussed the disagreement with the original biostatistician, and they would have come to an agreement on what was to be published. Without this rule, why would the Big Pharma sponsor agree to which data analysis was to be published?

Phil and I published an editorial in which Phil announced the rule and explained that the reason we instituted it was to assure that the statistician for the study had not been manipulated by his or her employer. We were clear that we didn't believe that university faculty biostatisticians were smarter or more honest, but that the study sponsor did not employ those faculty members and therefore had no control over them. Also, the reason we chose university faculty members was that if any question arose regarding the veracity of the analysis, we could refer the allegation to the faculty member's supervisor or dean for clarification. That was a role I had played when I was vice dean at Hopkins, and it had worked well there.

Despite that explanation, the rule for an "independent" biostatistician still caused consternation by some biostatisticians. They claimed that faculty members were no different than those who worked for Big Pharma. Obviously I disagreed, because unlike the sponsor-employed statistician, the faculty member's job was not at stake. In those cases, the golden rule was he who holds the gold (Big Pharma) rules, and that was simply not acceptable to me.

I knew this requirement for an independent biostatistician resulted in some studies not being sent to *JAMA*, but I thought that if the author or sponsor had something to hide, I didn't want to publish the paper anyway. A physician colleague sent me a copy of a letter from a Big Pharma executive to an author specifically stating that the manuscript was not to be sent to "DeAngelis at *JAMA*." That made me smile and convinced me that we must be doing something right in trying to protect the public from manipulation of medical literature.

The *New York Times* published an article in the summer of 2006, motivating another of my physician colleagues to send me a postcard. That postcard stated, "Cathy, the *NYT* reports that the pharmacology companies are out to get you. Remember, the basic rule for leaders, *'Illigitimus Non Carborundum*—don't let the bastards grind you down.'" Despite the misspelling of *illigitimi*, the message was heartwarming and made me smile. At least someone out there understood what I was trying to do. Actually, I received a lot of encouragement to keep on, and I did.

After I was hit by a CTA bus, I jokingly had told my friends and even a few of my friendly colleagues who worked for Big Pharma (yes, there are many such individuals) that the last thing I remembered before being hit by the bus was looking up at the driver, who was wearing a Big Pharma hat. Of course I was only kidding, but it made for a good laugh. While I still believe in the great worth of pharmaceutical and medical-device companies, I will continue to oppose the dishonest tactics used by some to enhance their profits while endangering patients.

ANOTHER NEW CONTRACT

December of 2008 was the scheduled time for my current contract, which went through December of 2009, to be reviewed and renewed if I wanted to stay on. Although I originally had planned not to extend my editorship beyond the current contract (i.e., a total of ten years), I knew l needed to stay on for another year beyond the end of the current contract to meet my remaining goals.

During the remaining two years (with my desired one-year extension of my current contract), I planned to work very hard to assure that the next in editor in chief would have the same editorial freedom and control of the journals as I, which I believed were essential to continuing the success of *JAMA*. I did not want all the gains we had made to be lost, in the case that the primary control of the journals resorted back to the business executives. I knew that was the desire of the SVP for business, the COO, and even the EVP/CEO. It was going to be a difficult task but essential to try very hard to not allow them once again to take full control of *JAMA* and the Archives journals.

Therefore, in early December of 2008, I asked Mike when we were going to meet regarding my contract, meet the requirement that we do so a year before the expiration of the current contract. He didn't seem very concerned about it and told me he'd have a meeting scheduled soon. On the one hand, I thought that attitude might mean that he had viewed the issue as routine and of no great concern. On the other hand, because I plan for the worst, especially in that kind of situation, I took precautions and kept a paper trail of my discussions with Mike about a new contract.

On the Friday afternoon before I was to leave for my usual annual December two-week holiday vacation, Mike scheduled a meeting for us to discuss my contract. The warning red flag I perceived, because the timing of the meeting was on a Friday afternoon just before I was to leave for two weeks, proved to be true.

When I entered his office, Mike was sitting behind his desk, as he did when he was playing the power game. He told me that he would not renew my contract. I asked him on what grounds he had made that decision, because all my annual reviews had been very positive, the impact factor of *JAMA* and most of the Archives journals continued to increase, we were publishing material that brought a lot of positive media attention to the AMA, and we were still financially very profitable, despite the general down trend in advertisement sales nationally. He said that those things were expected, but that he had decided it was time for a change in the editorship. Only when I suggested that his decision might be based on my going to be only two days away from age seventy when my current contract expired did he become somewhat anxious.

I knew the real reason for his not wanting to renew my contract was that he and the business executives wanted to hire a new editor who, as in the past, would report to the business department. After a cordial but clearly uncomfortable conversation, we agreed that there would be no decision about my contract until he and I had time to consider the situation over the holidays. "Oh yes, Cathy, and have a Merry Christmas." Of course, I intended to do just that, despite what had just occurred.

I went directly from that meeting to the Chicago airport to catch my plane to Baltimore. Jim was to pick me up at the Baltimore airport, where we were to meet with some good friends to have an early holiday dinner. Instead of thinking about the wonderful holidays ahead with my family and friends, my plane ride was spent planning how I was going to handle Mike's plan not to renew my contract. I still cannot figure out how someone who has achieved a high leadership position would not have learned about timing, if nothing else. Of course, that's assuming the timing was not deliberate, which it probably was.

At any rate, after discussing the situation with Jim and several of my close and wise colleagues, I called the president of the AMA and the chairman of the AMA BOT and explained what Mike had proposed. Both of them were surprised and very supportive of me. They told me that they would discuss the situation with Mike, for me not to worry, and to have a great holiday. I thanked them and did just that, after planning exactly what I wanted and how I would negotiate with Mike at our next meeting.

When I returned after wonderful holidays spent with my family, the meeting with Mike was one of the most interesting I've ever experienced, and that's saying a lot, considering many of the experiences I've had. Prior to our previous meeting before leaving for the holidays, I had planned to merely ask for a one-year extension of my contract and for all to live happily ever after. But because of the circumstances surrounding our first meeting, I wanted to see what Mike would propose, assuming the AMA president and the BOT chair had discussed the situation with him, after I had spoken with them.

When I met with Mike this time, he invited me to sit in an easy chair next to his in his office. I considered this to be a very good sign of what was to come. He then told me that, after he'd thought about our previous meeting (no mention of the discussion with the AMA officers), he decided to extend my contract for an additional year. There would be an official "good-bye" announcement at the AMA House of Delegates, and my name would be placed on the masthead of *JAMA* as a former editor in chief. In response, I told him that I appreciated the AMA House of Delegates' offer, but the official announcement really wasn't necessary, and because all former editors' names already were on the *JAMA* masthead, that was not an issue.

As for his proposed one-year extension, I told him I wanted a two-year extension, but that I'd leave the editorship and Chicago after a year and a half, on June 30, 2011. However, I wanted full pay and all benefits to extend for the full two years—i.e., until December 31, 2011. We could consider the last six months a sabbatical, during which time I would work on any editorial project the AMA would assign, providing I could do it from Baltimore. I knew he wanted me to step down from the editorship as soon as possible, hence the plan for the last six months.

After not much thought, he agreed, and we shook hands. Actually, as I went back to my office, I shook my head in disbelief at the entire episode, which could have been handled so much better and easier. All he needed to have done in the first meeting was to have approved my quite reasonable request for a one-year extension and have done so with grace and goodwill. After all, it had happened just before Christmas.

No matter the timing, fighting for equity is essential, but you make the best out of every situation. In this case, everything worked out very well for me and, I assume, for Mike and the AMA, because I continued to work very hard to assure the success of *JAMA* and the Archives journals.

The senior editors, to whom I had explained the entire story before going to the second meeting, were waiting for me after my meeting with Mike and followed me to my office. When I told them the results of that meeting, they were relieved and happy. Now we were ready to get back to expending all our work energies on the journals.

INTERACTIONS WITH DEANS OF US MEDICAL SCHOOLS

During my editorship, I had occasion to interact with four deans of US medical schools regarding the editorial behavior of one each of their faculty members, respectively. Three of these interactions went exactly as I expected, based on my experience from "the other side" when I was vice dean and had handled such issues. All three deans investigated the alleged problems.

One dean not only appropriately dealt with the faculty member, but he also issued a notice to all faculty members regarding how they should handle matters related to possible conflicts of interest. In addition to appropriately handling the faculty members involved, the other two deans each also developed a specific course in human research and mandated that all faculty members involved in human research take the course.

Obviously these deans and I interacted with mutual respect. I have a letter from one of them confirming his gratitude for our professional and respectful interaction. I was very happy to have kept that letter when the interaction with the fourth dean occurred. That incident caused me much unnecessary sorrow. I read the letter from the grateful dean almost daily during the unfortunate episode, which I will describe in the next chapter.

CHAPTER 17

Lemonade from Lemons

THE FOLLOWING RELATES TO THE only negative encounter I've ever had with a medical school dean. As will be evident, the negative episode involved much more than the encounter with the dean. However, it provides a way to display how conflict interactions, when managed in a professional manner, can lead to a reasonable ending. This episode was a true test of how equity, in this case primarily fairness, would prevail even though at times it seemed that would not happen.

On May 28, 2008, we published a study in *JAMA* by Dr. Robert Robinson, a very well-respected psychiatrist, who had performed a great deal of sound and important psychiatric research. This article dealt with the use of an antidepressant drug in comparison with problem-solving therapy, to possibly prevent depression in patients who have had a stroke.

The conclusion was that both treatments were more effective than placebo at reducing the incidence of depression over twelve months of treatment, but the problem-solving therapy did not achieve statistically significant results over placebo, whereas the use of medication did reach significance. It is important to note that the study had been funded by the National Institute of Mental Health and that no pharmaceutical company was involved.

Subsequently, on October 15, 2008, *JAMA* published four "Letters to the Editor" from readers who had questions or comments about different aspects of the study. Robinson's response to each of the letters was published in the same issue. This follow-up was not unusual for published studies, which frequently generated questions and comments from readers.

Several days after the letters and response were published, one author (a reader) of one of the published "Letters to the Editor" sent e-mail messages to the *JAMA*'s general mailbox, to *JAMA*'s managing editor, and to a *New York Times* reporter, alleging that Robinson had failed to disclose some financial remuneration he had received in the past five years from a pharmaceutical company whose drug was used in the study. That author (a reader) had not stated this allegation in his "Letter to the Editor" that had been published. It seemed that he was looking for media coverage rather than clarity.

About a week later, Phil wrote to the author of the e-mail messages, stating that *JAMA* would take necessary steps to investigate the allegation and make appropriate corrections. Phil also asked the author why he had not mentioned the alleged failure of Robinson to disclose in his published "Letter to the Editor, and why he "felt the necessity to notify the media about this issue." Fortunately, the *New York Times* reporter did not publish anything about the message he had received (class has many ways of being displayed).

At about the same time, and unbeknown to any of us at *JAMA*, a blog article entitled "Undisclosed Financial: *JAMA* editor hoodwinked once again" appeared online. What appears on blogs is sometimes truly amazing; no matter how untrue or outrageous, written material can be sent out on a blog with essentially no oversight or repercussions. The Internet has no ethical standard; anyone can say anything without proof. Truly this is freedom of press gone amuck.

In early December, Phil discussed the issue with Richard (remember, he was both a deputy editor and a psychiatrist), who had handled Robinson's published paper and the follow-up letters to the editor about that publication. Richard then contacted Robinson about the allegation of nondisclosure and followed up with him from then on.

Unlike almost all other journals that required a three-year disclosure from authors, *JAMA*, at that time, required disclosure of all honoraria and other conflicts of interest covering the past five years. Robinson had to search his files for information going back four years prior to submission of the paper. He allegedly failed to disclose an honorarium he had received in 2004, four years before the publication.

As it turns out, many individuals keep readily available financial records for only three years, probably for IRS purposes. Because of this incident, *JAMA* changed the timing of reports to three years, like all other similar journals required. Our five-year requirement apparently was stricter than other journals. Once we realized this difference, we didn't want to confuse authors or put them under unnecessary duress with our unusual policy.

Robinson sent a reply to *JAMA* on February 5, 2009, stating that in 2004 he had indeed received (which he failed to disclose) two small honoraria from a pharmaceutical company whose drug had been used in the 2008 publication in question. He said that he simply did not remember receiving the payments, and as soon as he made the discovery by reviewing his tax files he sent a correction and an apology as we requested. He also stated that the pharmaceutical company that manufactured the drug in his research study played absolutely no role in the 2008 published study, which was funded by the National Institute of Mental Health. His correction and apology were then scheduled to be published in the March 11, 2009, issue of *JAMA*, which was the first issue not already completed at the time we received Robinson's disclosure.

However, in the interim before that publication date, the *British Medical Journal (BMJ)* published a letter in its Online Rapid Response blog (yet another blog), about Robinson's alleged nondisclosure. The same reader who raised the question with Phil also published that blog letter because, as he told Phil, he was highly skeptical that *JAMA* would set the record straight. Phil then informed him about the upcoming correction and apology to be published in *JAMA*.

That didn't seem to satisfy the reader, and Phil was concerned because the reader continued to seek media coverage. After we discussed the issue, I told Phil that I would call the reader's supervisor, who also happened to be the dean of his school. I would try to enlist enlist the dean's assistance in getting the reader to understand our position about media involvement. I then spoke with the dean and had a very pleasant conversation about the issue, which he seemed to understand. During that conversation, he told me he would discuss the issue of media involvement with the reader as soon as he (the dean) returned to his office from a meeting he was attending.

Unfortunately, I later received several phone calls from the reader, who was incensed that I had spoken with his dean. He would not listen to me as I tried to explain my conversation with his dean, but instead kept screaming at me. I told him I would only discuss the situation with him when he calmed down. He could certainly call me anytime when we could have a professional discussion. We never had that conversation because he never called back.

I also called Fiona Godley, my colleague editor of the *BMJ* and explained what was happening at *JAMA* involving the Robinson publication. I told her that, as we had explained to the author of the letter published on her blog, that our March 11 issue would contain a correction and apology from Robinson, as was our policy. We ended our cordial conversation, both believing the upcoming *JAMA* correction and Robinson's apology would be the end of the issue.

As described below, that belief was naïve, and several weeks later, the editor of *BMJ* came to my office on her way to California from London. She wanted to express her concern about the result of her journal's having published the blog letter. I told her that I really appreciated her concern, but how could she or anyone have known how one letter, published on their blog site, could have caused such a kerfuffle (her perfect term for what happened)?

Another site published a blog on March 11 (the same day as the *JAMA*-published response and apology from Robinson), stating that I had made sharp comments to the author of the messages. The author of that blog (obviously a friend of the message author) called our media-relations office asking to speak with me to get my side of the story. As was my custom, I did not respond to that or any other blog author.

Rather, I sent a copy of that blog, along with a message from me, in an e-mail to the message reader's dean. I asked if he'd had an opportunity to speak with the reader. The response from the dean shocked me, because in response he accused me of threatening his institution. Only God knows how he reached that conclusion, because I had never said or done anything to cause that concern. In fact, in our first, very cordial conversation, I had praised his osteopathic medical school for training so many badly needed primary-care physicians.

I have no idea what the message author had said to him, but it probably had led him to his erroneous belief that I had threatened his institution. How I might have been able to do any harm to his institution is beyond me. I felt very bad about his reaction, but it seemed that any further contact with him might only worsen the matter. I tried to remember that you should never put your foot in your mouth and then shoot yourself in the foot, no matter how good your intentions are.

In the meantime, the blog site continued to make even more vitriolic, untrue claims about me. Several other bloggers picked up the message and called me a bully and a variety of other names. Needless to say, I needed very thick skin at that point. I tried to remember that I should not get all hot and bothered about what was happening. One of my favorite sayings is that a boiled egg is hard to beat, so if I was feeling boiled I would probably be hard to beat.

That same day I received a call from a reporter from the *Wall Street Journal*, who told me that he was working on the same story as what had appeared on the blog site. He wanted to know my side. He was one of the very few reporters with whom I routinely spoke without his first going through our Communications Office. I told him that *JAMA* had just published the correction and Robinson's apology, so "there is nothing to the story, and nobody would be interested in it." Those were my exact words.

The next day that reporter posted an article on his newspaper's blog, the headline of which read, *"JAMA* Editor Calls Critic a 'Nobody and a Nothing.'" It is amazing how playing with words can completely change the meaning of messages. I would never call anyone created by God a "nobody," because that would be against everything I believe in the worthiness of all people.

I still cannot understand why that reporter misstated what I'd said, especially because he was one of the very few reporters whom I trusted without clearance from our Communications Office. He knew that we had settled the Robinson issue by publishing his clarification and apology, yet the headline stated that I had demeaned a whistle blower.

I knew there were many cutbacks being made by newspapers at that time, and I assumed, perhaps erroneously, that he was worried about his job and wanted to gain some notoriety from the reports he published. A generous explanation is that he thought he had heard what he printed. (That process of processing what we hear and see is well described in the famous film *Rashomon*. That film is a psychological thriller concerning truth, based on what several people witnessed but reported quite conflicting accounts of what happened.) In any case I chose to doubt he wanted to cause trouble for me.

If I thought all that had occurred as described previously was a bad experience that was now ended, I was very wrong. The Kafka-esque episode was just heating up. On March 25, an eight-page letter from a group opposed to the use of all psychiatric drugs for any reason was sent to the senior officers of the AMA and to the chairman of the JOC. That group was known for sending similar letters with similar complaints about other individuals to other institutions. The letter to the AMA accused Phil and me of everything from unethical conduct to endangering the public health by failing to correct false information about comparative benefits and risks of an antidepressant drug. The letter called for, among other things, a public apology from us, and for our immediate suspension from duty.

On March 27, 2009, AMA acknowledged the complaint via a letter to the group, stating that the AMA takes such matters seriously and that the matter was to be investigated by the JOC. Not surprisingly, the next few weeks were filled with a deluge of media coverage on the matter. Obviously, the media had been alerted by the group that had made the complaint.

The JOC thoroughly investigated the matter, including inviting the author (the reader) of the letters, the reporter, and the author's dean to a meeting. All declined to attend, but the author and the dean sent e-mail messages to the JOC. Robinson also sent messages to the JOC, explaining what had happened from his perspective. The JOC also received phone calls, e-mails, and letters from the American Psychiatric Association, the American Academy of Child and Adolescent Psychiatry, the American College of Neuro-Psychopharmacology, and the American Association for Geriatric Psychiatry, all of which supported Robinson, Phil, and me. These organizations did acknowledge that Robinson should have disclosed the honoraria in his first disclosure, because he should have kept records going back as far as *JAMA* required.

Other groups contacted the JOC, noting the complaining reader's work as a reviewer for the official journal of an organization that criticizes the psychiatric medical model, which includes using medication to treat patients with major mental disorders. The complaining author had not disclosed this in his letters to *JAMA* or on the *BMJ* blog. These groups also pointed out that media coverage is "showcased" on that reader's CV, hence the media involvement in this case.

As part of the JOC investigation, JOC members interviewed Phil and me and asked used a number of questions. In addition, all of us were provided with copies of a very detailed notebook, prepared by attorney Joe Thornton, that contained copies of pertinent letters, telephone records, e-mails, journal articles, blog articles, and media coverage. The JOC then reported its findings to the AMA BOT.

Thereafter, Phil and I met with the BOT, at which Jordan Cohen, the chair of the JOC, and Joe Thornton were present, and during which

Phil and I responded to questions. Some of the questions and comments from the BOT members convinced me that not all members really understood how journals and editors function or how interactions with deans could be very helpful. However, after that meeting, the chair of the BOT graciously met with Phil and me, and Phil agreed to call the reader and apologize for the process having taken so long, and for not keeping him informed of how the investigation had been proceeding.

One important thing to note is that, after this episode, I continued as necessary to call deans for a variety of reasons with successful results. The best example is what happened with the only article retracted during my editorship, which I discussed in chapter 13. My conversation with that dean occurred after the episode just described. That retraction also took some time (more than a year), but was possible only because of the cooperation of the school's dean, who had taken the time to carefully examine the issue.

While the episode described above was stressful, I believe it is an excellent example of how such matters can be resolved. An institution (the AMA) had a mechanism for a proper, professionally conducted investigation. I am very grateful to Joe Thorton, who provided extensive data to the JOC and BOT to fully inform their investigations. I am also grateful to those members of the JOC and BOT and especially the chairs of both groups. Both of these gentlemen studied the facts and actions of all involved before and during the episode and made decisions based on a thorough investigation.

To paraphrase Abraham Lincoln, you can please some of the people some of the time, some people you can please all of the time, but you can't please all of the people all of the time. So such episodes are bound to happen to leaders, especially those who try to make progress. The experience solidified my belief that leaders must develop and maintain four *T* characteristics: tough-minded, tenacious, thick-skinned (very hard sometimes) and tenderhearted. These *T*s are essential because of another *T*: leaders often become *targets* of individuals who have other ideas or ideologies.

My Last Two and a Half Years as Editor in Chief

In addition to the usual time and effort devoted to assuring the continued success of *JAMA* and the Archives journals, much of my time and energy over the last two and a half years of my editorship was expended trying to achieve four important things I believed were essential for the success of the journals and the new editor in chief. Whereas I had been trying to accomplish these four goals over the past three years, I knew I had to expend much more time and effort now because the time for me to achieve them was growing short.

The four essentials included (1) the naming of a new fully engaged, experienced publisher; (2) obtaining funds for a content management system, which is a computer application that allows publishing and editing, including content modification and maintenance, to be managed from a central interface; (3) obtaining funds for the journals to be clearly displayed at important national and international meetings with materials such as exhibit booths to promote the journals to potential authors, reviewers and readers; and (4) as was the practice with other high-impact journals, funds for the editor in chief to interact with potential authors over lunches or dinners, where discussions could occur about why they should submit their best research to *JAMA*.

Achieving all these goals was going to be a very difficult task. Understanding the role and relationships of the editorial board and the publisher with the editor in chief is essential to understanding what happened next.

The JAMA Editorial Board

Virtually every journal has an editorial board composed of a variety of individuals who have different, pertinent expertise for the journal. The *JAMA* Editorial Board is composed primarily of physicians from various specialties and backgrounds and includes all of the Archives journal editors. For *JAMA*, every editorial board member is chosen solely by the editor in chief and serves for as long as the editor in chief chooses but ordinarily not longer than ten years. Members serve in an advisory capacity to the editor in chief and, despite what many authors believe, play no role in the everyday decisions regarding manuscripts. Also, the editorial board does not have any reporting relationship to the AMA BOT, AMA Officers, the EVP/CEO, or any other AMA person except the editor in chief (sorry, more alphabet soup).

The editorial board meetings were held annually in May in the AMA boardroom. I always invited the chair of the JOC to join us. When the JOC met for its annual meeting, usually just before the editorial board meeting, the JOC chair would often be able to attend. Others present at editorial board meetings were the deputy editors and other editorial staff, who would attend the open portions of the meetings.

At the invitation of the editor in chief, the EVP/CEO would attend at least the first part of the meeting to greet and welcome the board members on behalf of the AMA. The publisher and other publishing staff, including the advertising-sales director and the publisher responsible for the Archives journals, also attended, even though each Archives journal had its own, separate editorial board. We were functioning as a real family of journals.

The meetings usually consisted of reports by the editor in chief, the publisher, and various others who would present pertinent issues concerning *JAMA*. The most important part of the meeting, however, was the discussion and the suggestions and advice provided by the editorial board members to the editor in chief. These meetings proved to be very valuable over the years and especially so during the last three years of my editorship.

THE PUBLISHER

One partner essential to every editor is a good publisher. This was especially true for me because, unlike previous editors, I did not report to the publisher. It is important to remember that the publisher reported to the SVP for business, who reported to the COO, who reported to the EVP/CEO, but I reported directly to the EVP/CEO. Thereby, I had administratively "jumped" two steps in the AMA hierarchy compared to the previous editors.

I knew this reporting situation could engender problems with the publisher. However, successful journals have very good individuals in both the editor and publisher positions, who make great team decisions. The editor assures high-quality editorial content. The publisher provides the resources to make the editorial material available to subscribers and the public in an attractive manner, while assuring financial profitability to the owners of the publication, in this case, the AMA. The highest possibility for success occurs when the editor and publisher trust each other, and work and plan closely together.

During the first two and a half years of my editorship at *JAMA*, I had worked with three different publishers and one interim publisher. I had a very good working relationship with each of those publishers, but none of them served as publisher for a sufficient amount of time for us to establish ourselves as a team.

I understood the reasons for the first three publishers and the interim publisher having left the AMA, but it was rather frustrating. Therefore, I was very pleased when the fourth publisher, Naveen Gupta, was hired in mid-2002. He made it clear that he wanted to stay. Naveen was an experienced, knowledgeable, and fully engaged person who had many good ideas for the journal. He also had previous experience with the AMA by having worked there in another capacity. I very much enjoyed working with him, and we planned for the upcoming years at our frequent meetings. We frequently had lunch meetings together, often in my office or his.

He would set his annual budget, based on the plans we had made for the journals, with the approval of Bob Musacchio, the SVP for business, who was the publisher's supervisor. Unfortunately, there always seemed to be a reason why some of the approved planning funds were cut from the *JAMA* publisher's budget midway through the year or sooner. These funds were then used for other purposes in the business office.

This was very frustrating, because by that point in time we were competing editorially very successfully with the other top journals, especially the *New England Journal of Medicine (NEJM)* and the *Lancet*. Whereas *NEJM* had always been the top-rated general medical journal in the world, and the *Lancet* was the top-rated general British medical journal, *JAMA* was now ranking second or third, overall, depending on the year. The rank order of a journal was very important to authors, so it was essential that *JAMA* compete successfully.

I knew that to compete successfully required financial support from the publisher. Therefore, I checked the publicly available records for *NEJM* and discovered that its management spent well over half of their substantial journal profits to enhance the journal. *NEJM* used these funds for items such as having exhibit booths at key medical meetings, inviting potential authors to dinner or to receptions at meetings, putting ads at the airport and on buses in the cities where major medical meetings were being held, performing research to enhance readership, and upgrading their publishing materials. All of these things were essential in order to compete for the best articles and to market a journal.

I also knew that *JAMA* and the Archives journals made a substantial profit as well, but only relatively small amounts were used to enhance the journals. I knew *NEJM* is owned by the Massachusetts Medical Association, which is much smaller than the AMA, and therefore had fewer projects requiring funding. However, *JAMA* was supposed to compete with *NEJM*, so I believed it was essential that reasonable consideration be given to funding.

Naveen and I discussed with Bob the difference between *JAMA* and the Archives journals versus the journals with which we were competing. Bob said that as the SVP for business, he had to make the various adjustments to the publisher's budget depending on the goals of the AMA. I certainly understood that the AMA, as owner of the journals, had the right to use profits any way it wanted. However, it seemed wrong not to allow one of its "cash cows" (the journals) sufficient funds for research and development, or at least for development, if they expected the journals to remain competitive and so profitable. We all agreed that, going forward, the approved budget for the *JAMA* publisher would be preserved as much as possible.

Over the next few years, I continued to meet and plan with Naveen, and we were able to use some funds for exhibits at a few important meetings, but not much more. I continued to use my own money to take potential authors to dinner or lunch, where we would discuss their research and possible publication in *JAMA*.

Naveen and I also continued to discuss and plan for projects to advance *JAMA* and the Archives journals, including such ideas as having a magazine for the public using the material from *JAMA* and the Archives journals as the basis for articles, which would be reformatted for the public. I even suggested the name "Public Access *JAMA*," or "PA*JAMA*" for short. There is nothing wrong with having a sense of humor when planning. That project, like many others, never came to fruition, but I still think the idea, if perhaps not the title, is a good one.

Because I directly reported to the EVP/CEO, technically I could have made a big issue about funding with the EVP/CEO (Mike Maves at that time). However, despite my knowing how to play to win and having done so many times, the "power game" has never appealed to me as a means toward an end, especially because I was a woman dealing with male egos. And choosing when to use it is essential. I knew Bob had not been very happy that I was a direct report to Mike but that he and Mike had a good relationship regardless of reporting. I already had had too much experience with such matters, and I didn't want to rock that boat. I chose my battles, and this was not one I wanted to fight.

In any case, in 2005 Naveen, after another year or so of mostly frustration, decided to seek other employment. At that point, Bob proposed that he personally would assume the publisher's position, supposedly so we could work closely together to promote the journals. I did not especially like that idea, because it would mean that he would have yet another job responsibility in addition to already being very busy.

I did not want to argue the point until we had some experience with his proposal. Therefore, I agreed to try (note the word "try") this plan for a while. I assumed Bob would hire some supporting staff to cover his other responsibilities with the money saved from the publisher's salary. That would free some time, which he could spend on the journals.

That agreement proved to be a big mistake. When dealing with an experienced job survivor (as Bob surely was, having worked successfully at the AMA for many years in several senior positions) nothing is ever simply "tried." No matter the outcome, once an agreement to try something has been made with a job survivor, it will probably never change. In addition, the saved publisher's salary went to the bottom line for the Business Department, making the department and Bob look good in the eyes of the AMA hierarchy.

To be fair, at first this new arrangement seemed to work well. We started out continuing the weekly publisher and editor-in-chief meetings, and we even had a one-day weekend strategic-planning meeting for the editorial and publishing staff leaders. However, over time the weekly meetings disappeared, and the strategic plans never were implemented. Bob, who was now the SVP for business *and* publisher, became involved with yet another new major AMA initiative. This one was driven by his COO supervisor, and Bob spent almost no time with me or with *JAMA*-Archives matters. In fact, because the new AMA major initiative in which he was now involved required substantial funding, essentially none of our proposed initiatives came to fruition. Also, for practical purposes we essentially had no engaged publisher.

My relationships with the AMA Board of Trustees (BOT) members, which always had been enjoyable and cordial, began to erode. The COO and Bob had full access to them, virtually at all times, and their opinion held sway over anything I proposed. Remember that the BOT members served for a set number of years and required election and reelection, so there was some turnover constantly. After all, the COO and SVP for business were the senior staff responsible for AMA Business. The logical assumption by the BOT members was that the business senior staff knew best what funds needed to be allocated for the projects they felt were most important.

The one major project I knew *JAMA* and the Archives needed in order to progress and possibly even survive over time involved a content management system (CMS). As I mentioned in the previous chapter, that is a computer program that, among other things, would allow us to modify editorial content before publication and maintain it from a central interface. This system would provide procedures to manage workflow in a collaborative environment, which was very necessary, because at that point we managed editorially ten journals.

Such systems had been on the market since the late 1990s. When I proposed a CMS to Mike, he told me that it was a BOT decision, not his, and therefore I proposed it to the BOT at several meetings. However, it was always tabled because the COO and Bob convinced the BOT that the CMS was very expensive (which it was) and not really needed (though it was critically needed).

I knew it meant a penny now or a dollar later, but I guess if you think primarily of the present, the penny saved takes precedence. It seemed to me that economists and business people gave priority to the present, whereas pediatricians thought of the present but also its effect on the future. Perhaps that kind of thinking explains a great deal of why pediatricians are at the bottom of the list for physicians' salaries, but they fill many leadership positions in academic medicine.

I knew that without our getting a CMS soon, the journal's success would be in jeopardy, but obviously the BOT was convinced otherwise. The expensive CMS project competed for funds with a new AMA project that involved an electronic health-record system. This project had been approved by the BOT, and the COO and Bob played major roles. Whereas I never discussed it directly with the BOT, I believed this was a clear conflict of interest for Bob, who was also the publisher, but the BOT obviously did not see it that way. Further, the CMS issue resulted in my losing the confidence of some BOT members, who believed that I wanted something that was expensive and unnecessary for the journals.

The new AMA project for an electronic health system, as estimated, also was very expensive (at least ten times the cost of a CMS), but it was supposed to generate funds for the AMA and possibly even stimulate growth in membership. Obviously, these were two very high-priority goals. The cost of that project turned out to be even more than originally estimated but never did succeed in generating funds for the AMA. In addition, the project generated few, if any, new members. However, not having access to a crystal ball, who could have known the outcome at that time?

In any case, the result of the BOT's continued decision to table my request for a CMS contributed to my continuing frustration, because also I could not obtain the funds necessary for the other three items mentioned previously. Each of those were also needed to advance *JAMA* and fully compete with the other top general medical journals. I also felt very compromised that Mike and some members of the BOT favored the opinions of two individuals who were not really involved with the journals over my opinion and consequently thought less of me in this matter.

SEEKING A SOLUTION

I did not want to leave the editorship without having tried everything possible to assure the continued success of *JAMA* and the Archives journals and to leave them in pristine condition for the next editor in chief. I discussed my unsuccessful attempts to obtain the four goals with the editorial board at annual meetings, but now I believed it was time to get them fully engaged in helping to acquire at least some of the goals. I knew the main thing we needed for continued success of the journals was a fully engaged, experienced publisher. I believed that if we had such an experienced publisher, the other three goals would be much easier to obtain.

Since 2007, I had been discussing the special need for a fully engaged publisher with the editorial board members, who readily recognized the problem. At the May 2008 meeting, they became fully committed in trying to help convince Mike to hire a fully engaged publisher. The editorial board members prepared a letter discussing the reasons why a full-time, experienced publisher was essential, and we gave it to Mike at the next meeting. (Mike had been attending all the editorial board meetings in the mornings, to greet and welcome the members.)

We then discussed the letter with him, including having a selection committee to help in choosing the best candidate for the position. After the discussion, Mike told us that he would work on getting a publisher. We were very pleased with this outcome. However, much to our disappointment, a year later, at the May 2009 editorial board meeting, Mike reported that he was still working on the issue. Frustration was continuing.

A CONSULTING FIRM

I continued to discuss the needs of *JAMA* and the Archives journal with members of the AMA BOT. Obviously, some of them continued to be interested. I have no idea if those conversations had any effect. However, in 2009, they made some funds available for an outside consulting firm to review *JAMA* and the Archives journals and to complete a needs assessment. This consulting firm met with the senior editors, senior publishers, the AMA senior managing staff, the AMA officers, and other individuals who played important roles with the journals.

It was an interesting experience to hear what various individuals said at the general meeting, conducted with all involved in the process. For example, during the discussion about the subscription pricing of *JAMA*, which the consulting firm thought was relatively low compared to comparable journals, an AMA board member stated that perhaps that that was all *JAMA* was worth. I was shocked, but fortunately, the consultants provided data to show clearly that was not the case. It made me wonder whether that AMA board member actually had read *JAMA* with any consistency. In any case, I thought it was a peculiar statement from an AMA officer.

At the conclusion of the report, the consulting firm suggested five items that needed attention: (1) a full-time, experienced publisher, who should be hired as soon as possible, (2) a content management system, (3) funding for a visible presence of the journals at important meetings,

(4) funding for the editor in chief to meet with potential authors, and (5) an increase in the subscription price of the journals. Of course I ultimately was delighted with these suggestions, because I had been asking for four of the five items over the past few years !!

At first I was angry but I swallowed a lot of blood from biting my tongue. As I often did when upset, I took a walk outside and reminded myself to choose battles wisely. After I calmed down, I realized that, in fact, I had won the main battle with the suggestions. Who cares that it had been necessary to have spent a million dollars or so for a consulting firm to confirm these needs. However, I wished they had been contracted much sooner.

A New Publisher

In November of that year (2009), Mike, Bob, and the COO met with me to announce that a publisher had been chosen. I was very surprised, because there had been no search committee, and I had no knowledge about the selection process or any voice in the selection. In fact, I had never even met the new publisher even though she had been working with Bob on another AMA special project. Of course the selection was theirs to make, but I had expected to have at least met the person before she was hired. This was especially important because they had not appointed a selection committee, as we had discussed with Mike at the 2008 annual editorial board meeting.

Whatever the process, I was happy to finally have a publisher partner, and looked forward to planning for the needs of the journals with her. Over the next year or so, things seemed to be going well. We met frequently and exchanged ideas.

Our disagreements centered on the publisher's role in *JAMA*'s editorial process. For example, she saw no problem with her attending the manuscript meetings, where we decided on which manuscripts were to be published, or with her having access to the upcoming tables of contents. I explained that allowing her, or anyone else besides the editorial staff or authors, to know what articles were to be published would allow the perception, if not the reality, of the publisher selling advertisements against content. We agreed to disagree on that issue, but she never attended those meetings or received the tables of contents before publication. Consequently, the different roles of the editor in chief and the publisher were again clarified by both of us.

One other issue we discussed was the cover of *JAMA*. That was not a new discussion for me because Bob always had wanted to replace the cover art with the table of contents, emulating the *New England Journal of Medicine*. I had refused to do that, because I believed the art on the cover was distinctive of *JAMA* and added valuable enlightenment for physicians. Moreover, the art on the cover and accompanying story were one of the most popular features according to reader surveys. I remained steadfast in refusing to make that change.

Another issue that arose was making the Archives journals into *JAMA* specialty journals. That is, for example, instead of the *Archives of Neurology*, the journal would be called *JAMA Neurology*. I had no problem with the concept, because as discussed in chapter 13, I had made the specialty journals into a *JAMA* family of journals by changing the logos on the covers.

My reluctance to this proposed name change was that changing the names would cause the Archives journals' impact factors to essentially start from scratch and drop to zero. While we continued this discussion, for better or worse, the Archives journals remained the same throughout my editorship. The next editor in chief could choose whether or not the cover was to be changed and also deal with the possible Archives journals' name change.

There was one issue that I cannot discuss here that caused a substantial wedge in my relationship with the publisher, which I regret was never resolved despite my attempting to seek a remedy. In any case, she and I maintained a cordial working relationship throughout my editorship, and I was sad to learn that she left the AMA not long after I retired.

TIME TO CHOOSE A NEW EDITOR

Because I was going to step down from the editorship at the end of June 2011, the EVP/CEO and the AMA Board chose a selection committee for a new editor in chief about six months prior to my departure. As is frequently done, the committee was to choose and interview certain candidates and submit three names to the AMA senior managerial staff. I was fairly certain that the AMA senior managerial staff would prefer that the next editor not have as much independence as I had. That essentially would mean having the next editor in chief report to the publisher, as had those before me.

Of course I hoped that would not be the case, but the almost-immediate elimination of Phil and a senior editor of the *New England Journal of Medicine* as candidates provided an early warning sign. It seemed that the next editor in chief would very likely report to the publisher if the selection committee could find someone willing to accept that reporting arrangement.

I knew Phil had been eliminated as a candidate without even the courtesy of an interview, because I worked so closely with him and he had told me. I also learned about the same treatment of the *New England Journal of Medicine (NEJM)* senior editor from colleagues at that journal. They were angry because their senior editor had not even received the courtesy of an interview. That Phil had also been eliminated as a candidate with no interview only seemed to make them more upset.

I knew Phil would never have accepted a different reporting system than mine, and I was fairly certain neither would the *NEJM* editor. So, I thought that might have been one, if not the main, reason for their elimination for candidacy despite their vast experience and academic reputations.

As with many high-profile searches, rumors circulated about potential candidates. I learned the names of many potential candidates, often because people erroneously thought I had some voice in the matter, and they were probably seeking information. By early in March 2011, it was clear that the search committee had chosen three potential candidates.

I knew who the candidates were, having learned their names from several knowledgeable sources. For example, while I was having breakfast at the European Urological Association meeting in Vienna, at which I had been invited to speak, two of my fellow diners told me how wonderful it was that one of their nephrology members, whom they named, had been selected as a finalist. I knew the names of the other two candidates because of similar interactions with other individuals. The academic world is like a small town, where it is almost impossible to keep secrets no matter how hard one tries.

I had a great deal of experience with search committees, both as a member and as a candidate for other positions, and I knew how the system worked. In addition, George Lundberg, the previous editor of *JAMA*, had kindly provided me with valuable information before I had accepted the editorship. Therefore, I called all three potential candidates and told each one that I had heard that he or she was being considered for the editorship of *JAMA*. I said that if he or she was chosen as a candidate, I would be happy to answer any questions he or she might have. In addition, if any of them was chosen to be the next editor in chief, I would help in any way I could.

All three expressed their appreciation for the calls and said they would be sure to call if officially contacted to arrange for further interviews. I had assumed the candidates had already been contacted by the search committee, because so many others unaffiliated with JAMA were already aware of the names of the finalists. Those conversations with the potential candidates were nothing unusual. They clearly were in keeping with other conversations I had had both as a candidate and as someone who was stepping down from a prior position.

The day after I made those calls, however, Mike contacted me and was irate that I had telephoned the potential candidates. He said their names were strictly confidential. I told him about my conversations with various outside individuals, including those in Vienna. I said that in such matters, confidentiality is a dream. He then forbade (he actually used the word "forbid") me from speaking to any of the candidates again. I told him that freedom of speech was still a constitutional right in the United States and as long as I didn't break any AMA confidentiality policies, I would speak with whomever I wanted.

I then asked him what he was trying to hide by keeping me away from the candidates, and he responded there was nothing to hide. He simply didn't think I should speak with candidates. I thought that was peculiar but let the issue slide because Mike knew I certainly would respond if a candidate called me.

To my surprise, on March 11, 2011, I received a call from Mike's secretary to come to an 8:00 a.m. meeting in his office. At that meeting, Mike and the chair of the AMA BOT informed me that Howard Bauchner was to be the next editor in chief of *JAMA* and that he would be reporting to the publisher. They also asked me to gather all the senior *JAMA* and Archives staff for a meeting at 8:30 a.m. I did so, and at that meeting. Mike and the BOT chair informed us that we were expected to greet Howard at a reception in the AMA building, scheduled for later that morning.

I explained that we had a manuscript meeting scheduled at that same time with several contributing editors calling in from all over the United States. We couldn't cancel that meeting at this late date and reschedule another meeting necessary to keep the journal on time. Therefore, we would have to greet Howard in groups, because I could not attend with the others. At least a few editors had to be present when we discussed manuscripts.

The *JAMA* and Archives staff were as surprised as I was at how we had been informed about the new editor in chief. At that point, I told them to attend the meeting with Howard, and I would do so after the manuscript meeting. The lack of courtesy in this abrupt announcement was stunning but not surprising.

I had known Howard for many years while he was the editor of Archives of Disease in Childhood (A British journal) and the director of pediatric ambulatory services at Boston University School of Medicine. I had provided advice to him, at his request, on a number of issues over the years long before he'd become a candidate for the editorship. And of course he was one of the three potential candidates I'd called before he'd been chosen as editor, and he had been the only one who had asked questions during that call. I was amazed that he hadn't called me after being offered the position.

I also was miffed that he had agreed to report to the publisher, especially without discussing the implications of that vital issue with me. In retrospect, since the publisher was the individual who had made the final decision for the editorship from the short list of names provided to her by the search committee, reporting to her was probably an essential part of the offer.

Of course, it was Howard's right to make that decision, just as I had made mine. Still, I was disappointed and angry that he hadn't at least called me a day or so earlier, so I could have prepared the *JAMA* senior staff to welcome him. Therefore, my greeting to him that day was cordial but hardly warm. However, we discussed *JAMA* and other issues at a pediatric meeting several weeks later, and I sincerely wished him success. I truly hoped he would continue advancing the mission of *JAMA* and the Archives journals.

As someone once said, losing your eyes is not as bad as losing your vision. I knew that I had done my best to maintain the vision of making *JAMA* the best possible general medical journal. It was time for me to move on.

The Fondest of Fond Farewells

Over the next three months, we continued to work as usual, maintaining the same high standards for the journals. Amazingly, because of the outstanding staff I was blessed to lead, I never felt like a lame duck. Perhaps they believed that I had already been lame enough for a lifetime after being hit by the CTA bus.

One of my most heartwarming *JAMA* memories occurred on the evening of Thursday, May 12, 2011, as we held our scheduled annual editorial board dinner at a very nice club in downtown Chicago. The editorial board members, the entire *JAMA* staff, the publisher, several associate publishers who worked on *JAMA* and the Archives journals, and several of the AMA senior managerial staff attended that dinner.

That evening, as the crowd began to move toward the dining area from the reception area, Joe Thorton asked if he could discuss something with me in the reception area, where we might have some privacy for a little while. I saw no problem in doing so, but I simply cannot remember the topic of that discussion.

We then walked together into the private dining room, where the theme from the movie Rocky was playing loudly from the loudspeakers and a room full of people rose and cheered. I was completely overwhelmed as I looked around the room. In addition to the usual crowd, I saw my sister; my friend Phyllis; Roni, my former administrative assistant (and forever friend) from Hopkins; and a number of other individuals, who had made a special trip just for this event.

What proceeded was the best-orchestrated "roast" I've ever witnessed. Phil was the MC, and many of the *JAMA* staff had written and made very clever presentations. For examples, Rob Golub sang the words he had written to the tune of "Sloop John B"; Drummond Rennie read a poem he had written, as only he could write; Annette had a very clever presentation; Mike Johns and Joe Coyle also made funny remarks; and most surprising, Jordie Cohen acted out an "Uncle Guido" scenario. I waxed and waned between laughing and being choked up by the love displayed on that evening,

About a month later, I attended the annual AMA Board of Trustees dinner. A number of the members said very nice things about me and about *JAMA* and the Archives journals under my leadership. The board even gave me a standing ovation. I remain very grateful to them for that evening, in which they displayed care and appreciation. Also at that dinner, Dr. James Madera, the new EVP/CEO, was introduced, because Mike was to step down in July, the same time as I. The irony of Mike's unexpected departure at the same time as mine was unbelievable. Go figure on that note. The Great Comedian was at work once again.

Dr. Madera had been the dean at the University of Chicago, and I had known him for several years in several capacities. Both of us served on the University of Pittsburgh Health Science Center's Board of Visitors. I often wonder how the last few years of my editorship would have been if he had been the EVP/CEO. The important thing is that he now serves in the role of EVP/CEO of the AMA, which thrives under his leadership.

My last manuscript meeting was an occasion of mixed emotions for me. I was happy because I knew I had done the best I could to lead this magnificent team, and sad because I would no longer be with them on a daily basis. So many of them had a spirituality that touched me deeply. There was never a question of fairness, or equity, among them.

At that meeting I tried (it's hard to sing when you are choked up) to sing some of the words to the song composed by the Secret Garden duo, Rolf Løvland and Brendan Graham, entitled "You Raise Me Up." I believe the words to that song best describe my experience as the leader of those outstanding individuals: "I am strong when I am on your shoulders; you raise me up to more than I can be." AMEN.

CHAPTER 18

Hopkins Redux and Life's Lessons Learned

IN JULY OF 2011, AFTER eleven and a half years as the editor in chief of *JAMA*, I returned to my beloved academic home at the Johns Hopkins University School of Medicine. I knew I would dearly miss my colleagues from *JAMA*, but life goes on, and it was time for a new adventure for all of us.

It took several months for Jim and me to move and settle into our Baltimore condominium and to transfer our furniture and other possessions from Chicago to our house on the Delaware River in Pennsylvania, which we had purchased for our family when Poppie and Nannie became ill. It was September before I was able to begin working at Hopkins. Because of the generosity of George Dover, the Pediatric Department chairman, and Tina Cheng, the director of the division, I had an office in the Division of General Pediatrics and Adolescent Medicine, which I had started in 1978.

That program was located in a building on the other side of the medical complex from the dean's office. I soon found that, except for the General Pediatrics and Adolescent Medicine group, that location was very inconvenient for the many faculty, fellows, residents, and medical students I was assisting with their research and their manuscript preparations for publication.

I met with Paul Rothman, the new dean of the Medical School, who had been appointed while I was at *JAMA*, to discuss what I would be doing at Hopkins over the next few years. I had been on the faculty since 1978 but had officially retired from financial employment when I went to *JAMA*. We discussed what I was doing currently with the faculty, fellows, and students; the book I was editing on patient care and professionalism; the numerous national and international meetings, grand rounds, and seminars at which I was speaking; and the project I was working on with the Fetzer Institute that involved the medical schools in Myanmar, née Burma.

I told him that, although I would be available to help him in any way he felt I could, I did not want a salary because my desire was to be free to work on whatever I wanted and not constrained to be in Baltimore for long periods of time. What I did request was a different office closer to the dean's office, which was across the street from the hospital. He provided a very nice and convenient office (with two windows!), new furniture, and a parking place in the most convenient garage. A parking place at Hopkins is akin to a firstborn child, so I was very grateful for all the amenities. Most of them were arranged by Chris White, the person who essentially ran the dean's office, and with whom I'd worked when I was vice dean.

Also, the Hopkins University Board of Trustees approved my appointment as University Distinguished (Extinguished?) Service Professor Emerita. This appointment, which was completely unexpected, meant a great deal to me.

In addition to working with the Hopkins faculty, residents, and medical students, and providing some presentations in the School of Public Health, I also worked with the Fetzer Institute on one of their Faculty Advisory Committees. I had received funding from them for a special project, making it possible for Jim, an American physician who had been born in Myanmar, and me to spend one year (which became eighteen months) working with the minister of health and the rectors (deans) of the medical schools in Myanmar to upgrade their curriculum—there is essentially a single curriculum for all five of their medical schools.

Going forward, I am so very lucky because Jim and I continue to work at Hopkins with faculty, fellows, residents, and students. In addition, we frequently speak as visiting professors at many medical centers and conferences in the United States and abroad. We love to travel and to meet so many different people from a variety of nations and cultures, from whom and from which we learn more about life.

Life's Lessons Learned

Along the way in all my adventures, I learned some very important lessons that I believe are important for everyone, but especially for leaders in any field. They are as follows:

1. Good leaders require four characteristics that begin with the letter *T*:
    *   **T**enacity
    *   **T**ough-mindedness (not *tough*, *tough-minded* means to hold on to an idea as long as you believe it is good, no matter how tough that might be)
    *   **T**hick skin (the most difficult)
    *   **T**ender heart (essential to forgive those who have made you a **t**arget [the biggest *T*])
    *   Nota bene: If you have never been made a target by those who disagree with you, you probably have not accomplished anything of importance and are therefore not much of a leader.
2. Never underestimate the ability you have to change things that need to be changed. That means putting the four *T*s into practice, remembering that the results will be rewarding, if only to your social conscience and sense of equity.
3. Losing your vision is worse than losing your sight.
4. As stated so beautifully by David Brinkley, "A successful person is one who can lay a firm foundation with the bricks that others throw at him or her."

5. When you find yourself dealing with individuals who have proven to be untrustworthy, keep a paper trail and stay as far away from them as possible.

6. The longer you hold on to hostility or a grudge, the heavier and more onerous the load becomes. Let it go.

7. As some wise person once said, "People will not remember what you say, but they'll never forget how you make them feel."

8. Support that only comes from the top is actually a hanging.

9. Try to never put your foot in your mouth and then also shoot yourself in the foot.

10. To paraphrase Abraham Lincoln, you can please some of the people some of the time, and some people you can please all of the time, but you can't please all of the people all of the time. Give yourself some slack.

11. Plant an acorn (i.e., an idea or project), and with proper nourishment it will grow into a beautiful tree (i.e., something that will make the world a better place).

12. Every once in a while, allow yourself to act a bit nutsy. Constant normal is boring and can lead to missed opportunities for joy.

13. When you are feeling sorry for yourself or believe you are under too much strain, visit someone really ill, especially a child.

14. Find something or someone to make you laugh every day, even if it means only looking in a mirror.

15. Spend at least a full minute every day looking at something beautiful (a child, picture, flower, etc.).

16. Approach life in the basic anatomical position, facing outward with arms extended in an accepting stance.

17. To paraphrase Bishop Oscar Romero, there are many important things that can only be seen through eyes that have cried.

18. Every day ask yourself, "Who am I"? and then consider what you did that day to define who you think you are.

FINALE

My plan to return to Hopkins and live happily ever after, using whatever I can with my medical vocation continuing to pursue medicine with equity, seems to be on track. Over my professional lifetime, I have had the pleasure of perceiving and participating in the progress toward equity in medicine.

Since 1997, I have spoken at seventeen US medical school graduations and observed more and more women graduating with honors and as student leaders. Currently, half of medical school students are women. As male physicians are educated and trained with women, they will learn from experience about the intellect, creativity, and work ethic of women physicians. The likelihood of unwarranted biases and unfair treatment should decrease dramatically.

There are women professors and department chairs in every US medical school, and thirteen deans are women. These women leaders are in positions to assure equity for all physicians. They also have the ability to convince male leaders about the importance of equity for all physicians.

Except for the number of women medical students, very much more needs to be done to reach full equity in medicine, including equal payment for equal work. However, many advances have been made in cracking the glass ceiling. Now, the goal is to shatter the glass ceiling, and my plan is to continue assisting in that goal in any way I can.

And yes, life is a wondrous adventure, all according to the plan of the Great Comedian.

ONWARD.

Acknowledgments

MANY PEOPLE HAVE HELPED ME write this book either by just being there for me (far too many to name), or by directly assisting me with the manuscript. The latter include Professor Richard Macksey, Johns Hopkins University, who provided sage advice for the early drafts; Johannah Vondeling, who read an early version and encouraged me to publish; Dr. Howard Markel, University of Michigan, who read an early draft and suggested changes and encouragement; John (Jack) Hanley, New York who I expected only to read the manuscript and provide suggestions, but he copy edited the entire 110,000 words or so plus added suggestions; and the enthusiastic CreateSpace team, especially my editor, Lauren. Finally, and most importantly, my husband, Dr. Jim Harris, not only made many suggestions, but he put up with my various up and down moods while writing and encouraged me to keep writing. To all I give my sincere gratitude.

Made in the USA
San Bernardino, CA
30 April 2019